The Paradox of
Youth Violence

Social Problems, Social Constructions

Joel Best and Scott R. Harris, series editors

The **Paradox** of
Youth Violence

J. William Spencer

LYNNE
RIENNER
PUBLISHERS

BOULDER
LONDON

Published in the United States of America in 2011 by
Lynne Rienner Publishers, Inc.
1800 30th Street, Boulder, Colorado 80301
www.rienner.com

and in the United Kingdom by
Lynne Rienner Publishers, Inc.
3 Henrietta Street, Covent Garden, London WC2E 8LU

Library of Congress Cataloging-in-Publication Data
Spencer, J. William.
    The paradox of youth violence / J. William Spencer.
        p.   cm. — (Social problems, social constructions)
    Includes bibliographical references and index.
    ISBN 978-1-58826-788-7 (hardcover : alk. paper)
    1. Juvenile delinquency—United States. 2. Youth and violence.
3. Mass media and youth. 4. Juvenile delinquency—United States
—Prevention. I. Title.
    HV9104.S75 2011
    363.620835'0973—dc22

                                                    2011000084

British Cataloguing in Publication Data
A Cataloguing in Publication record for this book
is available from the British Library.

Printed and bound in the United States of America

The paper used in this publication meets the requirements
∞   of the American National Standard for Permanence of
Paper for Printed Library Materials Z39.48-1992.

5   4   3   2   1

Contents

Acknowledgments

This book has been a long time coming, and many people helped make it possible. First, I want to thank the Hudson Institute for their support in the early stages of this project through a Purdue–Hudson Institute Summer Fellowship. That support provided the needed time to get the project off the ground. I also want to thank my good friend James A. Holstein. Most notably, he was the source of the notion of paradox from which much of this project grew. Perhaps I can repay him someday with a few more gratuitous citations. In addition, the master's project of a former graduate student—Amy Crook—provided much of the early inspiration for looking at ambiguity and ambivalence. A number of other students helped along the way by searching for, assembling, and coding news articles. Others, notably Nathan Shippee, Elizabeth Sternke, and Steph Silva, proofread drafts, served as a sounding board for ideas, and generally put up with my ramblings about ambivalence, ambiguity, and paradox.

The book would not have been possible without the patience and support of my partner and wife, Alison Greene. She listened thoughtfully to ideas and provided critical feedback, and she helped me to create graphics and resolve word processing problems. Most important, she gave me the space to get this done. Last, but by no means least, I want to dedicate this book to my parents and my daughter. My parents, Tex and Ellen, were high-school educated and never quite understood what I do for a living. However, my father liked to brag to his friends that his son worked at Purdue and was writing a book. My daughter, Emily, spent much of her youth in the 1990s. In some ways, she is lucky. Both her parents are professionals, and she has had the benefit of attending good schools. Alison and I carefully monitored her exposure to violence, talked with her about things that mattered, and made sure she knew that we love her. She has made all the right choices along the way. She studied and worked hard at school and in sports. She has matured into a most wonderful woman, and she married a remarkable man (though I am all too often loath to admit that to his face). While they are still in the early stages of learning firsthand what it means to be parents, Emily and Matt are already well on their way to raising a terrific daughter who, I am sure, will make her own good choices. May they create a better world for their children than the one we created for them.

The Paradox of
Youth Violence

1

The Problem
of Youth Violence

The 1990s were the decade of the Clinton presidency and growing economic prosperity, the O. J. Simpson trial and the Rodney King incident and subsequent Los Angeles riots, the fall of the Soviet Union, and the FBI siege of the Branch Davidian compound in Waco and the Oklahoma City Federal Building bombing. I might argue that the 1990s were also the decade of youth violence. Almost all of us remember the shootings at Columbine High School in 1999. It was almost impossible to read a newspaper or magazine or turn on the television without encountering a story about the event. We learned about the offenders—Eric Harris and Dylan Klebold—and their backgrounds: The speculation about how these two young men could have come to this act seemed endless. We encountered stories about their victims and followed the local community's efforts to deal with the tragedy. We were also treated to, and most likely became part of, a wide-ranging debate on how such events could be prevented in the future.

Of course, Columbine was not the first event of its kind during that decade. Many of us may remember similar events in schools in Pearl, Mississippi; West Paducah, Kentucky; Springfield, Oregon; and elsewhere. And there was a seemingly endless string of events outside schools: A young boy in Chicago was dropped to his death from a fourteenth-story window by two other boys—ostensibly for refusing to steal candy for them. Also in Chicago, a young boy was shot to death days after he had killed a neighborhood girl. An older woman in New Jersey was killed by a teenager who lived in her neighborhood. There were stories about the "superpredator"—a new sort of violent youthful of-

1

fender who grew up in conditions of moral poverty and killed without conscience—and about the "gang problem" involving drive-by shootings and drugs. During the 1990s, all these exemplified the growing threat of youth violence. By the time the Columbine shooting occurred, the term "youth violence" had become firmly established in our cultural lexicon.

Over the course of that decade, talk about the problem of youth violence underwent considerable change—both in how the problem was framed and in our collective searches for causal accounts and solutions to the problem. Consider the following two *New York Times* articles. The first article appeared on January 31, 1990, and began:

> In a voice choked with emotion, a Brooklyn mother told a City Hall hearing yesterday that when she sends her children to school by public transportation each morning, she worries she will not see them alive again because of marauding groups of violent youths.
>
> "I might have to bury my child. No, I don't want that. I want my children to bury me," she said before a hushed audience at a hearing on the perils children encounter on the way to school—youth violence and "wilding."
>
> The hearing was held by City Council President Andrew J. Stein, and Family Court judges, probation officials and police officers also spoke. Mr. Stein said he wanted to focus attention on youth violence and wilding and to send the message that "if you hurt other people, you are going to be punished."

The second article appeared on June 6, 1999, and began:

> A bitterly divided House plunged into the nation's culture wars today, passionately debating long into the night whether school prayer, a clampdown on violence in entertainment, stiff prison sentences or gun control was the answer to the spate of school shootings that have left teen-agers dead. The debate was the beginning of a two- to three-day free-for-all as the House considered 44 amendments on cultural issues and crime and 11 gun control proposals. The House approved tough mandatory minimum sentences to combat juvenile crime. But in a blow to social conservatives, the House voted 282 to 146 tonight to reject a measure sponsored by Representative Henry J. Hyde, Republican of Illinois that would have made it a crime to expose children to movies, books or video games containing explicit sex or violence.

Both articles focus on the problem of violence committed by youth and a search for a solution to that problem. In both articles, the victims of this violence were, themselves, other youth. The talk in both articles is full of emotion. In the first article, a mother's talk is "choked with emotion" as she describes how she "worries" about her children. In the second article, debate among lawmakers is "passionate" and a "free-for-all."

However, these two articles also illustrate some of the ways in which public discourse about youth violence underwent significant transformation over the course of the decade. Notice how the first article casts the problem as a local one—the incidents occur in New York City, and solutions are being discussed by local officials and parents. In the second article, members of the US House of Representatives debate solutions to a national problem. In the first article, the problem appears to constitute "marauding groups of violent youth"—perhaps a reference to gangs or the "wilding" problem (Best 1999; Welch, Price, and Yankey 2002)—whereas in the second, the problem clearly constitutes the school shootings that dominated public discourse on youth violence in the last few years of the decade. The solutions proffered in the first article seem relatively simple, if not vague. There is talk of deterrence—"if you hurt other people, you are going to be punished," and in the absence of talk to the contrary, there seems to be a consensus regarding that. In the second article, the solutions are more clearly articulated, but they are also more complex—running the gamut from "mandatory sentences" to school prayer and a "clampdown on violence in entertainment"—and there is much debate and acrimony.

In the pages that follow, I examine the continuities and changes in talk about the youth violence problem over the course of the 1990s. My main argument throughout is that we confronted youth violence as a paradox, as a mystery, or simply senseless. At the most general level, the presumed innocence of youth was contradicted by their deadly—and malevolent—acts; that other youth were among the victims only added to the senselessness. Violence in suburban and small towns was a mystery— they were the last kids we'd expect to be killers. Not surprisingly, the emotions revealed in this talk were full of ambivalence: pity and sympathy versus fear and anxiety. Talk about the causes of, and solutions to, the problem was rife with complexity. Sometimes causes appeared to be taken for granted, but at other times agreement could not be reached. The search for solutions spawned hotly contested political battles.

The Context: Youth Violence and Social Reactions in the 1990s

Although official data suggest that rates of violent *adult* crime declined throughout the 1990s, it appears that *youth* crime, especially *violent* youth crime, reached its highest level in several decades. One official measure of violent crime is found in the FBI's *Uniform Crime Report*. As Figure 1.1 shows, based on these data, the juvenile arrest rate for the violent crime index (which comprises data on murder, aggravated assault, rape, and robbery) began to increase in the late 1980s and continued to climb until peaking around 1994. At that point, the juvenile violent crime rate was over 60 percent higher than it had been in the mid-1980s.

That rate declined until the end of the 1990s. Although higher than it had been in the 1970s, the 1999 juvenile arrest rate for violent crimes had returned to a level comparable to that of the early 1980s. The trends for each of the individual offenses that comprise the violent crime index were the same over the decade. For example, the juvenile arrest rate for murder peaked in 1993 at a level (14 per 100,000) more than twice the rate in 1980 (6 per 100,000) before dropping to around 4 per 100,000 in 1999. The increase and decline in the arrest rate for forcible rape was not nearly so dramatic, peaking at a rate of 23 per 100,000 in 1991 before dropping to 16 per 100,000 in 1999—the same rate as in 1980. Robbery

Figure 1.1   Violent Juvenile Arrest Rates, 1980–1999

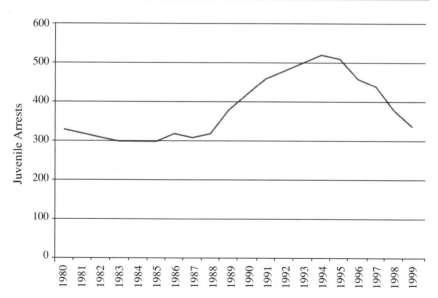

Source: Adapted from H. N. Snyder. 2000. *Juvenile Arrests, 1999.* Washington, DC: US Department of Justice.

peaked in 1994–1995 at a rate of 200 per 100,000, but by decade's end was below 100 per 100,000. Finally, the rate for aggravated assault peaked at around 300 per 100,000 in 1994—double its rate in 1980—and then dropped to around 225 per 100,000 in 1999.

The previous paragraph is, of course, only one of many different ways of "reading" or understanding these data. That is one of the grounding assumptions of this book: The "reality" of youth violence was—and is—in many important ways a matter of social definition. The numbers are important, but what we make of them (and the reality of youth violence more generally) is at least as important. We could see the rising rates of the first half of the decade—as many did at the time—as grounds for anxiety and fear. Alternatively, the falling rates might indicate that during the last half of the decade, significant progress was made in mitigating the problem. With a more historical perspective in mind, we could argue that the rates by decade's end were higher than in the 1970s, suggesting that we might be concerned about longer-term trends. We could suggest that the focus on violence by youth is misplaced, that this focus draws our attention away from much more common nonviolent crimes such as drug use or property crime. We might critique the use of official statistics to measure the problem, arguing that such statistics always underestimate the problem, thus suggesting the "problem" was even greater than what these facts suggested. Finally, it is possible that these statistics exaggerated the gravity of the problem and that all the anxiety and fear they generated were misplaced or unwarranted. After all, most kids behave themselves most of the time; violent crime like this is relatively rare.

Given all the possible ways listed above of orienting to the "facts" about youth violence, it is clear that most of the *public discourse* both reflected and fed a growing concern and fear of the problem. As we see in this book, the general view was that violence among youth was a serious threat and was growing worse. Reactions on the part of the federal and state governments, as well as the general public, were predictable. In 1993, the US Conference of Mayors and the Rainbow Coalition formed task forces to address the problem. The following year, violence prevention was designated as the theme of National Child Month by the American Academy of Pediatrics. In 1995, National Random Acts of Kindness Day was declared by the Kindness Movement. Mark Warr (1995, p. 300) has noted that public opinion about crime underwent "an unprecedented reassessment" in 1994—the year that the juvenile violent crime index rate peaked. Crime and violence came to head the list of perceived problems in a number of public opinion polls for the first time in more than a decade (Warr 1995).

With rising youth crime rates and growing public concern, it is not surprising that the juvenile justice system shifted to a more punitive stance (Colomy and Greiner 2004; see also Haydon and Scraton 2000 for a discussion of this phenomenon in Great Britain). A 1999 US Department of Justice report suggested "the 1990's have been a time of unprecedented change as State legislatures crack down on juvenile crime" (Snyder and Sickmund 1999, p. 87). According to this report, states responded to public concerns about youth crime with a flurry of legislative activity. For example, between 1992 and 1997, forty-seven states and the District of Columbia enacted legislation in one or more of the following areas: (1) making it easier to waive or transfer juvenile offenders from the juvenile court to the adult criminal court, (2) giving both sets of courts expanded sentencing options, and (3) modifying or removing traditional requirements that shielded juvenile court proceedings from public scrutiny. Thus, by 1997, twenty-eight states had passed laws that excluded certain offenders from juvenile court jurisdiction, meaning that their cases now *originated* in the adult criminal court. In twenty-four of these states, laws singled out for such statutory exclusion capital crimes, murder, and/or other violent offenses. For example, ten-year-olds living in Wisconsin could have their cases automatically waived to the criminal court. In five other states, the minimum age was thirteen.

These changes in violent crime rates and state-level juvenile justice policies provide part of the immediate context of this book. However, there is much more to the story of youth violence in the 1990s. These changes in policy were not simply a direct reaction to the increase in official rates of violent juvenile crime. As Ira Schwartz (1992) has suggested, juvenile justice policy is "usually made in an emotionally charged atmosphere" (p. 224). Similarly, Paul Colomy and Laura Greiner (2004) argue that a full understanding of juvenile justice policy must consider "analyses of the symbolic dimensions of crime, law, and punishment" (p. 5). Put differently, to understand how juvenile justice policy changed—indeed, to understand our broader collective search for solutions to the problem of youth violence—we need to understand the cultural meanings attributed to youth violence during this period. From this perspective, official rates of youth violence take on a different importance—they not only partially shape this search for meaning and solutions but also become part of the process. These numbers were part of the discursive "raw material" out of which the "crisis" of youth violence was constructed.

Youthful Misbehavior as a Recurring Social Problem

With a broader context in mind, the 1990s were certainly not the first time the misbehavior of youth had become an object of widespread concern and intense public debate. Indeed, recurring concern about delinquency can be traced back to the Progressive Era of the late 1800s and early 1900s. Social reformers of that time raised alarm at the untoward behavior of lower-class, immigrant children (Bernard and Kurlychek 2010; Hagan and Leon 1977; Platt 1977; Schlossman 1977). The child-savers, as child advocates of this time were known, saw these youth as largely responsible for dramatic increases in crime in our major cities. According to the dominant discourse of that time, the behavior of these youth was the result of three factors—inept parenting, the weak moral nature of the lower class, and the more general corrupting influences of the urban landscape (Bernard and Kurlychek 2010; Platt 1977). This discourse, and the shared understandings of which they were part, resulted in a host of different methods of training, treating, and rehabilitating these lower-class youth and their parents, ranging from houses of refuge in the early 1800s to the juvenile court systems of the first decades of the twentieth century.

The 1950s appear to have been another period of intense concern regarding juvenile delinquency. James Gilbert (1986) suggests that much of the discourse during this period expressed a deep concern for what was seen as an emerging middle-class teen subculture characterized by rock-and-roll music, new styles of dress (e.g., blue jeans and boots) and hairstyles, and even a new language. To many adults, the new appearance and lifestyle of teenagers signaled a troubling change—a transformation of traditional teen rebellion and high jinks to dangerous criminal behavior. According to Gilbert (1986), the discourse of the time identified several culprits responsible for this new and growing problem, in particular (1) the inability of middle-class parents (and for that matter, most of adult society) to properly understand and socialize children and (2) the influence of popular culture—specifically mass media in the form of movies, television, and comic books. This concern with popular culture was not new, but rather the most recent manifestation of anxiety about social change and its effects on youth that periodically surfaces. From the mid- to late 1960s through the early 1970s, young members of the baby boom generation (myself included) were objects of growing concern because of reputed drug use (marijuana and LSD in particular), participation in antiwar protests, and teenage rejection of marriage, school, and the world of work. More recently, in the 1980s Americans witnessed widespread concern regarding youth gangs generally and with violence and drug dealing in particular.

Although this book is not the place for a full history of delinquency as a social problem, I want to make several observations. Delinquency—and youthful misbehavior more generally—is an enduring feature of American society. There have always been children and adolescents who misbehave. However, only periodically has this misbehavior emerged as a *significant* public concern. That is, it is always around, but we discover or, rather, rediscover it from time to time. Second, each time we do rediscover it, we see it as worse than it has ever been. Thomas Bernard and Megan Kurlychek (2010, p. 13) refer to this as the myth of the "good old days." Third, delinquency is often—perhaps most of the time—rediscovered as a rather different sort of problem. In the Progressive Era, it was lower-class urban youth, in the 1950s, it was middle-class suburban youth, and in the 1980s, it was urban youth gangs. There are noticeable continuities in what gets defined as its origins—the usual suspects seem to be faulty parenting and other family problems; problems or dangers of the urban landscape; and mass media, as well as other aspects of popular culture. We come to these conclusions, in part, because our understandings of delinquency inevitably draw on deeply held cultural images of children, youth, and their environments; crime and criminals; and social change. However, within these commonalities, new or different origins or causes are invented. For example, although we commonly blame youthful misbehavior on popular culture, it tends to take on different guises with each rediscovery of the problem: In the 1950s, it was comic books and music, whereas in the 1990s (as we will see later in this book), it was video games and movies. More recently, the Internet and cell phones have taken their place in our concerns about youth. In sum, when the problem of youthful misbehavior (be it drug use or violent crime) is periodically rediscovered—that is, becomes the object of public concern—this problem is understood as a different sort of problem with different causes than previously.

The Theoretical Framework of the Book

I use a constructionist social problems framework for the basic foundation of this book. For constructionists, social problems are those phenomena that are *socially defined* as problematic (Spector and Kitsuse 1987; Blumer 1971). To say that pollution, violent crime, homelessness, and terrorism are social problems means that they have become socially defined as problems and, thus, objects of widespread concern. Whether a phenomenon is defined as a social problem is not necessarily related to its objective characteristics, such as its size or the potential harm it may cause. There are many phenomena that arguably pose serious threats that are not defined as problems, and, likewise, many others that are arguably rather innocuous that come to be socially defined as problems. Social definitions are found in, and arise out of, social discourse about problems. In constructionist terminology, social problems discourse both constitutes and produces the social meanings of problems. Such discourse, or talk, can be found in all sorts of places: in the news, on talk shows and popular television series, in congressional hearings and presidential speeches, or in our everyday discussion over the dinner table; when we talk about a phenomenon as a problem, we are defining it as one. Put another way, there are a host of discursive arenas in which social problems get constructed.

Discourse about a social problem is complex and multidimensional. Part of what gets defined—indeed, "created"—when we talk about a problem is the condition itself (Loseke 1993; Ibarra and Kitsuse 1993). For example, talk about "violent crime," "cigarette smoking," and "homelessness" as conditions typically establishes their "size," their negative consequences, and their causes. Thus, when we talk about "the homelessness problem," we often talk about how many homeless people there are on the streets and why or how they end up there. When we talk about the "smoking problem," we may talk about the unhealthy effects of secondhand smoke and the cancer rate among smokers. When we talk about violent crime, we may talk about the murder rate or the social and economic costs of violence.

In addition, the types of people who populate a problem get defined in this sort of discourse (Loseke 1993; Loseke and Best 2003). Thus, homelessness is populated with the "homeless person," and smoking is populated by "the smoker." Such conclusions may appear quite intuitive at first glance, but *how* these person-categories are constructed is important. Many, perhaps most, social problems involve both victims and victimizers (Best 1999; Loseke 1993; Holstein and Miller 1990). For example, the social problem of terrorism may include the "terrorist" and his or her "innocent civilian victims." The problem of "domestic violence" might be populated with the "battered woman" and her "abuser"

(Loseke 1992). Sometimes, the status of a person-category is subject to some debate. For example, is the homeless person someone who ends up on the street because of forces beyond his or her control? Or do people become homeless because they are lazy? Are terrorists freedom fighters (that is, victims of oppressive governments), or are they victimizers (killers of innocents)? Answers to these questions help us understand a final element of social problems discourse—the emotional orientations that surround a problem (Loseke 1993). Discourse that constructs victims and victimizers does not merely *name* these persons or groups. Rather, victims and victimizers are cultural categories—or labels—that carry both semantic and emotional baggage. The term "victim" typically means someone who is harmed and, more importantly, someone who does not deserve this harm. In other words, victims are—unless otherwise defined—innocent or blameless. Alternatively, victimizers are—in lieu of other information—assumed to have intentionally brought this harm to their victims; that is, they are to be blamed. Further, these images or meanings of victims and victimizers invoke predictable emotions: Outrage or anger may be common elements of the discourse about the victimizers in the problem of violent crime, whereas sympathy or compassion might be engendered for their victims.

Defining a problem has consequences. First, since a problem is by definition an object of public concern, there will be calls to do something about it. Indeed, such efforts are an important element of social problems discourse. The emergence of drunk driving as a social problem (Gusfield 1981) generated a host of efforts to ameliorate it. The same can be said about the problem of homelessness: In the mid-1980s amid widespread talk about the problem, Congress passed the McKinney Act—the first comprehensive federal legislation addressing homelessness (Sisco 2008). Despite decades of warnings by experts, global warming was slow to emerge as a social problem, and thus, little in the way of serious work was done about it. However, recently it seems everyone is pitching in to "save the planet"—from recycling to using less electricity to buying hybrid cars. Second, the specific nature of these ameliorative efforts is shaped by our particular definition of the problem. For example, defining aviary flu as a health threat would (and did) result in the production and stockpiling of large volumes of flu vaccine, examination of hospital emergency rooms and procedures, and all sorts of talk about rationing scarce medical resources related to the treatment of this condition. Defining this condition as a threat to US national security, however, would result in myriad efforts involving the Department of Homeland Security.

Social problems discourse is rhetorical, in the sense that it represents a preferred definition of a condition (Holstein and Miller 1990). In many instances, people debate whether a condition is "really" a problem. Even when people appear to agree that a condition is a problem, they may hold multiple views regarding the particular type of problem it constitutes or how to properly go about trying to solve it. Using the example of drunk driving from above, it seems that Americans are of at least two minds. At times we define it as a medical problem, the solution to which is treatment (Conrad and Schneider 1992). However, at other times, our penchant for demanding tougher jail sentences for drunk drivers seems to suggest we also see it as a crime problem. This same observation might apply to teenage pregnancy, which sparks perennial debates among advocates of abstinence, condom use, and sex education.

Constructionists often argue that public discourse—especially in the media—simplifies problems. For example, they suggest that the media (and by extension other arenas of public discourse) prefer monocausal framings of conditions (Fishman 1980; Gusfield 1981; Stallings 1995). That is, constructionists argue that the media construct problems in singular ways—violence as a crime problem or terrorism as a matter of national security. Similarly, the person-categories that populate problems fit into either of two types—victim or victimizer (Loseke 1993; Holstein and Miller 1990). Our analyses of emotional orientations likewise tend toward the simple—for example, we examine discourse for fear (of victimizers) or sympathy (for victims) (Loseke 1993; Altheide 2002). This simplicity in constructing problems contrasts with the complexity of the "real" world itself. For example, Donileen Loseke (1992) suggests that the relative simplicity of the organizational discourse at a domestic violence shelter allowed workers to make decisions about whom to admit to the shelter even in the face of the complexity and "messiness" of the lived experience of domestic violence. At a different level, in discussing the media, David Altheide (2002, p. 98) has suggested, "Entertainment abhors ambiguity, while truth and effective intervention efforts to improve social life reside in ambiguity. It is this tension between entertaining and familiar news reports, on the one hand, and civic understanding, on the other hand, that remains to be resolved." That may well be the case with many social problems, but the central tenet of this book is that youth violence has been constructed as a rather ambiguous and uncertain problem on multiple levels and along several dimensions. As a condition, it constituted a variety of specific kinds of problems—from individual acts of violence to gang violence and school shootings to the "superpredator"—sometimes in sequence and at other times in combination. Further, youth violence was understood as a paradox that juxtaposed two images—the evil of their predatory acts versus the naïveté and innocence of these youth. In turn, the evil nature of the violence was consistently drawn against the innocence and, at times, the bravery of the victims. As constructed, this violence withstood explanation, or at least an easy one.

It has become a major principle of contemporary constructionist theory that social problems discourse be studied in relationship to its broader—especially cultural—context (see, e.g., Hilgartner and Bosk 1988; Gamson and Modigliani 1989; Ibarra and Kitsuse 1993). Consider what Joel Best (1999, p. 186) has to say: "Just as no social problem exists in isolation, unconnected from the surrounding patterns of social life, so the way we talk about a given problem has many links to other, familiar social problems—and to the larger culture—and those links influence what we understand and how we respond." Jaber Gubrium and James A. Holstein (1998) make this point when they distinguish between "discursive practice" and "discourses-in-practice": The former refers to the "hows" of social problems discourse—almost literally, the language of social problems discourse and its various features; the latter refers to the "whats" of this discourse, including "recognizable categories, familiar vocabularies, organizational missions, professional orientations, group cultures, and other existing frameworks for assigning meaning" (Gubrium and Holstein 1998). Constructionists often call these "whats" interpretive resources—referring to the notion that these elements of the social context provide ways of making sense of this discourse. In a human service organization, they might include formal and informal protocols for processing its clientele (Loseke 1992; Spencer 1997). In the news industry, they might include shared ideas of what constitutes newsworthiness, as well as broader collective representations of situations and persons. For example, assumptions about gender often make it easier to construct men as violent criminals and thus to craft explanations for this violence. In news discourse about youth violence, broader cultural understandings of youth, violent crime, race, and class were at play.

Constructionist studies often approach social problems discourse at a meso-level of analysis—that is, as claims made by specific groups or institutions. One of the major analytic goals of this work is to explain the form and content of these claims by way of group or organizational values, interests, or power. For example, in her analysis of the eugenics campaign of the late 1800s and early 1900s, Nicole Rafter makes re-

course to the motives of one of the central claimants of the campaign—
Josephine Shaw Lowell. In turn, Best (1990) argues that claims about
threats to children in the 1980s were often shaped by the goals or values
of various interest groups, such as child advocates or law enforcement.
Philip Jenkins (1994) argues that federal law enforcement and the media
each had stakes in how serial homicide was constructed in the 1980s.
Constructionists are most fond of using the news to study social problems
construction, and it is common to understand this sort of discourse as reflecting that institution's values or interests regarding newsworthiness,
sensationalism, entertainment, objectivity, and even the profit motive.
Extending this argument, Altheide (2002) suggests that the contemporary culture of fear is in part shaped by the logic and technology of mass
media. From this perspective, although media discourse may be shaped
by broader cultural ideas, typically it is viewed as separate from those
ideas.

I don't contest this way of conceptualizing news discourse, but I find
it more useful to treat the news as a more truly *cultural* text—a discourse
that simultaneously is produced by, reflects, and acts upon culture. In
this way, analyzing news discourse tells us as least as much about culture
as it does about the news industry itself. This view is very similar to that
used in many contemporary studies of popular culture. For example,
Chris Barker (2003, p. 319) argues that the media "draw off as well as
constitute consensual assumptions about the world." Norman Denzin
(1995, p. 7) saw popular film as one way "a society cinematically represents itself to its members." Similarly, Robert Bulman (2005, p. 2) treats
films as cultural artifacts that "tell us truths about the culture that produces them." Put a bit differently, the news (along with other mass media
forms like film, popular music, and television) is a sort of window on
how our culture tries to make sense of youth violence. In this light, the
news is, in a way, authorless—less the work of individuals, groups, or
even an entire industry and more a part, and a product, of culture. To be
sure, the news is still an *institutional* discourse—partially shaped by a variety of beliefs, logics, values, and conventions relatively specific to the
news industry, such as concerns with balance or objectivity, newsworthiness, profit, and entertainment (Altheide 2002; Lester 1980). Admit-
ting that, though, still allows for a more cultural reading of the news,
where in addition to conditions specific to the news industry, the concern is with how broad cultural values, assumptions, expectations, and
the like are employed and, in turn, given specific shape and meaning in
this discourse. In this way, my perspective is like that of Denzin (1991),

who argues that Hollywood treatments of alcoholism and the alcoholic have been shaped by broader historical and cultural understandings. Thus, in this study of youth violence, broad cultural understandings of youth, gender, violence, and the city as a social place all serve as discourses-in-practice, or interpretive resources, that shaped how youth violence was constructed in the news. Likewise, news discourse about programs and policies regarding this problem presents a window on our collective search for solutions.

In using this constructionist perspective, I am not suggesting that the objective condition of youth violence—the "reality" of the problem—isn't worthy of study. Indeed, a considerable body of research and theory exists that focuses on the rates and correlates of youth violence, its origins or causes, as well as promising prevention and intervention programs. What I *am* suggesting is that discourse about the problem is equally worthy of serious study for at least two reasons. First, if we take seriously the notion that social definitions shape our collective reactions to problems, then to understand the ways we respond to youth violence requires that we recognize how we have come to understand it, which, in turn, means a serious study of public discourse about it. In Chapter 3, I examine discourse about our collective search for a solution to youth violence and show how this search—and the discourse about it—was shaped in important ways by our understandings of the problem itself. Second, a serious consideration of public discourse about youth violence requires an understanding of its wider social and cultural contexts. Talk about the youth violence problem was shaped by broader assumptions or understandings about youth, violence, race, class, and a number of other cultural beliefs and concerns. If we take this wider focus seriously, we can learn some important lessons about American culture. Consider what Bulman (2005, p. 8) has said about movies: "One way in which we collectively manage to cope with the complexity and confusion of social life is to package reality and represent it as fiction—to tell stories about our social world that make it more comprehensible." I am not arguing, of course, that the news and film are equivalent sorts of discourses. However, I do argue that the news may function in ways similar to popular film in that it represents one of the ways we collectively make sense of social life—in this case, youth violence. As seen through the lens of media discourse in the 1990s, we viewed youth violence as a complex, ambiguous problem—indeed, as a paradox. What does this understanding tell us about our views of youth and of violence? Why did we describe the violence of inner-city youth in ways fundamentally different from—and more understandable than—that of suburban or rural youth? Why, in our collective search for solutions, did we continually get caught up in debates over treatment versus punishment or prevention versus incarceration and, in the process, fail to seriously pursue alternative solutions?

Media Discourse About Violence Problems

Violence occupies a significant and highly visible place in American society. Our rates of violent crime are among the highest of all industrialized countries, and—perhaps not coincidently—violence pervades our popular culture. It is the fundamental basis of many of our most popular sports, from hockey and football to wrestling and, increasingly, basketball. It serves as the basic plotline for television shows and movies and has become a staple in video and computer games. References to violence can be found in the lyrics of many songs. Perhaps, then, it is not surprising that violence is the subject of considerable social problems talk. We discuss the "violence problem" at work and at home, and, of course, there is much of it in the news. Stories about specific violence problems, such as serial murder, rape, spousal and child abuse, freeway violence, and, more recently, terrorism, have been and continue to be commonplace.

A large body of research focuses on news discourse about violence-related problems. From reading these stories, we can glean a number of general themes or patterns in the way that the news portrays or presents violence. First, violent crime *dominates* media reports (Beckett and Sasson 2000; Gorelick 1989; Graber 1980; Kappeler, Blumberg, and Potter 2000; Sheley and Ashkins 1981), even though it comprises a relatively small proportion of the total rate of officially recognized street crime. For example, Robert Lichter and Linda Lichter (1994) find that 80 percent of news stories in 1993 featured violent crime. According to Sanford Sherizen (1978), 23 percent of crime news during 1975 in Chicago was about robbery and 45 percent was about murder. Stephen Gorelick (1989) found that robbery was featured in 50 percent of stories in the *New York Daily News* crime-fighting campaign druring 1982.

Second, in some instances and in some venues (such as newsweeklies and opinion columns), news discourse *thematizes* violence by crafting problems out of individual violent events. For example, Mark Fishman (1978) found that individual cases of violent crime in New York were organized into a wave of "crimes against the elderly." More recently, Best (1999) has illustrated how individual incidents, such as two seemingly unrelated shootings on Los Angeles freeways, or an assault on and rape of a jogger in New York's Central Park, were framed as instances of larger problems of "freeway violence" and "wilding," respectively. Similarly, Gorelick (1989) illustrates how journalists at the *New York Daily News* took a variety of news fragments and organized them around the theme of "crime fighting," which became part of a more general campaign against violent crime.

Third, violence problems are almost always characterized as *expanding, spreading,* or generally *growing worse.* We see this in Best's (1990) analysis of the rhetoric about threatened children in the 1980s. Violence is often depicted as random and unpredictable (Best 1999; Beckett and Sasson 2000). Relatedly, news discourse often characterizes violence as widespread—with no one being safe, irrespective of race, class, age, gender, and place of residence. All this is accomplished, in part, through the use of words such as "epidemic" or "plague" (Best 1999; Gorelick 1989), and, in a sometimes unfortunate mixing of metaphors, crime control may be likened to a "war" waged against a "plague"— defining violence as the enemy whose defeat will require extraordinary efforts and sacrifice (Gorelick 1989). Claims about violence problems often draw connections to other, more familiar problems and concerns. For example, Best (1990, 1999) has noted how new problems are "piggybacked" onto established ones, such as happened in constructions of stalking that linked it to the more established problem of domestic violence (Lowney and Best 1995). In more general terms, Gorelick (1989) and Best (1999) have both noted that constructions of violence problems draw on broad cultural concerns about social disorder and moral decay.

Fourth, perpetrators and victims of violence (Holstein and Miller 1990; Loseke 1993) are fashioned by media discourse into a type of morality play (Altheide 2002), with offenders as the evil, predatory villains and their targets as innocent victims. Typecasting of offenders and victims facilitates the fashioning of these morality plays. For example, news discourse focuses disproportionately on women, children, and the elderly as victims of violence (Kappeler, Blumberg, and Potter 2000), likely because they are more easily presented as vulnerable and weak (Best 1999; Gorelick 1989; Websdale 1999). Further, victims are typically portrayed as morally pure—not responsible for their plight and deserving of our sympathy and assistance (Loseke 1992; Holstein and Miller 1990).

Violent offenders, however, are often demonized. For example, media discourse focuses on violence committed by men and youth

(Reiman 1997). Violence by strangers garners more attention than violence between friends, acquaintances, or family members (Kappeler, Blumberg, and Potter 2000; Beckett and Sasson 2000). Quite often in this discourse, victimizers lack conscience and act without remorse. Neil Websdale (1999, p. 99) shows how the sexual predator is constructed as a "fiendishly dangerous individual," and Jenkins (1994) argues that during the 1970s serial killers came increasingly to be portrayed as monsters and savage animals.

The focus on individual offenders results partly from the media's tendency to decontextualize violence by backgrounding both the immediate situation as well as larger social contexts. For example, John Johnson (1995) notes that in talking about child abuse, the media fail to address everyday stressors that might account for the abuse (which in turn ends up attributing responsibility to the abuser) and do not attend to the immediate context of abuse, such as preceding events or interpersonal roles and relationships. From a different perspective, Websdale (1999) argues that constructions of the sexual predator do not connect the problem with battering of women, marital rape, and child sexual abuse. Similarly, Neil Websdale and Alexander Alvarez (1998) illustrate how constructions of lethal domestic violence fail to place it in the context of a history of battering on the part of the offender. In both instances, these constructions are seen as failing to confront, and thus reinforcing, patriarchal violence and other aspects of gender politics in the United States. This tendency to focus on the individual violent offender has to do with an American cultural orientation toward a "volitional" view of crime and criminals (Sasson 1995; Scheingold 1991), which accords considerable free will and choice to offenders—in effect, rendering them evil and immoral. Victims, however, typically have few choices and are most generally portrayed as weak and vulnerable. For example, Loseke (1992) shows how the "battered woman" was portrayed as someone who was *trapped* in her situation—economically, emotionally, socially, and psychologically. More generally, James Holstein and Gale Miller (1990) suggest a "victim" is someone who had no role in their plight.

Compared to the volumes of research literature on media discourse about violence problems, relatively little work has been done on how the media portray juvenile delinquency and youth crime. This is surprising because the news has always been a major vehicle or platform for our public concerns when we periodically rediscover youthful behavior as a problem. For example, Robert Shepherd (1997, p. 10) cites an 1857 *New York Times* editorial noting "the number of boy burglars, boy robbers, and boy murderers is so astoundingly large as to alarm all good men."

Likewise, James Gilbert (1986) suggests that popular magazines like *Life* and the *Saturday Evening Post,* in addition to popular films, were common vehicles for such discourse in the 1950s. Specifically, James Garbarino (2001, p. 83) notes a *Saturday Evening Post* article in which a child psychologist writes of "youngsters under 16 who rob at the point of a gun, push dope, rape and kill."

Partially reflecting more popular concerns of the decade, some academics turned to the study of news discourse and youth crime in the 1990s. Deena Haydon and Phil Scraton (2000) described a case in England in which two ten-year-olds, Jon Venables and Robert Thompson, were convicted in adult court and sentenced to prison for the murder of two-year-old James Bulger. Colomy and Greiner (2004) examined how the Denver media presented violent youth during the local 1993 "summer of violence." Jennifer Ogle, Molly Eckman, and Catherine Leslie (2003) considered how press coverage of the Columbine shootings sought to frame the incident and propose its solution. Finally, Ann Herda-Rapp (2003) explored how local media interpreted their own school violence threat in the context of national news constructions of the problem. These recent studies of youth violence suggest that media discourse portrays violent *youth* in ways sometimes quite similar to its portrayal of violent *adults.* For example, both Colomy and Greiner (2004) and Haydon and Scraton (2000) illustrate how youth violence is cast as a threat to the moral and social order. The media often demonize violent youth, framing them as acting randomly and without conscience (Colomy and Greiner 2000), and media campaigns often lead to important changes in juvenile and criminal justice policies (Colomy and Greiner 2000; Haydon and Scraton 2000; Herda-Rapp 2003). However, in other significant ways, how the media talked about youth violence in the 1990s differed quite a bit from how it constructed other violence problems.

The Social Construction of Youth Violence

In the chapters that follow, I demonstrate how the media constructed youth violence as a complex phenomenon attributable to multiple causes and solutions. Far from decontextualizing this violence, it probed almost every conceivable aspect of the social and cultural lives of these kids. The condition of youth violence was construed as a paradox in which the malevolence of the violence was juxtaposed against the youthful status of those committing it. The problem was framed and reframed over the course of the 1990s, as if we were facing not a single problem, but multiple ones that changed constantly. Even as the victims of this violence were consistently portrayed as innocents and their deaths as tragedies, violent youth themselves were cast in complex and equivocal ways, as *both* victims and as victimizers. They were to be held culpable for their acts. Their violence was almost always premeditated and intentional. However, at the same time, a plethora of causal accounts located the origins of this violence in their families, neighborhoods or communities, and even in our general culture. Extensive as these causal accounts were, talk often suggested we may not *ever* know why these kids were killing. In this way, youth violence was perhaps more of a mystery than it was a paradox. A host of complex and ambivalent emotions attended these images of youth violence and violent youth. These were, after all, just kids, so they were to be afforded some degree of sympathy and pity. However, this pity was always equivocal. The violence they committed spawned both fear and anger. What they did was horrible. In addition, how could anyone sympathize with violent youth while feeling compassion for their victims? These reactions resemble what Michael Adorjan (2009 and forthcoming) has found in his analysis of discourse on the youth violence problem in Canada. Specifically, he found that violent youth were subjected to emotional contests in which multiple, often conflicting emotions were presented, contested, and resisted (Adorjan, forthcoming). In addition, he also identified complexity and ambiguity in the ways that government officials presented and debated solutions to the problem as part of juvenile crime legislation (Adorjan 2009).

Complexity, uncertainty, and ambivalence in media discussions of youth violence were shaped by a number of broader discourses or cultural understandings that converged on this talk. However, two such discourses deserve special mention at this point. The first comprises a complex set of understandings and beliefs regarding children and youth. The second comprises a long-standing set of beliefs and stereotypes regarding the big city as a social, physical, and cultural place.

Youth as a Social Construction

The concepts of childhood, youth, adolescence, and adulthood refer to various points or stages along a continuum of human physical and psychological development. At the same time, however, they are also social or cultural constructions. These terms do not exist universally, but rather emerge and carry different meanings in certain cultures and at various historical moments. As such, youth and adolescence become social objects to which various meanings are attributed (Barker 2003; Levander and Singley 2003). The concepts of youth and adolescence are relatively new to the Western cultural stage. In the United States, their emergence can be tied to the vast political, economic, cultural, and demographic transformations of the nineteenth century (see, e.g., Aries 1962; Bakan 1971; Bernard and Kurlychek 2010; Empy and Stafford 1991). Prior to this period, adulthood began around the time of puberty. However, with the advent of mass, compulsory education, adulthood was postponed, creating a gap between childhood and adulthood (Barker 2003; Jensen and Rojek 2000). This development was reinforced by the passage of child protection laws that prohibited, or at least curtailed, children's participation in the workforce (Corsaro 1997) and their free time on the streets (Zelizer 1985). As a result of these social forces, children were gradually removed from the world of adults. People we now call teenagers were no longer adults, but historically they had never been considered children. Adolescence emerged as a "cultural space of transition" (Barker 2003, p. 375) that "filled" this gap, and teens began to spend an increasing amount of their time in the home, school, and on playgrounds (Corsaro 1997).

These cultural categories of adolescence in general and youth in particular came to be understood in ways that we now take for granted. Generally, we began to view youth as innocent and vulnerable and, therefore, needing special protection (Aries 1962; Empy and Stafford 1991; Jensen and Rojek 2000). These views form the foundation for almost all our legal and institutional arrangements related to children, such as child welfare laws, educational policies, and the juvenile justice system. These views also make youth ideal victims in social problems discourse (Best 1990; Corsaro 1997; Spencer 2000). Because we take these meanings for granted, they are rarely challenged. Constructionists would say that including youth-as-victims in the discourse about almost any condition carries considerable affective force. For example, it was easy to be emotionally moved in the face of the 1980s discourse about children being abducted, and often killed or raped, by strangers (Best 1990). The emergence of youth in the discourse of homelessness in the 1980s added a significant element to the discovery of the "new" homeless and subsequent policy changes aimed at ameliorating this problem (Spencer 1996; Sisco 2008).

Youth make powerful subjects of social problems discourse for another reason. Discourse about troublesome youth tends to be associated with anxiety about social change. Because youth signify the future of our society, cultural anxieties—especially about the future, social change, and the like—are often expressed as threats to children (Best 1990;

Corsaro 1997; Jenkins 1992). Thus, for example, concerns about technological change may be expressed in discourse about the risk posed to youth by the Internet. Likewise, anxiety about social change (such as an increasingly multicultural society) may be articulated in discourse about the spread of so-called urban problems like crime or gangs to the suburbs and small towns. In their classic treatise on social disorganization, Clifford Shaw and Henry McKay (1942) suggested that traditional systems of social control were weakened by new inventions for transportation and communication, such as the automobile and radio.

Although constructionist studies of social problems may suggest that youth are employed in relatively uniform ways in social problems discourse, the cultural meanings of "youth" are not so simple and unequivocal. At times constructionists seem to view youth as innocent and vulnerable, but there is more to this story. Since its inception, adolescence has been a site of cultural ambiguity, ambivalence, and confusion (Barker 2003; Sibley 1995). As commonly understood in American culture, youth are caught between the worlds of childhood freedom and adult responsibility. Legally, adolescents are accorded some, but certainly not all, adult rights and responsibilities, such as driving, voting, and working. At the same time, however, we require them to attend school and restrict their access to alcohol, tobacco, and R-rated films. But youth and adolescence represent even more than that—they are sites of cultural ambivalence. According to Barker (2003, p. 377), "Youth has become an ideological signifier charged with utopian images of the future. On the other hand it is also commonly feared as a potential threat to existing norms and regulations." In similar fashion, Thomas Hine (1999, p. 11) suggests:

> Our beliefs about teenagers are deeply contradictory: They should be free to become themselves. They need many years of training and study. They know more about the future than adults do. They know hardly anything at all. They ought to know the value of a dollar. They should be protected from the world of work. They are frail, vulnerable creatures. They are children, they are sex fiends. They are the death of culture. They are the hope of us all.

As both Barker and Hine suggest, cultural images of youth connect inextricably to concerns about the present and the future. That being the case, the ways that the cultural meanings of youth function in social problems discourse may be considerably more complex than the extant constructionist literature would have us believe.

Hine (1999), Gillian Brown (2003), Caroline Levander and Carol Singley (2003) and others have argued that many of these cultural discourses find expression particularly in the ways we think and talk about youth and their problems. That youthful misbehavior (variously labeled youth crime, delinquency, and the like) has been a recurring topic of American social problems discourse since at least the early 1800s is instructive. Its *endurance* as a social problem suggests that the misbehavior of youth articulates closely in some ways with salient cultural concerns and beliefs. According to Levander and Singley (2003, p. 3), the child is "a rich and varied site of cultural inscription . . . [that] comes to represent, and often codify, the prevailing ideologies of a given culture or historical period." Gilbert (1986) has made a similar observation regarding discourse about juvenile delinquency in the 1950s. He points out that this discourse reflected a deep-seated anxiety about social change, particularly the growing influence of the mass media. Likewise, Best (1990) notes how the rise of horror fiction featuring child monsters (such as *Rosemary's Baby* or *The Exorcist*) coincided with the youth-centered social crises of the late 1960s and early 1970s. He argues that these horror novels spoke to, or reflected, widespread anxiety regarding youthful rebellion, drug use, and sexual activity. I return to these and other related ideas in later chapters.

Place, Race, and Social Class

Talk about youth violence also appropriated long-standing assumptions and understandings about place, class, and race in American culture. Jeffrey Hadden and Josef Barton (1973) refer to these assumptions as an "anti-urban ideology." According to this ideology, the city is a dangerous place, filled with poverty, slums, and unemployment; rampant crime, vice, and corruption; and incivility and social disorder. Likewise, Lynn Lofland (1998, p. 108) suggests an "anti-urbanism" in which the city is compared to the small town and village: "This juxtapositioning of the moral and physical virtue and purity of small towns and villages and their rural or wilderness surroundings against the moral and physical vileness and pollution of the city is so common a device that each can be evoked by the other *even in the absence of the other.*"

In these understandings, place, race, and class are linked. According to these assumptions, youth violence was *supposed* to be limited to the big city, a place populated by the lower or working classes. Indeed, the first "discovery" of juvenile delinquency in the United States associated it with the urban environment and the immigrant populations that lived there (Bernard and Kurlychek 2010). During the Progressive Era, the middle classes, who were more familiar with the country and small towns, saw the big city and its working-class and lower-class immigrants as strange and dirty. From this era came not only the social problem of delinquency and youth crime (Platt 1977; Schlossman 1977) but a host of other problems, such as drinking, gambling, and prostitution (Abrams 2000; Flanagan 1986). (Indeed, the 1919 constitutional amendment that ushered in Prohibition can be seen as the culmination of a movement that began in the Progressive Era.) Delinquency was seen as so embedded in the physical and social environment of the city that many early solutions to the problem involved removing working-class and lower-class youth from their urban, and family, environments (Bernard and Kurlychek 2010).

Race, place, and class have played a role in the recurring problem of delinquency throughout the twentieth century. The association of youth crime with the big city and its immigrant populations shaped popular discourse until well into the 1940s (Gilbert 1986). The delinquency scare of the 1950s was also largely about class and, by extension, place and race. However, in the mass media, as well as in considerable sociological theorizing, the delinquency-of-concern in the 1950s was being committed by middle-class teens (Gilbert 1986). As manifested in iconic films of that decade (such as *Rebel Without a Cause*), it wasn't just social class—these were largely *white* kids living in the *suburbs*. Similarly, it could be argued that much of the great anxiety about the youthful rebellion of the 1960s was, likewise, about middle-class white kids. Alternatively, the gang problem of the 1980s—whether defined as a *youth* gang problem or not—was largely defined as a lower-class, urban, minority problem.

These cultural assumptions and beliefs were appropriated in 1990s talk about youth violence, in which place, race, and class were conflated. At times, the problem was located in the big city and involved working-class and lower-class minorities (largely African Americans and Hispanics). At other times, youth violence was located somewhere else, specifically in small towns and the suburbs. As juxtaposed against the big-city problem, this other—and at times more mysterious—problem was largely about middle-class white kids. Although at times popular discourse focused on one problem or the other, at other times it combined *both* into one problem. The conflation of place, race, and class allowed talk about one to reference talk about the others. That is, talk about youth violence in the suburbs suggested middle-class violence. Alternatively, talk about the big-city problem implicated lower-class and working-class minorities.

Assembling the Data

With the recent development of online search engines (e.g., Google and Bing) and databases (e.g., LexisNexis, EBSCOhost, Academic Elite), constructionists have found it increasingly easy to identify and assemble large bodies of news discourse for research purposes. However, even before these new technologies became available, constructionist researchers favored news discourse. Compared to other sites or arenas of social discourse (Hilgartner and Bosk 1988), such as testimony before government bodies and entertainment media, news discourse was among the most easily accessed, formatted, and analyzed. In addition, news discourse is a fundamentally *social* discourse. To varying degrees, the public not only attends to it but also participates in it (e.g., in the form of letters to the editor or on talk shows). The news is intimately related to how the public thinks and talks about a problem in other arenas (Gamson and Modigliani 1989; Sasson 1995). Further, the news is tied to popular media such as television and movies. In short, the news both shapes and is shaped by its broader social and cultural context.

As I have suggested above, youthful misbehavior has proven to be a recurring topic of public discourse—searches of the news using LexisNexis turned up a seemingly endless stream of "hits." That was both a curse and a blessing. Certainly, there was no lack of potential data for this project, but the sheer volume of available data forced me to make some hard decisions about how to systematically limit the study. First, I had to make choices regarding the *type* of news sources to focus on. I chose to focus on *national* news sources in both print and broadcast form. Thus, I collected items published in the *New York Times* and the *Washington Post* because these two newspapers carry a large body of stories of both local and national interest. For this reason, I also collected transcripts of stories appearing on the three major television networks (ABC, CBS, and NBC), television "newsmagazine" shows such as *20/20* and *Dateline,* and transcripts from National Public Radio (NPR). I wanted discourse about the origins of this social problem as well as talk about solutions. Although regular news stories contain this sort of talk, Katherine Beckett and Theodore Sasson (2000) and Theodore Sasson (1995) argue that media claims about causes and possible remedies for a crime problem are more likely to be found in newsweeklies and commentary sections of newspapers. Thus, in addition to news articles, I collected letters to the editors and editorials in the two papers. I also collected feature stories published in national newsmagazines such as *Time, Newsweek,* and *US News and World Report.*

I also had to make choices regarding the temporal boundaries of the study. My decision to focus on the 1990s depended on several factors. First, a graduate student I worked with had conducted her master's project on news constructions of youth violence using data from 1994 (Crook 1996). A surge of media interest in youth violence occurred from 1993 to 1994, spurred in part by several high-profile events, beginning with the so-called summer of violence in Denver in 1993, the trial of eleven-year-old Eric Smith for the murder of a four-year-old boy the year before, and the murder of an eleven-year-old girl in Chicago by nine-year-old Robert "Yummy" Sandifer and Sandifer's subsequent murder. In 1994, the *New York Times* published a fifteen-part series on youth violence titled "When Trouble Starts Young" (5/17/94). My student's project uncovered a wealth of interesting findings that promised useful avenues for future research, most notably the concepts of ambiguity and ambivalence. Searching further using LexisNexis, I found additional news discourse on youth violence that appeared to be rich and plentiful and extended in both directions in time. It seemed sensible to include the school shootings of the late 1990s since they garnered so much media attention, which extended the study to the end of the decade. Establishing the temporal boundary on the other end was more difficult. There appears to have been much media discourse in the 1980s about youth gangs and drugs (Best 1999; Reinarman and Levine 1995). News stories about youth gangs did not disappear, but they became less frequent as the 1990s wore on. For example, in 1990 the *New York Times, Washington Post,* and *Los Angeles Times* published at least seventeen stories focusing on youth gangs. By 1993, that number had fallen to ten. Still, the media used the idea of "gangs" to frame the problem of youth violence during the remainder of the decade.

Primarily using LexisNexis, I searched the news sources discussed above, from 1990 through 1999, initially using terms such as "youth violence," "violent youth," "teen violence," and "children and violence." When I found it useful, I also searched on names of specific places, persons, or special terms. For example, to ensure that I was finding all the stories about gangs, I used the term "youth AND gangs" or "youth gangs AND violence." To make sure I had collected all the stories on school shootings, I searched specifically for "school violence" or "school shootings." Likewise, to make sure I had all the stories about a particular school shooting, I might search on "Columbine" or "West Paducah." In one story, I came across a reference to a four-year-old—Eric Morse—who was thrown out of a fourteenth-story window by two other boys. To see if there were other stories about that event, I searched for "Eric Morse." On occasion, these searches would turn up items that appeared in places other than those forming the core database for this study. For example, discourse about the "superpredator" (a term referring to a type of violent young criminal) appeared frequently in news stories around mid-decade. The term was also mentioned in a book by John DiIulio and William Bennett; congressional testimony by DiIulio; and articles published in the *Weekly Standard, Texas Monthly,* and a handful of other print news outlets. I included them in my analysis. As one would expect, stories about the school shootings of 1997–1999 appeared in just about every newspaper in the country. Occasionally, to confirm my readings of the stories in the *Washington Post* and the *New York Times,* I would explore local stories about a shooting in, for example, Springfield, Oregon, or West Paducah, Kentucky. Eventually, this combination of strategies brought me more than 1,500 sources.

The Structure and Argument of the Book

The central themes of this book are that the media constructed youth violence as a rather complex, uncertain, and ambiguous problem and that these images of youth violence reflected the ways our culture came to apprehend the problem more generally. In the following chapters, I explore the various dimensions of these images. In Chapter 2, I examine the construction of the *condition* of youth violence and the person-categories that populate it, focusing first on the juxtaposition of evil and innocence. The evil of the violence was opposed to the innocence of its victims, a familiar opposition in discourse about violence. However, another opposition can be considered—the paradox of the evil and savagery of violent acts committed by otherwise innocent youth. Second, I focus on the ways the problem was cobbled together from otherwise rather disparate phenomena into four frames: youth violence, gang violence, school shootings, and the superpredator. I also explore the rhetoric of crisis, both by using statistics to show how the rate of youth violence was increasing and spreading across social space and by compiling "horror stories" (Johnson 1995) or "atrocity tales" (Best 1990). I show how broader cultural understandings of race, class, and place were used to assert that the problem was spreading beyond familiar boundaries. I argue here that the images of violence associated with minority, lower-class, inner-city youth were problematized by images of white, middle-class, suburban and rural youth. These images call into question our assumptions regarding not only who these violent youth were but also the causes or origins of this violence. Finally, I begin an exploration of the complex array of emotional orientations inspired by this condition. Certainly, there was horror at the savage acts of violence and sympathy for its victims, but also there was ambivalence regarding the offenders themselves—fear and anger over what they did, but also compassion for who they were and how they came to be that way.

In Chapter 3, I turn to the collective search for causes of and solutions to the problem. Causal accounts comprised talk of the multiple and complex origins of the problem, but the specific causes being talked about sometimes depended on what frame was being invoked. More importantly, the causes being discussed depended on whether we were talking about big-city or small-town violence. Accounts of big-city violence fit closely into frames found by Sasson (1995) in public talk about crime and typically comprised a contemporary version of environmentalism (Gilbert 1986) that focused on the social, economic, and cultural surroundings of the city. Alternatively, accounts of suburban and small-town violence focused on psychological factors as well as others often far removed from these environments—specifically, media violence and easy access to guns. Causal accounts of suburban and small-town violence were often hotly contested, whereas environmental accounts of big-city violence were rarely debated. Indeed, they appeared to be taken for granted to such an extent that they were sometimes left unexplicated. Bernard and Kurlychek (2010) have argued that our juvenile justice system cycles through periods of leniency, periods of harshness, and back again. In the 1990s, these two ideologies found simultaneous expression, which affected how the condition and its person-categories were constructed. There were broader cultural forces at work here as well. I use James Hunter's (1991) concept of "culture wars" to understand how the myriad solutions in this discourse were typically parsed into two competing camps—liberal versus conservative. In the context of legal and policy talk, that meant Democrats versus Republicans debating treatment versus punishment. These bifurcations provided a dramatic context to the search for solutions. They were not just alternative solutions; they were *competing* visions and were often treated as so many political tokens to be used in the battle for votes and power. In the news about law and policy debates, discussion of those differing visions allowed stories to do double work—to serve as talk about politics *and* talk about the youth violence problem. Not only did that reflect a tendency to talk about and understand this problem in dichotomous or bifurcated ways, but also it diverted attention from the search for solutions other than those two.

In Chapter 4, I examine the drama of what I call "iconic narratives of youth violence." Iconic narratives are more than relatively short and simple atrocity tales (Best 1990) and horror stories (Johnson 1995). They do not just illustrate the problem; they *symbolize* it. Combining the human interest narrative (e.g., Fine and White 1992) and "hard news," these iconic narratives run for weeks, months, or even years. Their first component—the first stories in the narrative—begins with the event itself and introduces other thematic plots: the violent youth and their victims, the local residents, and the court case. These first stories set the stage—or foundation—for how other plotlines would develop. As the narratives unfold, they explore the biographies of the victims and describe how the local residents are "coping" with the "tragedy." They follow the legal proceedings, in some instances from arrest to arraignment to testimony to final verdict and sentencing. As symbols or icons, these narratives both inform and draw on the more general images of the condition and its various framings, its person-categories, and the emotions discussed in Chapter 3. I also examine how understandings of race, class, and place are overlaid on these aggregate images to produce narratives of "communities" and narratives of "neighborhoods."

In Chapter 5, I explore what lessons we might learn from this study. I examine three main sets of lessons. First, I examine lessons for constructionist studies of social problems and ask three questions: Do uncertainty and ambiguity matter for constructionists? What might we learn about the forms and conditions of uncertainty? How might a focus on place, race, and class inform our analysis of other social problems talk? Second, I examine lessons regarding the ongoing search for long-term, viable policies regarding youth violence and again ask three questions: What policies did we pursue in the 1990s? Did these policies work? What policies could we have pursued and might they have been more viable in the long run? Third, I explore what this book might tell us about civic discourse about youth violence as well as race.

Finally, in Chapter 6, I briefly explore how—in and through public discourse—we are confronting today's challenges regarding youth violence. In what ways does our talk about youth and violence look or sound familiar? In what important ways does it differ from that of the 1990s? Do we still talk about the "gang problem"? In the relative absence of high-profile suburban school shootings, how do we talk about middle-class kids and violence?

2

Constructing the Problem

For several reasons, the problem of youth violence emerged and enjoyed considerable visibility throughout the 1990s. First, there was a seemingly never-ending supply of events (Molotch and Lester 1974; Fishman 1980) that served as its most recent examples or instances (Best 1999). Second, the problem was perceived to be worsening and spreading throughout the social and geographic landscape. Third, talk about the problem constituted a paradox in which the evil and horror of the violence contrasted with the otherwise innocent nature of the youthful offenders and victims. Finally, youth violence was never constructed as a simple or singular phenomenon. Rather, it was framed and constantly reframed as several complex, ambiguous problems involving different sorts of offenders with varying motivations who carried out their violence in different places.

What Sort of Problem Was It?

The concept of *frame* is a useful analytic tool in constructionist work. There are various definitions of the concept, but it is useful here to understand a frame as an interpretive package that organizes talk about a problem. Frames constitute ideas or images that provide meanings attributed to a problem—they define what sort of problem it is (Gamson and Modigliani 1989; Sasson 1995; Tuchman 1978). Four such frames dominated talk about the youth violence problem of the 1990s:

- youth violence,
- gang violence,
- school violence, and
- the superpredator.

Figure 2.1 shows how these frames were deployed over time.

As the figure shows, the school violence and superpredator frames were topics of talk only periodically throughout the decade. The school violence frame was dominant during the first and last thirds of the decade. During the first third, it was primarily cast as a big-city problem, although between 1993 and 1994, there was talk about the problem spreading to small towns and suburbs. Alternatively, during the last third of the decade, it was almost exclusively located in small towns and suburbs. The superpredator frame enjoyed its place on the cultural radar during mid-decade. The gangs frame was a frequent topic of talk for much of the decade, although its salience seemed to decline significantly around the time that school violence returned to prominence after 1997.

Figure 2.1   The Four Frames over Time

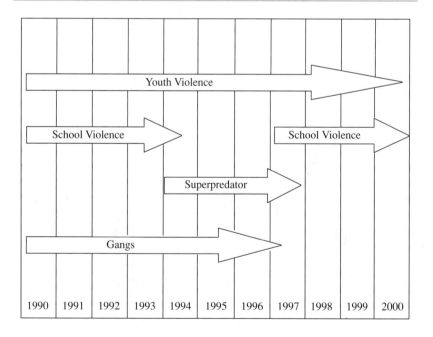

The youth violence frame occupied a salient and constant place in the news over the course of the entire decade.

As ways of talking about—and understanding—the problem, these frames were distinct from isolated events or incidents, although each might be built up from a series of events, and events often served as examples or instances of a frame. These frames comprised four interrelated elements. First, the talk that constituted a frame located the problem in a place or location. Second, it identified or cast violent youth as a particular kind of person. Third, a frame attributed (or searched for) particular motivations to these violent youth. Finally, each of these first three elements was associated with causal accounts and proffered solutions. (I save the discussion of this last element for Chapter 3.) Youth violence was the most general frame, encompassing the widest range of places and violent youth. The other frames—gangs, school violence, and superpredator—were "marked" in the sense that each identified a distinct combination of offenders, places, and motivations. These frames did not compete, at least not in the sense that they stood as contending definitions of the problem. Nor did they seem to replace each other over time, in the sense that one would disappear from talk while giving way to another frame. Rather, in the aggregate these frames constituted a rich, complex mosaic of understanding the problem of youth violence. One might rise and fall from view over time, whereas another might maintain a relatively constant presence. If they competed at all, it was for space or visibility in the media. At times it seemed as if youth violence comprised different sorts of problems simultaneously—for example, a gang *and* a school problem. At other times, we treated them as aspects of a singular problem—as though gang violence and school violence were aspects of the more general problem of youth violence. Let's examine each of these frames in turn.

Youth Violence

The relationship between the youth violence frame and the other three frames was not a simple one. In the sense that this frame was unmarked, it was the most general of the four frames and tended to exhibit the most variation in types of youth, motivations, and location or place. Sometimes, this frame comprised violence that was not framed in any other way. In this way, youth violence was something *not* associated with gangs, schools, or the superpredator. For example, even though gangs were often constructed as organized groups of youth, the youth violence frame might be used to capture groups that were defined as "unorga-nized"—or *not* gangs. A 1990 *New York Times* article told of "maraud-ing groups of violent youths" attacking other youths on their way to and from school in the subway. In this article, "youth violence" was linked to "wilding"—a form of youthful violence that garnered considerable media talk during the late 1980s (Best 1999; Welch, Price, and Yankey 2002). That violence was portrayed as spontaneous and not the result of organized activity. This general frame was also used to define "a national pattern of overt bigotry—ranging from shouted slurs and vandalism to physical violence and death threats—that marks a disturbing decline in civility among American youth" (*US News and World Report* 5/7/90). However, at other times, this frame subsumed one or more of the other three frames. For example, in an NPR story headlined, "Violence Among Youth Called the Epidemic of the '90s" (10/7/93), we learned, "Last year was the most violent in the history of the Philadelphia public schools. A series of shootings and stabbings in the high schools prompted officials to enforce gun-free school zones, increase security, and begin using metal detectors. Philadelphia's not alone in its youth violence problem." The story goes on to cite statistics from the National Education Association on the number of students taking weapons to school or being victimized on school grounds every day. In this excerpt we see that the Philadelphia youth violence problem *includes* violence in school. However, this local problem was not limited to school. The story also recounted the experi-ences of one youth: "The violence this youngster sees in his neighbor-hood often carries over into the very place you'd think he would be safe—school." In this example, the youth violence problem included vi-olence on the streets that surrounded the local schools. Note that this ex-cerpt does not implicate gangs. Although both the gang and youth frames located the violence in the streets (as opposed to, for example, in the schools), here gang violence was organized and youth violence was not. Indeed, the youth violence frame was often invoked by noting the ab-sence of organization. Consider an ABC *Primetime Live* story dated November 19, 1992, which told us guns were becoming an increasing problem in schools:

> Denver, Colorado, 7:30 am. These kids are gathering at a friend's house before going off to classes. . . . These are 14- and 15-year-old gang members. They share a few cigarettes, catch up on the news, and strap on their guns before heading off to school. Gangs aren't the only ones who have joined the arms race. These kids hanging out near a subur-ban junior high in Houston, Texas, *say they're not part of any organ-ized group.* (emphasis added)

The first part of this excerpt links school violence with gangs. However, by noting that the second group of kids was "not part of any organized group," this excerpt seems to invoke the more general youth violence frame. Taken together, these excerpts illustrate some of the various meanings of the youth violence frame: At times, it was a general rubric that encompassed other frames (such as school violence), but at other times, it was an alternative frame (such as when it was *not* gang violence). However, the latter understanding of this frame did not appear to treat it as competing with the others. Indeed, as some of the excerpts above suggest, frames were causally linked, such as when school violence was attributed to the intrusion of gang violence from the surrounding neighborhoods.

In the early years of the 1990s, youth violence mostly comprised local problems in big cities like New York City and Washington, DC. For example, we might learn that a local kid killed another kid and that this was the second such occurrence in the past month. Each was cast as an instance of an emerging—and troubling—trend. As constructed, youth violence was not necessarily new—indeed, this talk seemed to suggest violence in the big city was not surprising. However, now it was growing in both size and severity, as witnessed by a plethora of statistics periodically released by local officials. As talk about these local problems continued, talk about a nationwide problem of youth violence emerged. As early as 1991, stories provided recent statistics attesting to this new national problem, and soon such stories were common. For example, in 1993, a CBS story told us, "In California, a violent crime involving teenagers has a community reeling. And as Bill Lagattuta reports, violence by young people is on the rise across the country" (8/11/93). The story continued, "It's happening across America with a frequency that's chilling. Juvenile arrests for murder increased by 85 percent between 1987 and 1991." On the same newscast, a representative of the American Psychological Association, a member of Save Our Sons and Daughters, and a teenage boy all talked about "violence among America's teen-agers."

Youth violence became a subject for concern in other big cities, such as Chicago, Los Angeles, and Miami. No surprise there: Violence had always been assumed to permeate the big city. However, with increasing frequency, the problem now appeared in mid-sized cities. A 1991 *Newsweek* story told us, "In Milwaukee, for example, where the homicide count has leapt 126 percent in five years, the 1991 tally is up an additional 43 percent" (6/10/91). By 1994, it appeared that youth violence was reaching crisis proportions. The *New York Times* ran a special fifteen-part series titled "When Trouble Starts Young." As billed, it was "the fullest possible examination of crime among the very young" (5/17/94).

Although ostensibly about "crime," the series focused almost exclusively on *violent crime* committed by youth in the United States. Through statistics and individual cases, this series talked about the recent growth of youth violence nationwide, profiled the offenders and their victims, presented its causes, and proffered solutions. By 1996, youth violence was "America's scariest crime problem" (*US News and World Report* 12/23/96). The headline of a 1997 *Washington Post* story read "For Children, an Epidemic of Homicide" (2/7/97)—although it was unclear whether children were the victims or offenders or both. That same year, *People* magazine's cover read "Heartbreaking Crimes: Kids Without a Conscience?" (6/23/97). The inside story began by recounting familiar statistics on the increasing murder rate among teenagers. Using a series of recent cases, the rest of the story told us that "some teens these days are committing crimes of incomprehensible callousness." One such crime involved the "18-year-old high school girl who delivered a baby while attending her prom, left the infant in the trash and returned to the dance."

Although some of these quotes express concern about the rising tide of youth violence, of even greater concern was why and how these youth killed. The circumstances, the places, and the victims varied, but all the perpetrators had one thing in common. As constructed, they all acted with little regard for their victims. They lacked conscience and felt no remorse. They killed at the slightest provocation. From an adult perspective, none of this made sense. They would kill each other over a jacket or a pair of sneakers or for the money to buy sneakers. A boy might die because he quarreled with another boy over a girl. By contrast, adult violence, although deplorable, made sense. Even young gang members killing each other over drug turf made sense. But these kids threw a four-year-old boy out of a fourteenth-story window for refusing to steal candy for them. They killed a pregnant woman simply because she was in the wrong place at the wrong time. They gave birth and left the newborn in a trash can. Much of this would not have made much sense if committed by adults. However, these were the acts of children, some as young as six years old, so they were even less comprehensible.

Gang Violence

The "gang problem" was not new to our cultural landscape. Long associated with urban crime, gangs have periodically appeared as a social problem since the 1840s (Asbury 1927; Johnson 1979; Best 1999). Most recently, gangs had been an object of public concern in the 1980s, especially in association with crack cocaine (Reinarman and Levine 1995).

Perhaps as a result, gangs never appeared to attain the same level of visibility as did the other frames. They were not *new.* Although gangs may have been an object of some concern in the 1990s (Best 1999), the association of gangs with youth violence did not dominate concern over such violence. That said, there was some talk about youth gangs, and in many ways this frame intertwined with the others. As with the other frames, youth gang violence had traditionally been located in the lower-class or working-class areas of big cities and involved minority males. As a result, most of the talk about the problem located it in New York City; the Washington, DC, area; or in some other big city. Such talk was almost always prompted by a recent event such as a violent crime attributed to local gangs or a report on the problem released by local authorities. For example, in 1994 a host of stories related the account of Robert "Yummy" Sandifer in Chicago. In brief, Yummy—a nine-year-old African American boy—was a suspect in the death of a young neighborhood girl. According to these stories, the police found his body several days later and quickly arrested two other young boys for his murder. All three boys were reputedly members of the same gang. Although a story about gangs in Chicago was not all that new, what was particularly notable was Yummy's age. As a CBS headline noted, "Robert Sandifer, Age 11, Sought in Girl's Murder, Becomes Victim of Gang Violence in Chicago" (9/2/94).

This frame was often linked to other sorts of youth violence problems. Consider this excerpt from an NBC report: "The [federal] survey of 10,000 students nationwide indicates only a slight rise in violence or property stolen in schools when compared to 1989 figures. But there are troubling trends. Most are linked to gangs" (4/12/98). As this excerpt illustrated, gangs were linked to school violence, which was "troubling." As with the youth violence frame, gangs were assumed to be primarily a big-city problem. Consider the following excerpt: "Officials in Alexandria and Prince George's County agreed that *Thursday's clash did not involve organized gangs,* but local groups that nurse intense rivalries" (*Washington Post* 3/17/90; emphasis added). In this excerpt, the absence of gangs was *marked,* and that marking appeared to have accomplished two kinds of interpretive work. First, by noting the absence of "organized gangs," it invoked the youth violence frame. Second, and more importantly, it seemed to suggest that we might have otherwise assumed gangs were involved since this violence was located in two areas of Washington, DC, where, according to this talk, gangs were an established problem.

Although instances and official reports might occasion reminders about the problem, since we already "knew" gangs were a problem in the big cities, there seemed little need to devote a lot of talk to it—at least among inner-city, minority male youth. Instead, when the media did talk about gangs as a national problem, they tended to do so in two ways. First, the media talked about the gang problem spreading from its traditional haunts and transforming into a new sort of problem. According to this talk, gangs were beginning to appear in suburbs or small towns, and middle-class white youth were joining gangs. For example, "The US Department of Justice has reported that gangs and their drug operations, having matured in the big cities, have moved into places with smaller populations. Across the country, big-city-style gangs are flourishing in places where their existence seemed unheard of just five years ago" (NPR 7/23/96). The story went on to focus on the gang problem in Odessa, Texas, "which is far from the mean streets of L.A., Chicago, or New York." Another NPR story in 2000, headlined "Problem of Gangs in Rural Areas," related what was by then a familiar theme:

> Western Massachusetts is confronting an unexpected problem. The area is best known for rolling hills and picturesque New England towns. But organized gangs have moved in, and local officials and residents have been caught off guard. Rural communities like Amherst and Leverett are places where people are likely to know their neighbors and not so likely to lock their doors at night. And they're not places where people expect to find gangs. (10/18/00)

The language in both excerpts suggested surprise, even shock, at finding gangs outside the big city. The residents of these small towns and suburbs had been caught off guard. This talk looked the same—as early as 1990 and as late as 2000—and each time it suggested something "new" had happened. This rediscovery was one way to continually make news out of it, but it also suggested a certain reluctance to accept this problem as a routine aspect of the social landscape.

Second, talk about gangs also noted the emerging problem of girls in gangs. For example, the headline of a mid-decade CBS story read, "As the Turn of the Century Approaches, Girls Fast Becoming Members of Gangs" (9/4/96). The story continues, "We're looking at America's future through the eyes of the boys and girls just entering high school. Their tomorrow and ours may depend on the choices they make today as they face all kinds of temptations. One of the most dangerous is gangs, and they're not just for boys." According to a 1999 ABC story,

> You may think gangs are just a phenomenon in big cities. Wrong. Forty-eight hundred places in this country have gang activity, many of

them relatively small towns. In fact, police estimate there are 31,000 gangs operating across the nation with more than 800,000 members. It may surprise you to know that young women make up much of that population. We wanted to understand what draws females into that violent lifestyle. (2/11/99)

Both quotations illustrated how, just as we assumed gangs were a big-city problem, we also assumed that they were only a male problem. The second excerpt suggested we could no longer safely make either of these assumptions.

Why did kids join gangs? The most common explanations were familiar. Lower-class minority youth in the inner city joined gangs for protection. They joined because they lacked a stable home life and the gang provided a surrogate family. They joined gangs following the lure of money from dealing drugs. Likewise, the reasons for gang violence were also familiar: drug dealing and defense of gang "turf" and "honor." Sometimes, as in the youth violence frame, the violence grew out of seemingly minor things:

As dusk settled over East Hartford one day recently, Iran Nazario was at a stop sign near the Charter Oak Terrace housing complex. A pack of teenage boys swaggered by looking poised for action. "I know that look," Mr. Nazario said, nodding at the youngsters as they dipped their way into the projects. "All I'd have to do is give them that look back and say 'Yea,' and they'd be like, 'Man what do you mean, yea,' and before you know it, they'd be tearing into me. It doesn't take much." (*New York Times* 2/23/97)

According to a CBS story on President Bill Clinton's "plan to fight gangs and juvenile crime," "The truth is that all across the country children are still killing children. For shoes, for jackets, for turf, and we can stop it" (2/20/97).

As constructed, girls joined gangs for much the same reasons boys do. The assumption here, of course, was that we were talking about lower-class girls in the big city. Why would white, suburban, middle-class kids join gangs? In a story headlined "Not Just the Inner City: Well-to-Do Join Gangs," the *New York Times* described this new problem as "a dalliance that can be as innocent as a fashion statement or as deadly as hard-core drug dealing and violence. The development seems to defy the usual socioeconomic explanations for the growth of gangs in inner cities and it appears to have caught parents, teachers, and law-enforcement officers off guard" (4/10/90). The story goes on to tell us that sometimes these "affluent white youths" joined gangs for the same reasons their minority counterparts did—"pursuit of the easy money of drugs; self-defense against the spread of established hard-core gangs" and because "well-to-do families in the suburbs can be as empty and loveless as poor families in the inner city." However, these kids also joined gangs because of "a misguided sense of the romance of gangs" and to "shock their parents." Two things are important to note here. First, there was just as much talk about the gang problem outside the big city as there was inside. Second, and related, because it was assumed that gangs were a big-city problem, explanations for big-city gangs provided the standard against which explanations for middle-class gangs were measured.

As we moved on to the second half of the 1990s, this talk of a national problem—occasioned by stories of gangs spreading to the suburbs and small towns—was increasingly found only in the national broadcast media (CBS, NBC, and NPR). Even in these stories, for the most part references to the spread or growth of the problem merely served to occasion talk about solutions. The national media talked more and more about exemplary antigang programs in various places around the country—almost always big cities like Chicago; Washington, DC; New York; or Los Angeles. From time to time, we would hear stories from Texas or Utah or Washington State. In 1997, NPR reported a story titled "Gang Truce" from Washington, DC: "This past week, two rival youth gangs in Washington D.C. agreed to lay down their weapons. The truce was negotiated by a local group called the Alliance of Concerned Black Men, which met several times with the young men" (2/2/97). For their part, the *New York Times* and *Washington Post* still talked about the gang problem—but in the NPR story the problem was distinctly local. This talk about local gangs was almost always occasioned by an instance of violence, the prosecution of a "gang member," or the release of a report by city or county officials. Such stories seemed to serve more as reminders of this troubling problem than as something new. As in the broadcast news, these local stories also reported on solutions to this gang problem. For example, a 1997 *Washington Post* story was headlined "Alexandria Teen Gets 5 Years for Gang-Related Death; Judge Exceeds Sentencing Guidelines in First Major Test of State's Tougher Juvenile Law" (2/28/97). Here, as in other stories, one solution was to get "tougher" with gangs, but a wealth of other possible solutions were available, including truces, jobs programs and after-school programs, nonviolence training, and the like. This talk of solutions and causes is important, and I return to it in Chapter 3. However, my main point here is that amid all the talk about the gang problem, this frame never appeared to enjoy the same currency as another frame—that of school violence.

School Violence

There has been considerable research on the school violence of the 1990s (see, e.g., Newman 2004). It was perhaps the first time in American history that the problem of youth violence (or youthful misbehavior of any form) became so intimately attached to schools. Of course, the signature or defining aspect of this frame was location or place. It is tempting to assume that school violence did not emerge as a social problem until the highly visible shootings that began with Pearl, Mississippi (1997), and quickly came to include West Paducah, Kentucky (1997), Jonesboro, Arkansas (1998), Springfield, Oregon (1998), and, of course, Littleton, Colorado (1999). However, that was not the case. The first reference to school violence appeared in a *New York Times* story in 1990: "An 18-year-old Queens student took a sawed-off shotgun to school yesterday and fired two shells that sent pellets ricocheting through a stairwell, wounding another student and a teacher, police said" (3/6/90). As this excerpt suggests, there was no reference to a more general trend or problem, even a local one. Rather, this event appeared to stand on its own as a perhaps unfortunate but isolated incident. That would change with a *Washington Post* article the following month: "A 16-year-old became the District's latest victim of schoolyard violence yesterday when he was stabbed on the playground of Shaw Junior High School, police said" (4/6/90). As the second excerpt illustrates, *this* was not an isolated incident but rather the latest instance of an emerging problem in the local area. More specifically, according to this story, it was "the third stabbing victim at a junior high school in the District this year." By year's end, and well into the next year, more and more stories referenced increases in school violence in the two cities. Both the *New York Times* and *Washington Post* were talking about the problems plaguing their local school systems—drug dealing and drug use, verbal abuse, incivility and lack of respect, and, of course, physical violence. These problems were being met with tougher disciplinary measures, plans for alternative schools, metal detectors, dress codes, and the introduction of conflict resolution programs.

In 1992, a shooting at Thomas Jefferson High School in Brooklyn left two students dead. The *New York Times* ran a series of stories about the shooting, providing detailed narratives of the actions that led to it, the central characters, and what their motivations may have been. It was the first local event of school violence that received such extensive coverage. Rather than merely tying it to a local problem of violence in New York schools, however—or even a broader national one—the event was also constructed as a cautionary tale of life in the big city: "In the gritty, insular world of East New York, adolescent life can end over a book bag, a snide remark or a betrayal" (*New York Times* 2/27/92). It was clear that this was not so much a problem specific to schools as one of street violence encompassing a specific section of New York City and that the origins of this event—and presumably the problem itself—flowed from the problems plaguing the city itself.

This pattern—individual incidents interspersed with reports of instances of a local problem—continued until an episode of ABC's *Primetime Live* on November 19, 1992, the focus of which was "something every parent needs to know about the growing threat in America's schools." Using hidden cameras, this wide-ranging exposé involved interviews with teachers, administrators, and academic experts on "kids and violence," as well as discussions with youth. Like the more general problem of youth violence, school violence was an "epidemic." Further, like youth violence and gangs, it was not just an inner-city problem, confined to a few gangs in a handful of schools, as most of us had thought. To illustrate the scope of the problem, we were provided examples of this violence in schools from Texas, Colorado, and California. More to the point, ABC reported that "the serious incidents involving weapons on campus have occurred as much in suburban America, if not more so, than many of our inner cities. They are coming to a community near you." According to this same story, in addition to the easy availability of guns, there was, apparently, "plenty of blame to go around—a school system that is underfunded and in desperate need of reform, a collapsing family structure . . . the vacuum gets filled by gangs on the street or images from a culture infatuated with violence."

This national—as opposed to a local—problem emerged slowly. Although there was talk of the spread of the problem to suburbs and small towns, mostly the focus was on the big city. Indeed, the excerpt directly above mentions problems *always* associated with the big city, such as underfunded schools and collapsing families. Early in 1993, the *New York Times* ran a story about a shooting in a school in Grayson, Kentucky, headlined "Two Killed in School Shooting in Kentucky." Obviously, the crime was not committed in New York City—indeed, Grayson was a town of 3,500 people—and this event was not appropriated as an instance of a national problem. Indeed, there was no talk of such a problem—that would happen in a few short months. In April, a fatal stabbing occurred at a high school in Dartmouth, Massachusetts. CBS and the *New York Times* both ran stories using the event to propose that this problem was no longer limited to the big city: "Violence has almost become a way of life in some of the country's big-city schools, but now small towns in America are finding they aren't immune" (CBS 4/15/93). "But people in suburbs and small towns across the nation are increasingly confronting a somber truth about their schools: shootings, stabbings, and assaults are no longer confined to places like New York City, Detroit, and Los Angeles" (*New York Times* 4/21/93). In these stories, the problem of school violence itself was not new. As was common at the time, it was suggested that violence had long been a problem in big-city schools. However, now it was spreading, which appeared to make it more serious and certainly more worthy of attention than when it was limited to "minority kids from the projects" (*New York Times* 4/21/93). Those events that might have previously escaped the media's notice—or at least had been treated as isolated incidents—were now cast as examples of this new problem. In December, CBS reported the following: "And more school violence. In Gilroy, California, where a fifteen-year-old boy is charged with attempted murder in the shooting of another student. Police say the young suspect had been bullied by classmates. The victim is expected to recover" (12/17/93).

Although the event in Gilroy might have appeared in local papers or newscasts just a few months earlier, it is hard to imagine it appearing on a national news broadcast unless the national problem—a "new" problem—had not already been discovered. No one had died. Yet that event seemed to deserve mention as another example of a growing series of such events. Similarly, in June NPR aired a story headlined "Georgia Kids Suspected of Planning Teacher's Murder." According to the story:

> School is out in the southwest Georgia city of Columbus, where the memory of the last days of this school year probably will linger for some time. Last week, seven students, none older than 13, were arrested in connection with what police say was a plot to kill their teacher. While the midsized city of Columbus has had its share of school violence, the young age of these children has drawn national attention to the case. (6/11/93)

Like the event in Gilroy, California, this alleged plot—which did not result in death or even an assault—might have previously passed unmentioned in the national news. However, Columbus, Georgia, was a "midsized city"—one sort of place to which this new problem was said to be spreading—and the suspects were all younger than thirteen. Previous violence had involved older youth, so this instance was noteworthy and might be seen as a new and even more disturbing trend. In fact, this putative trend was part of another story: "The terrifying thing is that the nature of school crimes has grown more violent, the perpetrators steadily younger. A University of Michigan study reports that 9 percent of eighth graders carry a gun, knife or club to school at least once a month" (*US News and World Report* 11/8/93). We were now talking about an "epidemic" of school violence, a plague, a "rising tide" (CBS 12/17/93). National conferences of educators addressed the problem. Increasingly, talk about the nation's schools focused as much on metal detectors, knives, guns, and conflict resolution as it did on educating American youth.

This national problem emerged slowly over a few years, but then it disappeared from our cultural radar for most of 1994–1996. Occasionally, the media might talk about the nationwide problem, as in a story headlined "National League of Cities Survey Indicates School Violence Is Spreading" (CBS 11/02/94). President Clinton suggested that "uniforms might curb school violence" (NPR 2/24/96), which seemed to reference more of a national than a local problem. However, more common were stories about school violence as a local problem, such as a 1994 NPR story headlined "New York Teachers Want Protection from Violent Kids" (5/2/94) or a CBS story that California schools might soon require uniforms in order to reduce "gang violence by keeping gang colors and symbols out of schools" (8/24/94). In both stories, the problem was a local one, and the talk was about local solutions, although certainly the problem was more widespread in California than in New York City. Similarly, a CBS story in 1995 told us of a high school in East St. Louis that required students to show an ID before entering. Here, the talk of youth violence returned to the big city. In this story, as in many earlier stories set in the big city, violence was cast as just one of a number of serious problems in inner cities and their schools. For a few years in the mid-1990s, the national problem that was spreading from the big city fell from view. Two instances of school violence in 1995—one in Blackville, South Carolina, and the other in Lynnville, Tennessee, merited stories but were not linked to renewed talk of a national problem. A 1996 shooting in a school in Moses Lake, Washington, was cast in a *New York Times* story as an isolated event. Although this event prompted several stories in the local papers in Washington State and Oregon, it was not terribly visible in the national media. Likewise, a shooting in a Bethel, Alaska, high school was treated as an isolated event in a handful of stories in the national media.

All that began to change on October 2, 1997, in Pearl, Mississippi, when a teenage boy killed his mother and then went to school, where he killed two students and wounded seven others. This single event made headlines in the *New York Times* and the *Washington Post,* as well as CBS, NBC, ABC, and NPR. Previous school violence had typically been talked about as the work of a single student, but this event was constructed otherwise. Story after story speculated about a "plot" or "conspiracy." As in other social problems, the notion of a conspiracy was compelling (Best 1999). This shooting was the work of a "secret society" (ABC 10/15/97), a "cult" (*New York Times* 10/15/97), or a "satanic campaign" (*New York Times* 10/17/97). Despite all this attention and all the talk, however, the Pearl shooting was *not* treated as an instance of a national problem. Just two months later, a shooting in a West Paducah, Kentucky, high school generated intense media interest. An NPR story suggested that "there are growing fears about an increase in school violence following the killing of three high school girls on Monday. The shootings in Kentucky are just the latest of the past few months. Such incidents have increased recently, but research shows that from 1992 to 1994, cases like these were rare" (12/4/97).

Some of the early stories on West Paducah cast it, as they did with Pearl, as an isolated event. Even though these two recent incidents "raised fears" of a growing national problem, we were assured that "cases like these are rare." Yet a few days later, Americans learned that "President Clinton today took on the problem of violence in schools" (NBC 12/6/97). He had "ordered Government officials to produce an annual report on school violence" (*New York Times* 12/7/97) and stated that these events were a "wake-up call to every parent, every teacher, every religious leader, every student." That sounded like a call to arms to address a national problem. Even though the national death toll wasn't necessarily rising, "something else is new": "The age at which youngsters are bringing weapons to school is becoming younger. It's not simply a high school problem. It's down in the middle school and occasionally in the elementary school" (NBC 12/6/97).

Violent incidents in schools were no longer considered individually: West Paducah was being coupled with Pearl and other similar recent events. It was a problem on a *national* scale. The federal government was getting involved. Experts were talking about national statistics and trends. These trends continued in March 1998 after the school shooting in Jonesboro, Arkansas. Like the ones immediately preceding it, this event garnered considerable media interest. Once again, the media referred to a growing national trend as well as to the youthfulness of the shooters. It was "the fourth multiple killing at a school by a youth under the age of 16 in the last six months" (ABC 3/25/98). A *Washington Post* headline read, "Local Schools Shaken by Killings; Same Could Happen Here, Warn Students, Parents, Educators" (3/26/98). National statistics became an increasingly common part of this talk. According to an NBC story, "This has become all too familiar, of course, in the past half year, kids killing kids. Just last week the White House released a report on violence in America's schools, which in recent years has escalated into terrifying proportions" (3/24/98). However, just two days later, the *Washington Post* reported: "Data gathered around the nation show that the incidence of violence in schools has remained relatively stable over the past two decades, and that the deaths this week are a horrific aberration" (3/26/98). A *Newsweek* cover story recounted the growing list of recent school shootings and added "like adult homicide, the number of killings by kids 17 or younger has actually declined nearly a third since the early 1990s. And a new report from the US Department of Education suggests that violence is still mercifully rare in the nation's schools" (4/6/98).

The *Newsweek* and *Washington Post* stories appeared to contradict the NBC report. Was school violence becoming more common, or wasn't it? Were rates increasing or declining? The contradiction went unnoticed—as if it were a statistical artifact. One way or the other, violence in schools was clearly—once again—a national problem. We were talking about trends and the statistics and events that illustrated them. Much of this talk included an almost obligatory inventory of recent events: "Over the past two years, boys as young as 14 have mowed down classmates or teachers in Pacudah, Ky.; Pearl, Miss.; Moses Lake, Wash.; and Bethel, Alaska" (*Newsweek* 4/6/98). In testimony before the House Subcommittee on Early Childhood Education, Youth, and Families in 1998, the executive director of the National School Safety Center recounted an even longer list that included Grayson, Olathe, Blackville, Lynnville, Moses Lake, Bethel, Jonesboro, Pearl, West Paducah, and now Edinboro (4/28/98). What is noteworthy about both of these reports is that they included school shootings in Grayson, Moses Lake, and Lynnville, which, as I noted above, did not seem to generate much, if any, national attention when they occurred. Changing definitions of the importance of past events are reminiscent of what ethnomethodologists have called "retrospective interpretation" (Garfinkel 1956), which refers to a process in which past behavior or events are "continually evaluated to coincide with the current situation" (Cavaglion 2009). In this case, before there was a "problem," events such as Grayson or Lynnville were merely incidents, but after the emergence of that problem, they and similar events became instances. The emergence of the problem served to redefine these events, and, in turn, these events reinforced the gravity of the problem.

With the rediscovery of this national problem, talk emerged about the origins of these shootings. These events were no small mystery: "The shootings in Jonesboro, Ark., on Tuesday—coming only a few months after multiple shootings in West Paducah, Ky., and Pearl, Miss.—have galvanized public concern about school violence, and left parents, psychiatrists and politicians alike *wondering what prompts youngsters to open fire on their classmates*" (*New York Times* 3/26/98; emphasis added). People speculated about easy access to guns and even a "Southern gun culture" (*New York Times* 3/27/98). Experts on developmental psychology told us about the "harsh growing pains of youth," coupled with a wish for revenge (NBC 3/27/98) fueled by video games and lack of adult supervision.

In May, the shootings in Springfield, Oregon, further intensified concern. According to the *New York Times,* "It is no longer possible to pretend that fatal school shootings are an aberration that can be shrugged off as too hard to control. The latest shooting spree—by a 15-year-old in Springfield, Ore., according to police—cries out for national guidelines to handle these cases" (5/22/98). School shootings were "fast becoming a baffling, tragic new crisis in education" (*Washington Post* 5/23/98). The origins of this "new crisis" were now much broader than media violence, gun access, or teenage angst—we now needed to look more closely at ourselves, our culture. According to President Clinton, "We must face up to the fact that these [school shootings] are more than isolated incidents. They are symptoms of a changing culture" (*Washington Post* 5/24/98). A *Washington Post* editorial suggested that American adults needed to take a good look at themselves. Comparing the recent shootings to the canary in the coal mine, the article claimed that children were "products of a toxic society." More specifically, "We behave in our civic and political lives as though anything goes, so long as it fits our side of the issues. And we are endlessly surprised when our children show themselves to be heartless teasers, graceless winners, bitter losers, self-centered jerks—and occasionally killers" (5/25/98). Annual back-to-school stories beginning in late July 1998 focused on school safety and, as in an NBC story, how the communities of Springfield, Pearl, and West Paducah were doing now that they were about to begin a new school term. By the end of 1998, school violence became increasingly visible in the national discourse on youth violence. By the end of the 1998–1999 school year, yet another event would push this discourse even further. That event occurred, of course, at Columbine High School.

Until this point, as these events accumulated, more and more talk framed the problem as one of school violence (particularly in suburbs and small towns) that cried out for explanation and solutions. Columbine changed the dialogue both quantitatively and qualitatively. It came to be defined as a watershed event. For example, the *Washington Post* said that "we must make Littleton a turning point" (5/12/99), and the *New York Times* called it "a rampage that helped focus national attention" (10/4/99) and a "summons to action" (5/12/99). Columbine even became a warrant for talk that linked school violence to the more general frame of youth violence. The *Washington Post* argued, "'Columbine' has become shorthand for wanton youth violence" (4/13/99). In many important ways, this event—and the more general problem of school violence—quickly became *the* topic of talk. In a *USA Today* listing of the twenty-five biggest news stories of the past quarter century, Columbine ranked eleventh, and Associated Press reporters rated it the second-most-important news story of 1999—second only to the impeachment trial of President Clinton. According to a Pew Research Center survey, Columbine was the most closely followed news story of that year and ranked third among all news stories in the 1990s. This intense coverage of Columbine was shaped in part by the fact that national news outlets arrived on the scene shortly after it began and thus were able to provide live coverage of the event as it unfolded. Another likely factor in this regard was its death toll, which according to most accounts made it the deadliest school shooting in our nation's history. Finally, 1999 had already witnessed a growing crescendo of talk about school violence—indeed, according to the Pew Research Center, the Jonesboro and Springfield shootings were the first and second most closely followed news stories of the preceding year. Columbine may have simply brought another level of concern and urgency to this talk.

How the news media talked about Columbine has been examined extensively by academics (see two special issues of *American Behavioral Scientist,* May and June 2009), and I will not repeat that research here. However, it is important to note that by the end of the decade, "school violence" came to define the youth violence problem in many important ways, and Columbine was at the center of this talk. The media examined what seemed like every conceivable aspect of Columbine and, by extension, school violence in general. A growing number of stories in the *New York Times* and *Washington Post* linked Columbine to respective *local* events and concerns: How did local kids, their parents, and their teachers feel about it? What were local school districts doing to help prevent this sort of thing happening in *our* schools? In turn, talk about "youth violence" was almost always premised by a discussion of Columbine. This talk covered a wide range of possible causal factors—media violence, access to guns, bullying, and family problems. In turn, there was considerable talk about solutions to this new problem, including gun control, ways to mitigate the effect of mass media violence on kids, and of course, stiffer legal sanctions. There was even talk of allowing schools to post the Ten Commandments. Much of this talk had already been going on for years, but it now seemed more intense, and there was much more talk about legislation and the role of the federal government—especially regarding gun control and the mass media. The decade had begun with talk of the local problems of school violence in New York City and Washington, DC, and it ended with talk of a national problem of school violence.

The Strange Case of the Superpredator

On September 22, 1995, a new frame—and a new way of understanding violence among our nation's youth—was introduced with the publication of an article by John J. DiIulio, Jr., in the *Weekly Standard,* a political magazine based in Washington, DC. That article warned of "The Coming of the Super-Predators." Even though DiIulio had already presented the concept in public (e.g., at a district attorneys' association conference in May 1995), the publication of the article marked the introduction of this new problem into wider public discourse. According to the article, we were facing a new kind of juvenile offender who was so violent and so lacking in conscience that seasoned criminal justice workers and even hardened adult convicts were scared. The superpredator was younger and more violent than previous generations of violent youth and was born of a social environment termed "moral poverty": a condition full of "deviant, delinquent, and criminal adults in abusive, violence-ridden, fatherless, Godless, and jobless settings" (p. 25). According to this article, the superpredator problem was going to get worse—much worse. Using a few basic criminological and demographic principles, DiIulio argued that by the year 2000, the United States would have "at least 30,000 more murderers, rapists, and muggers on the streets" (p. 24). The only tractable solution to this impending problem was not the usual government program or policy—"liberal social engineering was bad; conservative social re-engineering will prove worse" (p. 26). We would, of course, need more police, judges, and prisons, but the only real hope of mitigating this problem was religion, and that would require public funding of religious-based programs in orphanages, drug treatment centers, day care centers, and preschools, as well as with regard to "other vital social and economic development functions" (p. 28).

On the same day as the publication of the *Weekly Standard* article, a CBS report announced, "Epidemic of Youth Violence Continues to Explode; Expected to Worsen by 2005." According to the story, "More and more children have guns. They say violent crime is down overall, but not for teenagers. In the last decade, the murder rate for young black males has tripled; it's doubled for young whites. And by all accounts, it won't soon improve" (9/22/95). Some of this talk was, of course, not new. Americans had heard about the rising rates of juvenile violence for several years. However, the CBS report added a second voice to the emerging discourse on the superpredator:

> James Fox, a Northeastern University criminologist, is raising an alarm. There are now 39 million American children under 11 years old, and the majority, Fox says, do not have full-time adult supervision. It's the recipe for a coming crime wave.
> Prof. Fox: I'm predicting that, by the year 2005, we may very well have a bloodbath of teen-age violence.

The talk in this CBS report, as well as in other news stories, was presented in a less academic style than was the *Weekly Standard* story, but the argument was the same: Youth violence was worse than it had been, and it would get even worse. In ten years we would be facing a "bloodbath." The superpredator had found its way into the mainstream news.

The following year William J. Bennett, John J. DiIulio, Jr., and John P. Walters added to this discourse, in a considerably more elaborate form, in a book titled *Body Count: Moral Poverty . . . and How to Win America's War Against Crime and Drugs.* DiIulio's coauthors were well established on the Washington scene. William Bennett had served as the so-called drug czar under President George H. W. Bush and secretary of education under President Ronald Reagan, and Walters had served as Bennett's deputy under Bush. According to *Body Count,* the basic elements of the superpredator problem were the same as those outlined in the original *Weekly Standard* article. The violent juvenile crime problem in the United States—and especially the problem of youth violence— was bad and would get worse. Crime statistics supported that idea, and police and prosecutors confirmed it. Statistics from the FBI's *Uniform Crime Report* were used to demonstrate the increase in violent crime committed by youth, and demographic trends showed us how the number of violent youth would increase in the coming decade. Thus, "A new generation of street criminals is upon us—the youngest, biggest, and baddest generation any society has every known" (p. 26). At several points, we were told that recent polls showed the public was concerned about youth violence. And they *should* be concerned.

These kids—these "superpredators"—were described as "stone-cold" killers, acting impulsively and without remorse (p. 2). The authors suggested that as useful as the statistics on youth violence were, they could not provide a window into the minds of these superpredators. Instead, the authors provided a long line of testimonials by street-level experts such as cops, judges, and victims regarding the behavior and mentality of the superpredator. By interchangeably using terms like "superpredator," "gangbangers," "drug users," "street criminals," and the like, they seemed to want Americans to conclude that *all* youthful violent criminals were superpredators—or least potentially so—and that we were (or would soon be) surrounded by them. The talk of "moral poverty" as the origin of these superpredators was presented as a more valid alternative to what were called "liberal" and "conservative" fallacies regarding crime. Liberals, we were told, blamed poverty, racism, and the availability of guns for crime, whereas conservatives blamed a lenient criminal justice system that didn't deter or incapacitate. The solution to this problem was to be found in a twofold approach focusing on jails and churches that involved locking up serious juvenile offenders to protect law-abiding citizens and relying on community-level, especially faith-based, institutions to provide a moral environment designed to combat moral poverty.

Shortly after the turn of the twenty-first century, the authors predicted that a wave of young, violent criminals would flood our streets. This was classic scientific discourse, filled with statistics and based on two putatively simple facts, each of which was grounded on "well-established" research on violent crime and delinquency. First, citing "scientific kiddie-crime literature," we were presented with a simple formula—"6 percent do 50 percent." That is, 6 percent of any cohort of boys will always account for 50 percent of all serious crimes committed by juveniles. The second fact was that each generation of these crime-prone boys is more dangerous than the one before it. This second "fact" was demonstrated in familiar, popular culture terms: "The difference between the juvenile criminals of the 1950s and those of the 1970s and the 1980s was about the difference between the Sharks and Jets of *West Side*

Story fame and the Bloods and Crips of Los Angeles County." By extension, this new generation of "young male predatory street criminals" would make the Bloods and Crips look tame. However, the problem of the superpredator had "yet begun to crest" (p. 23); it was a "demographic time bomb" (p. 23).

The superpredator would become a decidedly visible image in public discourse from 1996 to 1998, and DiIulio (and to a lesser extent Bennett and Fox) became almost inextricably linked with the concept. He was quoted or named in articles published in *Newsweek, US News and World Report,* and the *New York Times,* as well as stories on CBS, NPR, and even CNBC's *Rivera Live.* Even when DiIulio was not directly cited, the term "superpredator" found its way into more local or specialized outlets such as *Texas Monthly, Nation's Business* (published by the US Chamber of Commerce), *Architectural Record,* and the American Bar Association's *ABA Journal,* as well as magazines and newsletters published by self-defined conservative (e.g., *American Spectator*) and liberal groups (e.g., *American Prospect*). The specific focus of the stories in these secondary media outlets varied. In a *Texas Monthly* article, a local overnight crime spree by two young Hispanic males was presented as an atrocity tale that illustrated the national superpredator problem. An article in the *Architectural Record* offered a critical analysis of the "get tough" response to juvenile crime from the perspective of prison design, suggesting that media hype of the superpredator phenomenon had led to the construction of more and more places to warehouse youth. Observations like that were common during the 1990s, but this article explored the consequences of this hype for the architectural profession. Apparently, this prison boom for kids was not necessarily a good idea. Succinctly put, the question was asked: "Should [architects] design better kid warehouses, get out of the business, or help change the political climate?" (*Architectural Record* 12/98).

Perhaps more significant than the mass media, two congressional hearings in 1996 served as forums for the superpredator discourse. On February 28, 1996, DiIulio testified before the Senate Judiciary Committee regarding "the current state of youth violence, focusing on its changing nature . . . and programs designed to prevent increased violence" ("The Changing Nature of Youth Violence," 1996). On June 27, 1996, the Subcommittee on Crime of the House Judiciary Committee hosted hearings on two bills: *Violent Youth Predator Act of 1996* and *Balanced Juvenile Justice and Crime Prevention Act of 1996.* With all necessary hyperbole, chair Bill McCollum of Florida introduced the pro-

ceedings by telling us that "the coming storm of violent youth crime"—
a "storm of unprecedented proportions"—was the "most pressing law
enforcement issue of our day." We would need to reform an "anachro-
nistic" juvenile justice system to more adequately deal with this coming
"storm." State legislatures had already begun the reformation of their juvenile courts system into a more punitive system, but this act would reform the ways district courts handled juvenile cases by having, under
certain circumstances, the case automatically tried in adult court. In turn,
this act would serve as a model for the states to reform their own juvenile justice systems. Given the title of the act itself, the language used to
characterize violent youth, and the predictions of an imminent tidal wave
of such youth, it is clear that the specter of the superpredator loomed
large over these hearings.

Although much of the talk about the superpredator was new, much
of it also bore a striking resemblance to images of violent youth that pre-
ceded it. The superpredator was cold, calculating, and remorseless and
was born of an environment rife with gangs, delinquency, and crime;
drug use; and abuse. In this respect, at least, the superpredator appropriated and reinforced not only existing imagery of violent youth but also
the assumed link between the big-city and youth violence. The concept
of moral poverty played on long-standing fears of inner cities filled with
poor minorities, gangs, drugs, fatherless families, and wanton street violence. Images of lower-class families harkened back to a 1965 report
titled *The Negro Family: A Case for National Action* (the so-called
Moynihan Report), which portrayed a female-headed, unstable black
family whose sons were growing up without moral steerage because their
mothers were having kids as teenagers and out of wedlock. However, as
originally defined in the *Weekly Standard* article, the poverty described
by DiIulio was not just economic but moral:

> the poverty of being without loving, capable, responsible adults who
> teach you right from wrong. It is the poverty of being without parents
> and other authorities who habituate you to feel joy at others' joy, pain
> at others' pain, happiness when you do right, remorse when you do
> wrong. It is the poverty of growing up in the virtual absence of people
> who teach morality by their own everyday example and who insist that
> you follow suit. (*Weekly Standard* 9/22/95, p. 23)

We had seen these images before, but now we had a name for this
problem and we had a seemingly simple "theory" for its origins. This
imagery found in these hearings, the book, and the news—imagery of

moral poverty, sociopathic youth, and a coming tidal wave of violence—
provided the discourse with much of its rhetorical and affective force.
Testimonials from criminal justice personnel to academic researchers to
victims provided legitimacy or credibility. However, amid all the scientific talk of research and theories and formulas, the discourse was also
about right and wrong, morality and immorality, responsibility and irre-
sponsibility. It was certainly not a discourse of moral pluralism. The title
of the book itself suggested that the United States faced a battle. Reinforcing this metaphor, the words "body count" strongly suggested not
merely a skirmish but an all-out war whose severity could be counted in
the lives that were being, and would be, lost. It was a discourse of child
development, founded on assumptions that children become what they
experience blended with talk of "proper" moral training. In this talk, children who became superpredators were almost feral, lacking feelings for
others and therefore unable to feel remorse for their violent acts.

Although much of this imagery appropriated earlier talk of youth violence, four aspects of the superpredator discourse differed from other
discourse—and frames—and deserve special attention here. First, the superpredator appears to have been the brainchild of a small and select
group of primary claims-makers: DiIulio, Bennett, Fox, and a handful of
others. Second, the superpredator brought years' worth of discourse about
youth violence into sharp relief by focusing and codifying it—providing
specific names for familiar, established images. In doing so, it seemingly
created a new problem. Third, the superpredator discourse was in large
part future-oriented. Although this discourse was partially grounded in
claims about the past and present (that is, it was far worse in the mid-
1990s than in prior decades), its dire predictions about the future were
distinctive. Fourth, even though talk of the other three frames waxed and
waned, they never fully disappeared from public discourse. The superpredator, however, fell from view and did not return. That said, although
we could understand the superpredator as a story of the rise and fall of a
social problem, it is more appropriately read as a story of its rise and putative failure.

In many respects, the superpredator appeared to have all the elements of a long-lived social problem. It gave a specific form—and
forum—to earlier, and quite scary, images of youth violence. In some respects, the image of the superpredator resembled the evil child of popular
fiction fame (such as *The Omen* and *The Bad Seed*) and thus presumably
promised mass appeal. It was a problem that would putatively grow
larger and more menacing until it became a tidal wave of bloodshed

sometime after the turn of the new century. This discourse represented an artful blending of emotions and statistics, of unabashed moral rhetoric and staid academic analysis drawing from credible sources. Science informed the discussion, and criminologists and other experts—usually academics—were often quoted. There were theories and research findings, but the discourse was also impassioned. Consider testimony by DiIulio before the Subcommittee on Crime of the House Judiciary Committee, on June 27, 1996: "The need to rebuild and resurrect the civil society (families, churches, community groups) of high-crime, drug-plagued urban neighborhoods is not an intellectual or research hypothesis that requires testing. It's a moral and social imperative that requires doing— and doing now." There were police officers and district attorneys whose daily work lives brought them into contact with violent offenders. We had hardened criminals, usually doing time in prison for violent crimes, who were scared of these young offenders. And, finally, we had victims and their families who told of the horrors of this violence and its aftermath. These forms of knowledge and expertise gave this discourse a considerable degree of credibility. Further, the forecasts could not be fully tested for close to ten years. This combination of elements seemed to make for a long-lived, highly visible problem. Indeed, it might have provided all the elements necessary for a full-fledged moral panic (Cohen 1980) or scare (Reinarman and Levine 1995). However, that did not happen. By all indications, the problem enjoyed its place in the limelight for no more than a few short years, although the superpredator image would linger in the public discourse for a number of years after that, as would sketchy predictions of an increase in the size of the violence-prone age cohort, described in a 1997 *Washington Post* editorial: "youth violence, particularly homicides committed with guns. The victims, as well as the perpetrators, are largely concentrated among minority males in urban centers, where the risk of being killed in a lifetime is an astonishing one in 25. *That age group will grow over the next 15 years*" (1/05/97).

That said, why was this problem so short-lived? Robert Stallings's (1995) analysis of public discourse about the earthquake threat might provide some hints. He argues that earthquakes are a partially constructed problem (pp. 203–205), which means that although there has been claims-making about this threat as well as policy action, this claims-making has never generated "grassroots" public attention or support. He argues that the future orientation of the claims causes the problem—the threat *may* come to fruition at some point in the future. In other words, it is not happening *now*. Further, he argues that the causes of the earthquake threat are impersonal, suggesting that there isn't much that can be done about it. The future orientation of the superpredator discourse may have had the same effect. This problem, despite its putatively serious nature and consequences, would not reach its apex for another ten years. In addition, its seemingly infallible logic—based as it was on formulas and scientific theory—may have rendered an impression of inevitability. Thus, despite talk about more jails and public funding for faith-based programs, it seemed there wasn't much we could do to prevent the coming bloodbath—all we might do is mitigate its effects.

Also consider the language used to describe the problem of the superpredator. Images of cold, calculating, and remorseless youth had been in the youth violence discourse for much of the decade, but this new problem constituted a "storm" or "army" of teenagers whose violence was like nothing we'd ever seen. We were called to go to all-out "war" against this army. War metaphors abound in discourse about other social problems (Gorelick 1989; Best 1999), but the only time they surfaced in the discourse about youth violence in the 1990s involved talk about superpredators. Strong language and powerful images granted this discourse considerable rhetorical and affective force. However, it is also possible that this discourse did not resonate well with the more general American ambivalence regarding youth violence: We may be scared of our youth; we may fear for their, and our own, future given how they often behave, but also we take great pains to express our desire to nurture and protect them. Perhaps we just could not stomach a "war" against our own kids.

Another factor in the short life of the superpredator was the lack of specific instances of the problem. A report of a violent event in a school was cast as an instance of the school violence frame. An event involving organized groups of youth served as an instance of the gang problem and violence committed by an individual youth was typically cast as an example of the more general youth violence problem. There seemed an unending supply of events that served to keep the other three problem frames "new" or, rather, "newsworthy." However, this left the superpredator without such grounding. It became "old news." The superpredator finally fell from view after reports in 1996–1997 that official rates of youth violence were declining. While these reports sometimes occasioned talk of a lull before the storm, for the most part they were used to declare the end of this putative threat. By 1997, talk of the superpredator had all but disappeared.

Constructing the Condition

A social problem comprises two main elements: a *condition* and the *person-categories* that populate it. As constructed, irrespective of the particular frame being invoked, the condition of youth violence was serious and getting worse. Two metaphors familiar in talk about almost any social problem routinely appeared in this discourse—crisis and epidemic— and together these metaphors captured the sense of the gravity of the condition. Sometimes this crisis was local. Other times, it was national: "The country is facing a *crisis of violence* among young people" (*New York Times* 5/16/94) and "Violence among the young is a *crisis*" (*New York Times* 12/12/94). Talk of solutions also referenced a crisis, as in a 1998 *Washington Post* story headlined "Educators Pursue Solutions to Violence Crisis; As Deadly Sprees Increase, Schools Struggle for Ways to Deal with Student Anger." Here we read that "what was once unthinkable in the classrooms of West Paducah, Ky., or Jonesboro, Ark., and now Springfield, Ore., is fast becoming a baffling, tragic new *crisis* in education" (5/23/98). Violence among youth was also an epidemic:

> "We are witnessing a tragedy of *epidemic* proportions," said Senator Herb Kohl, Democrat of Wisconsin. "A 15-year-old Madison, Wis., girl shooting her teenage boyfriend, the drive-by shooting of a 12-year-old Milwaukee boy, a 14-year-old Milwaukee boy shooting an elderly woman who was walking her dog, an Anacostia student shooting his 13-year-old classmate in the locker room of their junior high, a 4-year-old D.C. girl killed in the crossfire of a brutal gang shootout." (*New York Times* 11/10/93)

Another *New York Times* article reported on a nonviolent conflict resolution program in Chicago schools: "Financed by the National Institute of Mental Health, the Chicago project is only one of thousands of anti-violence programs that have sprung up in schools, clinics, churches and neighborhoods around the country in the past few years in response to the *epidemic* of violence among young people" (12/30/94). According to NPR, an outlet not often given to hyperbole, "People are calling it the *epidemic* of the '90s, and I think—and that's valid. I know at a national level, violence is the leading killer of young African American males. It's a very high leading cause of death for all adolescents, often higher than problems that seem to get more attention, like AIDS" (10/7/93). Metaphors such as these are convenient because they can convey the gravity of the condition in a single word. However, metaphors are accountable; a metaphor must be accompanied by supporting facts. Here, their use was occasioned by, and in turn occasioned, putative "facts" regarding the condition. In other words, it seemed the simple invocation of these metaphors wasn't sufficient—we needed some way of knowing how big this epidemic was or how widespread the crisis had become. Put simply, it was a crisis (or an epidemic) because it was serious and it was getting worse, but in what ways?

When academics talk about how serious a problem is, they often measure it with numbers or statistics. For example, when we talk about crime, we quite often talk about crime rates. Epidemiologists will talk about the incidence rates of a disease. In like fashion, the news quantified youth violence by marshaling numbers to describe almost every conceivable aspect of the condition. In fact, it might be said that at times we were drowning in numbers. There was talk about the numbers of offenders and rates of offending; the numbers of victims or rates of victimization; and how both differed according to race, class, and geographic location. People reiterated how rates had changed over time. The frequency with which numbers were used to describe this problem and the variety of numbers that were used can be seen as a rough indicator of the status of youth violence as a problem. Put simply, the more concerned we were, the more we quantified the problem. Consider the following:

> Last year, researchers at Xavier University in Cincinnati interviewed administrators in 1,261 school systems. Fifty-four percent of the 294 suburban school officials said violence in their schools had gotten worse in the past four years; 43 percent of the 344 small-town officials said violence was up, and 34 percent of the 413 rural officials said the same. (NPR 6/17/93)

In this excerpt, statistics were used to describe the growing severity of the problem. The story provides specific and detailed numbers from a study on school violence, including the sample size and how these numbers vary by type of school district. Of course, not all talk about statistics was so specific and detailed. Much of the time, we were merely told violence rates had increased.

Not only statistics, but also the ages of offenders and victims highlighted the seriousness of the problem:

> The move to lower the age at which juveniles can be tried as adults in Massachusetts began when a judge ruled that a 16-year-old should

be tried as an adult for killing a woman who lived next door. (*US News and World Report* 3/25/96)

The march [the Stand for Children Rally in Washington, DC] comes in the wake of news reports involving very young criminals; a six-year-old boy in California charged with attempted murder in the beating of a one-month-old baby. (NPR 6/1/96)

Indeed, the age of offenders was an almost obligatory part of any atrocity tale about an individual event, and the younger the age, the more horrendous the tale. Surely, violence involving adult offenders and victims was something to be concerned about, but the offenders and victims were *younger* than we had seen before, which rendered the condition much more troubling and serious.

The seriousness of the condition was also captured in more qualitative fashion. For example, in some atrocity tales a violent youth might have accumulated an impressively long arrest record. More common were qualitative comparisons between the contemporary condition and that of some prior time period. As we saw in the superpredator discourse, this generation of youth was more violent than previous cohorts. If the Crips and Bloods of 1980s Los Angeles were more hardened than the Sharks and Jets of *West Side Story,* then the violent youth of the 1990s were worse. In a story about the 1998 school shootings in Jonesboro, Arkansas, we were told: "In the last year, a trail of bloody school-yard shootings had led up to a new definition of school violence. It's no longer about fists or knives or single victims" (CBS 3/25/98). And with a bit of repetition, the *Washington Post* told us "We've gone from fistfights to gunfights" (3/3/96).

Likewise, qualitative descriptions of the growth and spread of youth violence were common. As I suggested above, early in the 1990s the condition was a local one set mostly in New York City and Washington, DC, in stories in the *New York Times* and *Washington Post,* respectively. National broadcast media such as NBC and NPR reported on the condition from other big cities such as Los Angeles, Chicago, or St. Louis. These stories expressed concern about the extent and seriousness of local problems. However, a growing sense of concern was associated with talk about a *national* condition. In three of the four frames—youth violence, gang violence, and school violence—the condition transformed from a local one into a national one. Sometimes the process built gradually on the accumulation of series of events, whereas at other times the national problem seemed to appear overnight. What did it mean to say it was a national problem? In this talk, it appeared to mean something both geographically and socially. Geographically, youth violence no longer appeared in just a few places—rather, it was found throughout the country. It many respects, it seemed to spread from a few big cities to all big cities, then to smaller cities, and ultimately to small towns and suburbs. Socially, the problem was no longer confined to the people who, in this talk, lived in the big city (lower-class and working-class inner-city minorities, almost exclusively African Americans and Hispanics). As the condition spread, violent youth came to include middle-class whites who lived in suburbs or small towns. The recasting of youth violence from a local to a national problem was done largely without the use of statistics, but it was nonetheless powerful talk, perhaps more powerful than numbers alone could have been. I return to this point later in this chapter.

Constructions of Violent Youth and Their Victims

In addition to the condition, the youth violence problem also comprised talk of the person-categories (Loseke 1993) that populated it. In youth violence, as in most social problems, the two most basic and seemingly universal person-categories were victims and their victimizers. As we saw above, there was talk of the numbers of violent youth and rates of victimization. They were almost always boys. However, most of what we learned about these two types of people, we learned in the context of stories about single violent events, usually atrocity tales (Best 1990; Bromley, Shupe, and Ventimiglia 1979) or horror stories (Johnson 1995). These stories were almost always brief—perhaps a few lines or a paragraph—and served to illustrate the problem of youth violence. However, these tales also served to personalize it (Colomy and Greiner 2000) by providing the names, ages, biographies, and other personal attributes of the characters involved.

Work by Holstein and Miller (1990), Loseke (1993), and Loseke and Best (2003) shows us that the term "victim" typically carries some specific semantic baggage. Victims are people who are injured or harmed and in a not inconsequential way. Indeed, this harm is typically serious and often lifelong, even fatal (Johnson 1995). In the ideal case, victims are innocent—they did nothing to bring this harm on themselves—which usually means they did not deserve this harm. So it was with victims of youth violence. Atrocity tales of youth violence established the innocence of its victims and the tragedies of their victimizations. For example, in one tale a sixteen-year-old girl was gang-raped by six teenage boys while traveling from her mother's house to visit her father. Another story illustrated the spread of youth violence from big cities to small towns: "In the middle of a silent country night last August, 17-year-old Michelle Jensen was shot to death. Her body was left along a dusty rural road, near a cornfield not far from the center of the city" (*New York Times* 5/18/94). Other tales provided the grim details of an event, as in the following excerpt from the tale of fourteen-year-old Wilfredo Feliciano: "As he struggled, screaming into the lobby of his building, a slash of the razor-sharp cutter opened an enormous wound across his back. He felt the sting and the blood, and then felt the blade slicing into his forearm" (*New York Times* 12/1/94). From these two tales, we learned the victims were teenagers and were told their names. In the first tale, we were told that the victim was fatally shot and her body left—rather callously—along a country road. In the second tale, we were provided the grim details of the attack. We could almost feel the blade slicing his skin. In these excerpts, the victims' youth mattered, serving to reinforce their innocence. That the first victim was a teenage *girl* reinforced it even further. Other details—such as names, the particulars of the attack, or even the context of the attack—personalized the problem in ways statistics alone could not.

Of course, other types of people were counted among the victims. In one tale, the victim was a pregnant mother of three, and in another the victim was a woman who volunteered as a school crossing guard. In another tale, we were told:

> Charles Conrad didn't have a chance. He was 55 years old, crippled by multiple sclerosis and needed a walker or wheelchair to get around. The boys who allegedly attacked him earlier this month were young— 17, 15 and 14—and they were ruthless. Police say that when Conrad returned to his suburban Atlanta condominium while they were burgling it, the boys did what they had to do. They got rid of him. Permanently. (*Newsweek* 8/2/93)

Charles Conrad was an adult man—the sort of person not normally counted among the victims of youth violence in the news. Adult men are not as easily accorded sympathy as are women and children. However, this adult man was older and physically disabled, and he was only one person counted among the victims of youth violence. Entire families were victims of drive-by gang shootings. Teachers were victims of school violence. In the more high-profile school shootings, the media often provided detailed stories of victims' heroism under fire, their selfless activities, and other features of their backgrounds that rendered them exemplary individuals. If such details did not reinforce their innocence, they certainly established the tragedies of their deaths.

The images of the youthful offenders who populated this problem stood in stark contrast to those of their victims in two respects. First, victimizers often got more press than their victims. Second, in contrast to the simple and singular discourse on victims, the discourse on violent youth was paradoxical and multilayered. Violent youth were simultaneously victimizers *and* victims. When we focused on their acts, they were victimizers: Their violence was intentional, inflicting serious injuries on their victims. Even worse, they appeared to act without remorse and often on the slightest provocation. In those two ways they resembled the superpredator, but the characterization of violent youth as uncaring persisted throughout the 1990s, irrespective of any particular framing of the problem. It bore striking resemblance to cultural portrayals of the adult sociopath—the cold, calculating offender who acted with little or no regard for victims (Spencer 2005). For example, a 1998 *New York Times* story on the recent series of school shootings reported, "We are seeing an increasing number of violent, callous, remorseless juveniles" (6/14/98). Likewise, in a 1999 story headlined "Death in Amarillo," NBC related an atrocity tale in which a "prep" football player stood trial for the murder of a "punk" classmate and received ten years probation rather than the maximum twenty years in prison for the crime. According to the tale, the "prep" had shown no remorse for the killing, which in the eyes of people interviewed for the story rendered the sentence an "injustice," "sent the wrong message," and even "compounded the tragedy" (11/28/99).

When talk focused on their violence, it all but demonized these youth. However, when it focused on their status as youth, they became victims. Adult, especially male, violence is often decontextualized (Johnson 1995; Websdale 1999)—that is, isolated from broader situations. The effect is to limit the violence to the individual offender, resulting in an image of bad, even evil, people doing evil things. That was *not* the case with violent youth. Most atrocity tales provided detailed descriptions of these youth and their lives. Their status as youths was established in a number of ways, almost always by noting their ages, but also through categorical descriptors such as "boy" or "baby." References were made to their physical size and appearance. An eleven-year-old gang member was described as a "4-ft. 8-in., 68-lb. runt of a child" (*Time* 9/9/94). A fourteen-year-old accused of killing a neighborhood four-year-old was described as a "baby-faced teen-ager [with] aviator glasses perched on a freckled nose [lost] in the shadow of the burly deputy who escorted him" (*New York Times* 8/2/94).

Biographical details of their lives often served as causal accounts for their actions. To be sure, those accounts were neither moral nor normative—they did not seem to excuse the violence or render it less horrific. Rather, they provided answers to a central question in this talk: How did these kids—who were supposed to be innocent and vulnerable—come to commit such terrible violence? The answers were varied and plentiful, including gangs, bullying, physical or sexual abuse, family problems, or even psychological problems. Sometimes these kids had been made violent by violence in the movies or television or video games. Sometimes that simply left them numb to violence, led them to see violence as normal or acceptable. In any event, rarely was this violence talked about in the absence of some context.

The resulting image was a duality. These youth were assumed to be naïve and vulnerable, but they also committed violence that was shocking and horrific. That duality was captured in the terms used to describe them. Sometimes they were "lost youth" who had been "robbed of their innocence." A 1997 PBS story on "little criminals" related the case of a six-year-old charged with kicking, punching, and beating a one-month-old baby. According to the story, this "was a case that shattered the very idea of childhood. How could someone so young be so violent?" (5/13/97). A 1996 *New York Times* story headlined "Prison for Young Killers Renews Debate on Saving Society's Lost" followed up on the death of a four-year-old dropped from the fourteenth-story window of a Chicago housing project by two brothers—one ten years old and the other eleven years old. Relating the sentencing of the two brothers, the story describes them as more like "predators" and "hardened criminals" than children. In their defense, these boys had been "ignored, neglected and failed for most of their lives by parents, teachers and social workers" (1/31/96). Finally, consider the simple headline for a 1994 story in *Time* magazine: "Murder in Miniature" (9/19/94). This duality of images is similar to what Johnson (1995) called ironic contrast: a way of portraying a story as a tragic example of "man bites dog." These violent youth were a paradox. They were among the most vulnerable of all of us—the very persons we talked about protecting from such acts of violence—yet they committed acts of horrible violence. They were simultaneously vulnerable and feared, victims and victimizers.

As the evil image of these youth stood in contrast to the image of their innocence, so it stood in contrast to images of their victims. These violent youth were as evil and bad as their victims were good and innocent. Indeed, these two images mutually reinforced each other. The malevolence of the actions of the two young brothers who dropped their victim from a fourteenth-story window contrasted with and reinforced the innocence of their four-year-old victim. The vulnerability of the pregnant mother of two made the actions of her two killers even more depraved.

Ambiguity in Talk About Youth Violence

The central theme of this book is that youth violence, as talked about and understood in the 1990s, constituted a social problem fraught with uncertainty, ambivalence, and ambiguity. In concluding this chapter, I highlight how this complexity manifested in both the condition and the person-categories that populated it: (1) uncertainty regarding the problem itself, (2) ambivalence regarding violent youth, and (3) ambiguity resulting from the conflation of place, race, and social class.

What Problem Was It?

It seems obvious that the problem of youth violence in the 1990s actually comprised multiple problems—a patchwork quilt cobbled together from various frames that themselves were occasioned by unpredictable events. Partly for that reason, the problem stayed on our cultural radar throughout the 1990s—there was always something happening that occasioned talk about violence among youth, and that talk was always about something noteworthy because it was "new"—or rather, "news." That prompts the question raised by Peter Ibarra and John Kitsuse (1993): If the way we frame a condition changes, then doesn't that problematize what the condition "really is"? Constructionist analyses suggest that the dynamics of frames are of two sorts. First, an issue or problem may be reframed. For example, as Best (1999) points out, a problem can be linked to, or piggybacked on, an already existing problem. In the case of stalking, this new "problem" was piggybacked onto the already familiar problem of domestic violence, thereby reframing the older problem in new and more serious terms (Lowney and Best 1995). Second, competing or rival framings of an issue might be proffered by different claims-makers. In their analysis of nuclear power in media discourse, for example, William Gamson and Andre Modigliani (1989) identified several competing frames or packages, each associated with a group or groups with an interest in the nuclear power issue. The progress frame—associated with the nuclear energy industry as well as the government—suggested that even though nuclear power could be used to bring about worldwide destruction, it also promised a future with cheap energy that could bring economic development. That frame was challenged by a variety of other frames, such as the soft paths frame—offered by a number of environmental groups—that argued for alternative forms of energy that were more in harmony with our environment.

Neither of these dynamics seemed to be at work in the case of youth violence. Ibarra and Kitsuse (1993) offer an alternative way of orienting to this situation. They argue that when we find different terms or frames in social problems discourse, it indicates more than alternative understandings of a single phenomenon. Instead, they argue, the use of different language problematizes what the problem is about:

> In the case of the so-called abortion issue, for example, one side dramatizes abortion's status as a symbol of sexual permissiveness and murder. Legalized abortion becomes, in turn, a signifier of a more diffuse sense of moral decay. Is the social condition (or the social problem for that matter) abortion, murder, licentiousness, or moral decay? It is semantically ambiguous, perhaps even, as deconstructionists would say, "undecidable." (p. 27)

That is a useful way to examine the discourse on violence among youth. At times, it was "about" the "problem" of "youth violence"—an unmarked or general sort of problem. However, at other times it was about the problem of "gang violence" or "school violence" or even something called the "superpredator problem." Each of these last three problems was "marked" and thus "about" a relatively specific phenomenon. It is tempting to subsume all that discourse under what would seem the more general—and unmarked—rubric of "youth violence." After all, we were always talking about acts of serious violence committed by youth. When we examine each frame, we see a type of offender committing acts of a particular kind in a particular setting or context and driven by certain motivations; at times, there is considerable continuity across frames.

However, when we looked at this discourse more closely, it appears that rather different sorts of problems were being constructed. At times, one frame or another might dominate media discourse, or a frame might wax and wane in the public limelight. To be sure, as I described in Chapter 1, using "youth" and "violence" as search terms in LexisNexis produced a seemingly never-ending supply of items that often included stories about "gangs" or "schools." Although not a perfect indicator, those search results suggest that the language in the stories often combined ways of describing the problem. Other search terms, however—"gangs" or "schools"—were often just as productive. Empirically, almost all the items produced by these searches contained discourse about youth committing serious acts of violence. However, analytically, the situation is much more complex. It's tempting to treat "gang violence" and "school violence" as alternative framings. But are they alternative (even competing) framings of a single problem or separate problems? At different times, they were treated as alternative framings and at other times as separate problems. Even more troubling, what do we do with the category of "youth violence"? Is it a broader and perhaps more inclusive problem—one that encompasses gangs and schools? The discourse used all three terms: youth violence, gang violence, or even school violence. It was, arguably, three problems in one. Even when these frames intertwined, it was as if one problem infringed upon another, such as when we talked about gangs being found in schools. Thus the media discourse of the 1990s did not use competing frames or a series of changing frames but rather multiple frames that at times existed separately but at other times became entangled. The result was not a condition of youth violence that might, at one time or another, come to be framed or reframed as "gangs" or "school violence." Instead, the result was considerable uncertainty regarding what condition—and problem—was being talking about.

Victims and Their Victimizers

Talk about violent youth and their victims was simultaneously predictable and filled with complexity and ambivalence. Women and children—common victims in social problems talk of all sorts—were recurring characters in this problem. As in most other venues, these victims were constructed as innocents, which makes sense given the ways women and children are commonly viewed in American culture. Compared to adult males, they are assumed to be relatively powerless, vulnerable, and thus deserving of considerable sympathy (Clark 1987; Loseke 1993). Pregnant women and especially young children were viewed as possessing extra innocence. As occasional victims of school violence, teachers were also constructed as selfless and heroic. They led exemplary lives. In atrocity tales, these teachers were dedicated to their students. They were caring beyond the call of duty. They made significant sacrifices for them. In the midst of a school shooting, they put themselves in harm's way to protect their students, often at the cost of their own lives. In this respect, the imagery of the youth violence problem was straightforward. It was a most serious problem, worthy of our considerable concern and anxiety not only because of the growing number of victims but because of who they were.

The imagery of violent youth was not nearly so simple or straightforward as that of victimizers in most other social problems talk (Spencer 2005). First, talk about these youth depended on whether the focus was on their age or their acts (Spencer and Muschert 2009). When the focus was on their status as youth, they were *victims*. They had been abused or bullied, or they had been exposed to violence (both real and virtual). They came from broken families, or they were depressed. Sometimes they were "lost youth" (Spencer 2005) whose innocence had been stolen by tough childhoods. When the focus was on what they had *done,* however, they were in many respects the worse sort of victimizers. They killed other children and pregnant women. They shot and killed students and teachers. They tortured their victims. They were members of gangs or satanic cults or worshiped Hitler. Their violence was intentional, and their intentions were malevolent. Thus, violent youth were simultaneously victims *and* victimizers. Youth violence—and violent youth—constituted a paradox. This condition juxtaposed seemingly incompatible images or ideas. Children were *supposed* to be innocent and vulnerable and playful. They were supposed to be riding bikes or playing sports rather than wielding guns and knives. The more innocent their victims, the more cruel their acts, and the younger they were, the greater the paradox. Certainly, they were the sorts of persons we normally *protect from* the very violence they were committing, not struggling to figure out how to protect us from *them.*

Given these images of violent youth and their victims, it is perhaps unsurprising that talk about the problem was infused with a mixture of complex and often conflicting emotional orientations. Often these emotions were left unstated, meant to be inferred. Such ambivalence typically appeared in talk about the broader condition. For example, as the condition was spreading and growing, it made sense that we were to feel afraid, perhaps even surprised or shocked. However, in the talk that comprised atrocity tales, the malevolence of the offenders and the innocence of their victims came into sharp relief. In so doing, these tales sometimes constructed emotions associated with the problem itself. Here, emotions were typically established in more explicit ways. Sometimes the story told us what the appropriate emotions were, as in an ABC story in the aftermath of the Columbine shootings: "Two teen-age boys filled with rage killed 13 people, *leaving behind a legacy of fear*" (12/17/99). Or as a CBS story put it: "A jogger murdered in New York's Central Park, a little girl gunned down in her family's car in Los Angeles—*crimes like these are terrifying,* partly because they seem to erupt out of nowhere" (9/12/95). At other times, someone close to the event or those with knowledge of such matters told us how they felt. In a 1997 CBS story, an "unidentified girl" was quoted as saying: "I am scared, and I know there's a lot of other people around that are scared, petrified that we don't know who's running around and who could've done such a horrible thing to somebody" (10/1/97). An NBC story provided this summary: "Needless to say, the shooting has left parents and children in Jonesboro *shocked, outraged, and very afraid*" (3/25/98).

The emotions mentioned above are not unlike the emotions surrounding most other violence problems. However, the youthful status of the offenders left Americans feeling more conflicted emotionally. Fear and horror accompanied a host of other, "softer" emotions. Talk about these youth always focused on their age and almost as often on their small size and innocent appearance. How were we supposed to feel? Consider the following two excerpts. The first is from a 1997 *New York Times* story about the shootings in West Paducah, Kentucky:

> Both the town and the school appeared to hold little hatred for the young boy who had brought so much grief to them. At the end of the day, there was a handwritten sign in front of the school that said, "We forgive you, Mike." And all around town there were other signs of sympathy, not just for the families of the victims, but also for the family of Michael Carneal. (12/3/97)

The second excerpt comes from a 1998 NPR story about the Jonesboro shootings. A substitute teacher at the school was quoted as saying that "it's the babies that are dead and babies that did it" (3/26/98). In the same story, a writer for the Associated Press reported: "I helped cover the shootings in West Paducah, Kentucky, in December. And in that case, there was just an immediate outpouring of sympathy and forgiveness for the family of the shooter and the shooter himself." As we see in both excerpts, sympathy was accorded the parents of these violent youth—after all, like the parents of their son's victims, they had lost a child as well. In addition, forgiveness and sympathy were accorded the killers. The second excerpt shows the linking of the killer's youthful status with sympathy: Even when they were violent offenders, "babies" could be accorded "sympathy and forgiveness."

Most of the time, however, sympathy for violent youth was less forthcoming. For example, a 1993 story in *US News and World Report* stated: "Townsfolk share a pervasive fear that Convery's expected defense of insanity—or at least 'extreme emotional disturbance'—will work and that sympathy for 'poor Scott Pennington' will stand in the way of what they consider justice" (11/8/93). Or consider this excerpt from a 1994 *New York Times* story relating the history of the juvenile justice system:

> In earlier times, delinquent children were treated like most other criminals, tried and sometimes jailed with adults or condemned to workhouses or reformatories. By the turn of the century, compassion prevailed as separate juvenile courts were created to intervene in the lives of troubled children. Now, fear is swinging the pendulum back to the days when youth was no protection from stiff punishment. (5/16/94)

In both excerpts, while "compassion" and "sympathy" are mentioned, they appear to be contrasted with other, unexplicated emotions. It seems reasonable to suspect they represent the opposite of compassion: coldness, or at least indifference, if not disdain or hostility. Consider, for example, this excerpt from a 1994 CBS story about a young boy who killed a neighborhood girl and was then killed by his fellow gang members: "The execution-style slaying of an 11-year-old suspected killer is forcing the country to examine the failings of our juvenile system: the failure to protect the Robert Sandifers, and the failure to protect the rest of society from the Robert Sandifers" (9/7/94). What were we to feel about Robert Sandifer? Certainly some degree of fear—we needed to be protected from him and those like him. However, there was more. He had been failed by the system that was supposed to protect him. Didn't that render him a victim? What were we to feel about any other violent youth? The media told us they were young and vulnerable, and thus we might infer that they deserved our compassion, but the tension between what they were and what they had done made sympathy difficult. In most cases they were neither wholly demonized nor painted as entirely sympathetic. And it wasn't true that the innocence of these youth somehow mitigated our fear of or anger toward them. Their youthful status did not provide for a "discount" on our antipathy. In the end, the emotions embedded in this problem were always ambivalent.

Place, Race, and Class

In their study of news reports of school violence, Charles Menifield, Winfield Rose, John Homa, and Anita Cunningham (2000) found that urban and rural school violence were portrayed by the media in quite different ways. Compared to urban violence, stories about rural incidents tended to run on the front page more often, were longer, were accompanied by more photographs, and were more likely to offer explanations. Urban school violence was treated as more commonplace and seemed to need little by way of explanation. Menifield and his colleagues found that these stories made few explicit connections to black teenagers. These findings articulate closely with what I have found more generally across the decade and across the four major frames. Although we deplored the violence in the inner city, we had some understanding of why it happened, and thus it was often unnecessary to offer explanations. Place and race were conflated, so there seemed little need to actually *say* they were minority kids. However, violence outside the big city—in small towns and suburbs—needed explanation precisely because it was unexpected. Because race was implicated in this talk, there seemed little need to explicitly say these were white kids. Of course, in this talk of youth violence, small towns and suburbs were the same kinds of places—they were *not* the big city and they were both populated with the same sorts of kids—and thus were painted with the same brushstrokes.

Early in the 1990s, the problem was largely confined to the big city, but as time went on, it moved from the inner city to suburbs and small towns and changed from a local problem into a national one. The only exception among the youth violence frames was the superpredator. During its short life, the superpredator was always confined to the big city. That was rarely noted, but the images of moral poverty were unmistakably those of the inner city. The spread of violence outside large cities was not merely a geographic change; it was a social and cultural change accompanied by talk about the problem in terms of social class. As a big-city problem, youth violence was understood as a lower-class or working-class phenomenon. However, as the problem grew and spread, it became a middle-class or even an upper-class problem. Middle-class kids were joining gangs in small towns. Suburban and rural schools were no longer immune from violence. As with place and race, this conflation of place and class was sometimes explicit, but most often it was partially hidden.

Not only were place and class conflated, but both were conflated with race. Thus, even when race was not explicitly implicated, in talk about inner-city violence, the implication was clear—these were minority kids. But as the problem spread—and concern increased—it became just as clear that the problem now involved white kids. As conflated, place, class, and race could stand for each other, so that talk about class could also mean race and place. Alternatively, in talk about class and place, the subtext would be race. An important aspect of this conflation is that any of these three could be implicated in this talk but still remain hidden from view. In this way, over and above the four major frames, much of the time it appeared that there were two problems being talked about. Beyond the dimensions of place, race, and class, big-city and suburban or small-town violence were constructed in rather different ways.

This conflation of place, race, and class appropriated, and gave specific meaning to, cultural assumptions and beliefs about the city. Horror stories of big-city violence were replete with vivid descriptions of dirty and dangerous streets. There were abandoned buildings and graffiti and trash on the streets. There were broken homes and abuse. At the same time, this talk appropriated these images of the city; it reinforced them. Certainly, stories about the big-city violence problem reinforced what we already "knew"—that it was a place where violence belonged. It was *expected* there. Although we might be concerned or even horrified at the level and nature of this violence, it seemed there was little surprise.

However, if the city was a dangerous place—filled with chaos and social disorganization—then as the violence spread, what did that say about the small towns and suburbs of the white middle class? Did this talk problematize our assumptions about place, race, and class? Youth violence, gangs, and school violence were not supposed to happen in *these* worlds. Consider the following excerpt from a 1998 *Washington Post* story on the school violence occurring in small towns: "They are all schools in quiet towns where violence is rare, the last places where anyone expects students to explode into a rage, show up with guns and fire ruthlessly at every classmate and teacher in sight" (5/23/98). As constructed, these "quiet towns" like West Paducah and Jonesboro were the "last places" we'd expect this sort of thing. The same could be said, and *was* said, about small towns in upstate New York and the suburbs of New Jersey, where such violence also occurred. If these places were now experiencing the same violence we traditionally associated with the big city, what did that say about these assumptions? Were American assumptions about the white, middle-class world now in question— were we *all* in danger, as President Clinton once claimed, of descending into "chaos"? That violence in small towns involved different sorts of problems than violence in big cities seemed to suggest two different sorts of explanations. The explanations for big-city violence did not seem to work for white, middle-class kids. But it was more than that. The search for an explanation for the latter sort of violence—and for solutions—held more urgency. It is to these two searches—for causal accounts and for solutions—that I now turn.

3

The Search for Explanations and Solutions

Talk of explanations and solutions were a common feature of news discourse about the problem of violence. That should come as no surprise. Social problems, by definition, are conditions serious enough to demand some sort of remedy or solution. Additionally, the problem of youth violence was typically constructed as a paradox that contrasted the evil of the behavior with the presumed innocence of youth. In this way, youth violence often seemed to defy solutions—or at least easy ones. To be sure, solutions talk was a relatively constant fixture in the news throughout the decade. Talk about explanations, however, was different. The visibility and volume of this talk rose and fell over the course of the 1990s. At times, there was a lot of it; at other times, there wasn't. At times, this talk was explicit in stories, whereas at other times it was only embedded in stories of the problem or its solutions. In the latter case, the causes of the problem were left to be inferred.

Causal Accounts: The Search for Explanations

In Chapter 2, I demonstrated how, along several dimensions, youth violence was constructed as a variety of problems. At times it was a local problem, at other times national; sometimes a big-city problem, at other times it was said to have spread beyond the big city to suburbs and small towns. Finally, the problem was variously designated as "youth violence," "gang violence," the "superpredator," or "school violence." Each of these frames, or designations, appeared to enjoy prominence at different times.

In the early years of the decade—roughly from 1990 to 1993—the *New York Times* and *Washington Post* constructed the problem primarily as a local one in their respective cities. Whether it was youth violence generally, or gangs or schools more specifically, little talk offered explicit explanations. However, that didn't mean that Americans were uninterested in finding explanations. In the early years of the decade, causal accounts were mostly found in atrocity tales. Here we found talk that *sought* explanations, and at times the rudiments of an explanation were offered up. Consider, for example, a story relating how youths "saw their friend and classmate fatally stabbed in the subway in December as the result of a dispute that had started with two students simply giving each other hostile looks" (*New York Times* 1/31/90). A *Washington Post* story that same year described a "brawl" involving two groups of youths at a local recreation center: "Although the exact cause of the melee remained uncertain, one thing seemed clear: It wasn't anything much. According to Alexandria police and city officials, Tyrone King died when a teenage dispute—possibly involving a girl, neighborhood pride or a petty drug debt—spun violently out of control" (3/17/90). Both excerpts exemplify talk of how instances "started" or about their "exact cause." Such talk remained either ambiguous or speculative, leaving us to ponder the exact nature of such "hostile looks" or the precipitating factor that "wasn't anything much," but two things seemed clear. First, according to this talk, the seriousness of the violence did not seem to match up to the seemingly mundane nature of its provocation. Second, and perhaps more importantly, such talk did not address the question of *why* it was that such small provocations could result in deadly violence. In other words, this talk begged the question: Why would youth resort to violence over something as simple as a "hostile look"? I suggest that this question was left begging because it was assumed we *already* knew the answer; we took the answer for granted. Consider another example. In 1992 a series of stories focused on a fatal shooting in a Brooklyn high school. In some of the stories, the shooting occasioned talk of a nationwide problem of big-city school violence. In other stories, the focus was on the more local problem in New York City. In either case, the explanation for the shooting could be found in the neighborhood surrounding this school—or *any* big-city school—an environment rife with drugs, gangs, and violence. However, there was precious little talk of *why* these neighborhoods were like this.

Although some causal accounts of youth violence were found in talk of instances, other accounts were found in talk about the problem itself.

In a *New York Times* story of students being attacked going to and from school on the subway, the recently appointed New York City Schools chancellor Joseph Fernandez addressed this problem. In the context of discussing how he was "growing more familiar with the city, . . . Mr. Fernandez said he grew upset when he heard suggestions that poor parents did not care about their children. New Yorkers," he said, "have to develop a deeper understanding of the difficulties faced by young poor mothers who may have been neglected as children and now have trouble dealing with their youngsters" (3/22/90). No *explicit* causal account was offered here, but it was clear the talk described children of poverty. There was no mention of fathers, so we might assume that these children of poverty came from female-headed households. Their mothers were "young" and faced "difficulties" that appeared to have been exacerbated by the neglect they suffered at the hands of their own parents. Once again, all we saw were the rudiments of an account of this local problem of youth violence in the city.

Similarly, talk of the "gang problem" in New York City, Washington, DC, and other large cities delineated the extent and size of the problem but offered little regarding its origins. However, in what proved to be a harbinger of talk yet to come, a 1990 *New York Times* story mentioned "well-to-do" youth joining gangs:

> The development seems to defy the usual socioeconomic explanations for the growth of gangs in inner cities. . . . Police experts and social workers offer an array of reasons: a misguided sense of the romance of gangs; pursuit of the easy money of drugs; self-defense against the spread of established hard-core gangs. And they note that well-to-do families in the suburbs can be as empty and loveless as poor families in the inner city, leaving young people searching for a sense of group identity. (4/10/90)

The first part of this excerpt talked of "the usual socioeconomic explanations" for inner-city gangs without explicitly telling us what they are. As with the excerpts above, the lack of an explicit or detailed account suggested that the explanations might have been assumed. However, the middle-class counterparts to these inner-city gangs did need explanation, and several accounts were offered, including "empty and loveless" families, which, it seemed, was something we already knew about the inner cities but not about the suburbs.

The pattern we saw in this last excerpt continued through 1993 in the context of growing talk of the spread of youth violence beyond the big city. For example, a *New York Times* story reported the spread of violence to "suburban and rural schools":

> Bullying, threatening and fighting have been facts of life at schools everywhere, at least as far back as "Tom Brown's School Days." But they are far more pervasive than they used to be, for a variety of reasons; experts cite the increasing number of students growing up in single-parent homes and the great many movies and television shows that feed the impression that striking out against authority is the appropriate way to settle disputes. And with the proliferation of gangs, guns and knives, behavior that was once merely nasty has turned life-threatening. Dartmouth was just the most recent example. (4/21/93)

The first aspect of this account deserving of note was its complexity. In sharp contrast to the earlier accounts of big-city violence, it contained several elements and was set in *historical* context. In the first part, "bullying, threatening and fighting" were identified as having a long history as "facts of life" in schools *everywhere*. What had changed recently was an increase in "single-parent homes" and "movies and television" that define violence as a way to "settle disputes." These two factors, however, did not necessarily explain why the "bullying, threatening and fighting" had turned deadly. That was explained by the "proliferation of gangs, guns, and knives." The reference to "Dartmouth" alluded to a fatal stabbing in a suburban Massachusetts high school widely constructed as an instance of the spread of school violence beyond the confines of the inner city. In short, this excerpt was about a growing national problem—a problem that was "everywhere," including Dartmouth.

In the early months of 1994, more talk emerged about youth violence as a growing national problem. Much of it located the problem in big and midsize cities. In this context, we witnessed the emergence of a *cultural* account of youth violence. For example, on CBS's *Face the Nation* (1/2/94), two such causal explanations were offered. According to one account, "Violence is now glamorous and popular. Children admire violence. That's the way we've raised them. We've got to change that." In another story offered in the same broadcast, the notion that "Americans loved their children" was critiqued as nothing more than "rhetoric." Although we might love our *own* children, our concern did not extend to children of *other* families. In the context of talk about the spread of the problem beyond the city, it is tempting to read that statement in terms of place, race, and class: that "our" meant middle-class suburban whites and "other" meant lower-class and working-class urban minorities. I return to this discussion in Chapter 4. For the moment, it is important to note that both these accounts illustrate a more general cultural way of explaining the problem—one that has to do with a general acceptance of violence, how "we've raised" our children, or with a culture that did not value children. This sort of account was sometimes extended, as in a CBS story (4/14/94) in which the Montana attorney general used a recent school shooting in his state as an occasion to address the "myth" that youth violence was a big-city problem: "I think, as a society, we have to address the fact that violence is an acceptable response, and it's becoming so at younger and younger ages. We have dysfunctional families, troubled youths who come from difficult backgrounds." As in earlier excerpts, the notion that violence was an "acceptable response" was again being implicated in the problem, as were "dysfunctional families" and "difficult backgrounds." Remember that these factors were being talked about in the context of the spread of the problem beyond the big city. The implication seems to be that the factors historically associated with big-city violence were now being found in suburbs and, in this instance, rural areas.

In 1994, the *New York Times* fifteen-part special series, "When Trouble Starts Young" (WTSY) (5/17/94), devoted a significant amount of column space to the problem. These stories were unique. Other than magazines such as *Newsweek* and *US News and World Report,* few periodicals had offered anything in the way of systematic and detailed descriptions of the "growing" problem of youth violence. And there was even less talk of big-city violence. In this series, the problem was almost exclusively populated by big-city, lower-class, minority youth. What earlier accounts left unsaid or assumed, WTSY articulated in vivid detail. The first installment of the series offered a horror story of two New York City youths, Jacob and Damien. The term "superpredator" had not yet been coined, but these two youths were portrayed in ways that foreshadowed that frame. The two shot and killed a pregnant mother of two for $20, which they promptly spent on a chili dog and toys. These two boys were born to teenage mothers and raised in a disorganized inner-city neighborhood full of drugs and violence. Later in this story, we read, "The causes are complicated and involve social, moral, and economic shifts in society that make it harder for parents to rear children and harder for children to grow up safely . . . more guns . . . and a culture that glorifies brutish behavior" (*New York Times* 5/16/94). Note that we again see a cultural account—"a culture that glorifies brutish behavior"—coupled with "social, moral, and economic" factors, in addition to "more guns." Later installments of WTSY would implicate children from broken homes "seeking older friends in place of the father they barely know"; parents who were "inconsistent," abusive, and addicted to drugs; the "neighborhood equivalent of an arms race" in which youth got guns because others had them; poverty and unemployment and the lure of the drug trade; and crack addiction, which further weakened the "bonds of family and community" already made frail by all these other factors.

An entire installment of WTSY (12/14/94) was devoted to the effects of televised violence. The notion that drugs, broken families, street violence, and poverty were partially responsible for the problem did not cause controversy. However, there was no lack of debate over whether media violence was implicated. Such debates featured complex arguments and a variety of participants. This installment of WTSY cited Leonard Eron's classic longitudinal study (see Eron et al. 1972) of the effects of exposure to television violence on later aggression. Although Eron and his colleagues were said to stand by their original findings of a connection, other studies, we were told, "have shown no link at all. Further, "those that deal firsthand with youth violence and its consequences: the police, prosecutors, probation officers, and even criminals themselves" seemed to believe this notion was "something made up by social scientists." Perhaps not surprisingly, television executives were said to claim that it was "society at large that bears responsibility." The final installments of WTSY focused primarily on the causes of, and especially solutions to, the problem. We were told once again that this "violence has complex roots" (12/30/94), and all the usual suspects were offered up. Over the course of the year, WTSY generated more than its fair share of letters to the editor. Some of them contributed new explanations for the problem, whereas others reinforced ones that were already part of the discourse. One letter writer (who happened to be the president of Nike) talked of "the effects of poverty, drugs, and broken families" (5/26/94), and another writer mentioned attention deficit disorder and mental retardation (6/1/94). The director of the American Civil Liberties Union (ACLU) rejected claims that television caused violence in favor of "the easy availability of guns, the loss of hope or relentless deprivation" (6/15/94).

By now, accounts of youth violence were becoming more complex along several dimensions. More and more causal factors were being offered—indeed, with increasing frequency, the problem was being described as "complex." Youth violence wasn't simply the result of access to guns *or* drugs *or* child neglect *or* poverty—it combined these factors. In addition, these accounts now considered *how and why* certain factors resulted in violence. For example, when street violence was offered as a cause of further youth violence, the accounts focused on how kids learned to view violence as an appropriate response to problems or how they resorted to violence simply to defend themselves. Last, and no less important, accounts were now being problematized. Increasingly, they were contested or critiqued, they didn't seem to "work" anymore, or there wasn't enough knowledge to assess them. With increasing frequency, we were told that "poverty" or "economic explanations" did not seem to explain the spread of violence outside of the inner city.

Media violence had become an increasingly common and salient element of causal accounts, which asserted that exposure to media violence desensitized kids to violence. However, with growing regularity, that account was contested by others. Indeed, the earliest causal accounts in 1995 were about media violence. A *Washington Post* story (1/8/95) reported on a PBS episode of *Frontline* that looked at the "link between TV and violence." According to the story, "Television is so pervasive in America that many critics blame it for an increase in violence in the society." Only a few lines later, we read "many writers and programming executives . . . say that television is a scapegoat and merely reflects modern America, a place with millions of guns in private hands." It seemed that no claim regarding the causal role played by media could go unchallenged.

Throughout 1995, the reasons given for violence became, once again, less explicit. Rather than causal accounts being the focus of stories, they were to be inferred from talk of the problem and its solutions. For example, a letter to the editor in the *New York Times* proffered local, neighborhood-based solutions such as youth centers, mentoring, and prevention programs, presumably based on the notion that "youngsters who have productive alternatives do not commit violent crimes" (12/15/95). The implication here seemed to be that kids became violent because they did *not* have productive alternatives. A *Washington Post* story describes a local program in which kids could trade their "violent toys" for "peace certificates" (2/23/95) that could in turn be redeemed for books and fast food. According to the story, these "violent toys" "encourage play at hurting and killing others." An ABC story (9/7/95) on "teen boys battering their girlfriends" mentioned "anger and insecurity" but did not explain why the boys were angry. Another ABC story (9/14/95) featured LeAlan Jones, who with a friend would later produce a Peabody Award–winning documentary about their neighborhood—the public housing projects on the South Side of Chicago. The story provided a "portrait of America told from the inside out" through Jones's own commentary as well as through interviews with people who lived in "our slice of the American pie." This story was not ostensibly about youth violence, but the topic always seemed to be just below the surface. This "slice" of America was full of drugs and guns and fourteen-year-old girls having babies. Fathers did not stick around very long, and kids dropped out of school at a young age. As was common, this portrait of the big city implicitly accounted for the violence endemic in this world without actually coming out and saying so. In a CBS story (10/23/95) about violence in St. Louis schools, one teacher related how the parent of one of her students attacked her. The president of the local school board suggested "this is a problem that needs to go back to parental responsibility. . . . What in the world are you teaching your child if . . . you charge up to the school . . . and strike the teacher?" Once again, there seemed to be no explanation for why these *parents* would act this way.

Talk about the superpredator emerged in 1995. Recall that the superpredator problem was going to be a "tidal wave" of youth violence that would crest by 2005, driven principally by an increase in the numbers of high-risk teenagers. The superpredator frame served as a site where preexisting images of youth violence coalesced. Images that had been part of talk for some years—inner-city, minority youth who killed without remorse—now came together. In much the same way, causal accounts of the superpredator were not necessarily novel; they simply found a new package or frame. They were considerably more explicit and detailed than those offered in prior years—especially those offered for big-city violence. For example, in a CBS story cited above, we were told "More and more, children have guns" and also "they have far too much time to kill" (that pun did not appear to be intended). There was talk of absent fathers and inadequate child-rearing, which was not new. However, in the *Weekly Standard* article, these factors were brought together in a "theory of moral poverty." I discussed this "theory" in Chapter 2, but it bears repeating here: "In the extreme, moral poverty is the poverty of growing up surrounded by deviant, delinquent, and criminal adults in abusive, violence-ridden, fatherless, Godless, and jobless settings." Thus the superpredator frame briefly resurrected causal accounts based on dysfunctional families, guns and drugs, and local environments. However, by mid-1996—as the superpredator receded to the background—causal accounts of the big-city problem of violence became less and less visible.

Beginning in 1997 and continuing into 1998, talk turned from what were by now the usual suspects of broken homes, poverty, street violence, and drugs to different sorts of accounts. Ordinarily, these new accounts were still "complex," but they became increasingly problematized. The sociologist Amatai Etzione suggested that the school shootings in Jonesboro, Arkansas, could be explained by "four or five factors and there's enough blame to go around for practically everybody. Take the ready availability of guns and the upbringing and there's the fact of the movies and there's the absence of parents and the various subcultures" (NPR 4/26/98). In that same story, a "professor of criminology" suggested that the connection between "watching violence on television and committing acts of violence in real life" was not "clear-cut." Guns remained a ubiquitous topic in accounts. Indeed, in a story reporting on the demise of the superpredator, the *New York Times* suggested that "virtually all the increase [in recent years] in homicides by juveniles was attributable to crime committed with handguns, not to a change in the nature of teenagers" (12/10/98). Although guns and broad cultural influences had long been elements of causal accounts, this talk seemed to take on a new flavor, turning cultural influences into regional accounts. Several stories in March 1998 speculated about "gun availability in the South" (NBC 3/27/98) or "southern culture" (ABC 3/29/98). In these accounts, the South was a unique kind of place, where kids grew up around guns and fathers taught their children how to hunt at an early age. In this place, learning how to use a gun was almost a birthright—especially for boys—and it seemed to represent a marker of manhood. However, this sort of regional cultural explanation was a popular topic only for a short period of time and quickly disappeared. The topic of guns, however, remained, albeit embedded in a different sort of talk—with a different edge. For example, on NPR, Scott Simon pondered the following:

> It is impossible, and perhaps irresponsible, to conclude that stricter gun control laws would have necessarily prevented any of this year's schoolyard shootings. But when people a thousand years from now read a few simple facts about us, I wonder, will they notice that as we Americans tell nations that more nuclear bombs in this world make the chance of some disaster greater, we often tell ourselves that more guns in our homes have nothing to do with the disasters that strike in our streets, our homes, and our schoolyards? (5/23/98)

In a *Washington Post* editorial, William Raspberry suggested, after granting that gun access was a factor in the violence: "We behave in our civic and political lives as though anything goes, so long as it fits our side of the issues. And we are endlessly surprised when our children show themselves to be heartless teasers, graceless winners, bitter losers, self-centered jerks—and occasionally killers" (5/25/98). Simon talked of a lack of gun control, and Raspberry lamented a general cultural acceptance of incivility. In one form or another, both accounts had long been part of the discourse on youth and violence. However, as these two excerpts illustrate, talk that implicated them now took on a more *critical* edge—now there seemed to be a profound sense that American culture was hypocritical: We talk arms control in international politics but allow guns to run rampant within our own borders; we behave like "jerks" in our adults lives but expect our kids to somehow do better.

Perhaps more importantly, the causal accounts of the last three years of the decade began to add new elements. On the heels of Jonesboro and previous school shootings, a *New York Times* editorial (3/26/98) asked, "How is it that teen-agers, living among adults and supposedly part of a school community, can become so alienated from life that they will shoot into a crowd?" It went on to suggest that "the fragility of a young personality, anger that goes unnoticed by parents and teachers, easy access to high-powered rifles and an entertainment world that desensitizes some children to death make killing possible. These Jonesboro killings are frightening because those ingredients are everywhere, in good schools and bad, in urban centers and rural enclaves." In an NBC story on the shootings at Pearl, West Paducah, and Jonesboro, the reporter asked, "What's going on in the lives of young people that could lead to this kind of violent outburst?" A therapist answered, "Troubled teen-age boys with hormones raging have learned from music, TV, and movies to deal with being bullied and ostracized by killing" (3/27/98). This rather complex account combined biology, mass media, and bullying. All sorts of new factors were being offered. During the final third of the decade, accounts that had previously included guns and media, as well as poverty, drugs, and family dysfunction, now incorporated teenage alienation, fragile personalities, and "troubled" teens. As these excerpts suggest, it is not clear whether these psychological accounts were referring to *all* teenage boys or just some of them.

What *was* clear, however, was that new accounts were emerging after the shootings at schools in Pearl, West Paducah, Jonesboro, and Springfield. Even though this violence occurred *in schools,* the talk was often about a new kind of *youth* violence and a new kind of violent youth. Older accounts provided little help: This new problem *demanded* an explanation. As a result, the search for new accounts had a decidedly desperate edge to it.

During the first few months of 1999, the talk—and desperation—seemed to have waned. Causal accounts returned to schools, gangs, and youth violence more generally. But that all changed on April 20—when talk came to focus almost exclusively on the shootings at Columbine High School. Once again, the talk was almost frantic, seeking explanations for yet another "horrific tragedy." In many of the accounts occasioned by Columbine, talk focused on patterns said to be common to all the recent shootings. In part because people sought explanations for a specific pattern, much of this talk was about school violence. During this time, "school violence" was used almost interchangeably with "youth violence," but now Columbine itself came to serve as a symbol of a more general and unmarked problem of youth violence. Indeed, almost all the talk about this more general problem cited Columbine as an "impetus" for a search for explanations. As with Jonesboro or Springfield or West Paducah, some of these accounts were specific to Columbine itself. Many stories posed the question "Why?"—that is, why did Eric Harris and Dylan Klebold do this? Goth culture and its local chapter—the "trench-coat mafia"—received considerable attention. Likewise, many accounts focused on "the complex social taxonomy" of the school, the cliques and social hierarchy and inevitable ostracism, teasing, and harassment. The role of the Internet was also a frequent topic of talk, because Harris and Klebold had supposedly learned to make bombs from Internet sites. Some stories asked, "Where were the parents?"—turning Americans' attention to the issue of parental supervision. It is important to note, however, that this last sort of account never gained much popularity. This stands in stark contrast to earlier accounts of big-city youth violence, in which the failure of family and parents was both visible and salient.

Other accounts occasioned by Columbine appeared to generalize to *all* youth. A *New York Times* story began by talking about Littleton but eventually suggested that "kids are affected by a set of factors that is simply mind-boggling in its complexity" (5/4/99). A *Newsweek* story offered an account based on the classic "nature-nurture" argument:

> There isn't one cause. And while that makes stemming the tide of youth violence a lot harder, it also makes it less of an unfathomable mystery. Science has a new understanding of the roots of violence that promises to explain why not every child with access to guns becomes an Eric Harris or a Dylan Klebold, and why not every child who feels ostracized, or who embraces the Goth esthetic, goes on a murderous rampage. The bottom line: you need a particular environment imposed on a particular biology to turn a child into a killer. (5/3/99)

As this excerpt illustrates, biology was becoming a more integral part of these causal accounts. Likewise, NBC's *Dateline* (5/18/99) spent an hour probing the question, "Why are boys always the ones to commit teen violence?" The answer was to be found in "the way our brains are built." However, it wasn't just that *all* boys are wired differently than girls. According to this story, some boys—like Harris and Klebold—had brains that fixated on violence and were less able to control this predisposition. Biology wasn't destiny, however: "We may never know exactly what causes a boy to commit a violent act. And while there are a lot of theories about the biological roots of violence, most now agree it takes a combination of nature and nurture, our biology and our environment together influence aggression." Once again, we view this problem as a mystery, but it seemed we might be on our way to deciphering it. This "nature *and* nurture" account was relatively rare in 1999, although as we have seen above, biology was implicated at times. However, these two sets of excerpts illustrate two important points. First, they show the tendency to use the Columbine shootings to generalize about youth violence more broadly and from two violent youth to all boys. Second, these accounts emphasized complexity, but it comprised different causal factors than earlier accounts based on street violence, family failure, gangs, and drugs.

Not surprisingly, most causal accounts not only focused on Columbine but set that event in the context of the much-talked-about school shootings dating back to 1997. Consider the following excerpt from a *New York Times* story in which, it was concluded "the details of school slaughters follow a pattern." What was that pattern? "Once again, a mixture of heavy firepower, alienated youths whose threats were largely ignored, and popular culture with a violent and nihilistic message is prominent" (4/22/99). A commentary appearing in the *Washington Post* began by noting that all the school shooters were *boys* and continued, "To really help boys, we need to think not only about issues such as the violence they are exposed to and the availability of weapons; we also need to widen the lens and look at their daily lives, both in and out of school, and examine the expectations and messages they get from us" (5/9/99). Here we see a complex causal account comprising guns, troubled youth, and popular culture and, in the second excerpt, gender roles. Added to this mix were the high school clique system, the Internet, Goth subculture, and perhaps even teenage biology.

Although in the aggregate these accounts were rather complex and variegated, in the midst of talk about the complex etiology of youth violence were two *central* factors—the availability of guns and violence in mass media and popular culture. It wasn't just that guns and the media held a prominent or salient place among talk of all the other factors, although they certainly did. Rather, talk tended to focus squarely on one or the other—or both. For example, around May 10, a host of stories appeared about a "White House Summit" called by President Clinton to discuss "the growing problem of youth violence." Clearly, this summit was occasioned by Columbine. According to these stories, Clinton initiated a wide-ranging discussion that covered both causes of and solutions to "a vastly complex societal problem. So many factors were identified—the Internet, movies, parental responsibility, domestic violence, lack of religious faith, a coarsening of the culture" (*New York Times* 5/11/99). However, despite the summit being cast as wide-ranging, most talk about the summit and its aftermath focused on the putative roles played by guns and media in the problem of youth violence. On May 11, CBS asked why President Clinton wasn't "pointing the finger of blame" at Hollywood. Likewise, a *Washington Post* story from May 16 suggested, "After days of targeting the gun industry for its role in facilitating youth violence, President Clinton today took sharp aim at what he said is the other half of the equation: Hollywood." Clinton was "trying to move the national debate beyond whether unwholesome cultural influences or easy access to guns is responsible when young people turn violent." What did that mean? In this story, it meant moving "toward a recognition that the two work in tandem," rather than suggesting other causal factors might be at play.

Accounts based on guns and mass media continued long after the summit had run its course as a news topic. For example, an ABC "special two-hour broadcast on kids and guns," hosted by the White House, addressed "accessibility of kids to guns, parenting, and whether this is a culture that glamorizes violence" (6/4/99). Despite occasional references to other causal factors (such as "parenting" above), in almost all this talk, accounts focusing on "guns" were set against accounts based on "culture," as we see in this headline from a CBS story on June 16: "Democrats Argue Guns Are Killing the Nation's Kids While Republicans Claim It Is Cultural Collapse." On June 20, NPR aired a story on a "summit on school violence" in Colorado. Much of this story focused on "guns" and "violence on TV, in movies and video games." Although most accounts based on "culture" had to do with mass media, they sometimes also included talk of religion and how "we've excluded the religious principle long enough" from public schools. According to the logic of these accounts, America was in the midst of a moral collapse. This collapse was manifested in, and fueled by, two things: a media industry that glorified violence and the removal of religion—and more specifically the Bible—from public schools.

Talk of guns and media continued through the rest of the year. From time to time it would wane briefly, only to reappear in a cluster of stories that were almost always occasioned by political events such as an impending congressional vote on a piece of legislation or a White House announcement of an initiative to combat school violence. For example, from June 8 to June 12, CBS, NBC, ABC and the *Washington Post* all ran stories on a White House proposal that would require teens entering R-rated films to provide proof of age. A range of voices contributed to this flurry of talk—President Clinton, representatives of a national association of theater owners, parents, and teenagers themselves. Later in the same month, a series of votes on a juvenile crime bill in the House of Representatives occasioned a number of stories focused on guns.

During the last half of 1999, three other accounts became interwoven into all this talk of guns and mass media. One account—which we had seen before—focused on the "informal social world of high schools" (*New York Times* 5/30/99). It comprised a variety of cliques and peer groups, all of which had their place in the social hierarchy. These status distinctions were often manifested in teasing, bullying, and ostracism—all of which played a role in the problem of youth violence. According to this account, this world had been a fixture of schools, but recently something about this social world had changed. A *New York Times* story told us "the moods, the cliques, the barely repressed violence" had all changed since the 1950s, and "American society has failed to come to terms with those changes." Using the same account but reaching a different conclusion, a letter writer to the *New York Times* talked of his own experience of being bullied in the early 1970s and suggested that it did not appear things had changed much since then. Still, the writer concluded, if contemporary victims of bullying felt the same way he had, he could understand their violent reactions.

A second account focused attention on teenage mental illness. It resembled earlier ones having to do with teenage alienation and the fragility of teen psyches, but with this difference: Mental illness—primarily in the form of depression—was a common element in most, if not all, of the school shootings over the past three years. It often went undiagnosed or was ignored or explained away by parents and teachers alike. According to a *Time* story occasioned by a school shooting in Conyers, Georgia, "We have suspected for some time that our young people suffer more depression and other mental illness than any previous generation. Perhaps we are now seeing the proof—and the long-term results" (5/31/99). A *Newsweek* commentary suggested, "Let's stop dismissing mental illness in kids as a character flaw" that can be corrected by a "good spanking" (11/29/99).

Third, and no less common, was an account that focused on the connection between teens and adults. As might be expected, this talk ranged far and wide, but at its core was an argument that the problem of youth violence was the result of a failure of teenagers to connect with adults or the adult world. There was considerable talk about parents, and other adults, failing to take active roles in the lives of children. For example, a *Washington Post* story about a youth summit on youth violence held in Denver quoted teens as repeatedly saying that "parents and school administrators alike need to be more supportive, more caring, and more nurturing" (6/20/99). NPR dedicated an entire story (9/20/99) to a study of children's relationships with working parents. In an indirect response to talk that so-called latchkey kids might be more prone to violence and other problem behavior, the story suggested the important thing was that a "parent is really connected to the child, the values that the parent has, and whether they care about the child." A CNN story (10/18/99) echoed such talk. Relating what kids were saying about "why teens resort to violence," the story suggested there were many answers, the most common of which was having supportive adults in their lives—not just parents, but other adults as well. Bill Cosby, who lost his son to youth violence, told us in an ABC interview that the problem had to do with how we raise our boys. An NBC story on August 11, told us of a teenage boy who, much to his parents' unhappy surprise, had a serious drinking problem. The implication appeared to be that parents who think they know their children should think again and should take time to get, and stay, closer to their kids.

The Search for Solutions

The discourse about solutions to the problems of violence among youth was as complex and variegated as that of causal accounts. During the first few years of the 1990s, most of this talk concerned programs and policies used or proposed in response to the local problems of school violence in New York City and Washington, DC, generally "strict" or "tough" disciplinary policies. For example, a *New York Times* story in the Education section talked of a program in a local secondary school that set "very strict rules about violence" (11/7/90). According to the story, "the rules are clear. No fighting, not even 'play fighting.' No threats of fighting or fighting back on or off school grounds." This policy, we were told, had been very successful. A *Washington Post* story dated July 28, 1990, described the discipline program in Prince George County as "the most severe in the region." There was also talk of dress codes, school uniforms, and tighter security. For example, the *Washington Post* reported on a new security plan, occasioned by several incidents of violence in local junior high schools, that included metal detectors (3/21/91), and other stories talked of placing security guards on school campuses. At first, these solutions went largely unchallenged. However, during 1992, as the school violence problem transformed from a local problem in New York City and Washington, DC, to a more general big-city problem, talk of security began to invite some criticism. Stories on NPR and CBS identified a national trend of a "transformation of high schools into fortresses guarded by metal detectors" (NPR 3/1/92), which would make schools "look more and more like prison yards than school yards" (CBS 3/2/92). As these two quotes suggested, there seemed to be a growing disillusionment with this approach, which, it was said, did not address the root causes of the problem. These criticisms aside, metal detectors and guards became closely associated with school violence in the big city. It was as if talk of this sort of solution *assumed* we were talking about big-city schools. In 1993 the Dartmouth school stabbing began to occasion talk of the problem spreading beyond its traditional urban boundaries. According to one story, this event was unexpected because "No graffiti mar the brick walls at Dartmouth. There are no security guards and no metal detectors. There has never been a need for them" (*New York Times* 4/14/93). The following week, another *New York Times* story suggested:

> The rising tide of violence has forced suburban and rural schools, like urban ones, to take a wide variety of new measures to protect themselves and their students. Metal detectors, once largely confined to city schools, are now used in more and more suburban schools. Some districts, like the Cypress-Fairbanks Independent School District near Houston, have gone so far as to form their own police forces. (4/21/93)

Another thread of solutions talk described various programs that taught children and teenagers nonviolent ways of resolving conflicts. This sort of solution was present from very early on. For example, in a series of *New York Times* stories about students being attacked traveling to and from school on the New York City subway system, the city's school district was said to be "exploring setting up programs to teach how to resolve conflicts without violence" (3/22/90). Later that year, a *New York*

Times (12/20/90) story mentioned local "reconciliation" programs, and the *Washington Post* (12/20/90) reported on "conflict resolution." According to these stories, although no data showed such programs were effective, they were catching on both locally and across the nation. A *Washington Post* editorial later that month praised such programs as being "more creative" than disciplinary policies. According to an NPR story in 1993, the National Education Association was calling for Congress to pass a bill that, among other things, would fund programs to "train students how to mediate their own disputes" (1/23/93). Again, the effectiveness of these programs was hard to validate, but according to one principal, "as long as we believe that we're preventing [violent incidents], as many as we can, we have to continue" (NPR 1/23/93). Not only was this sort of solution a pervasive topic of talk, it was, according to many stories, "the most popular" or part of "the best programs" (*New York Times* 4/21/93).

Beginning in 1994 and continuing through 1996, the problem of school violence gave way to the more general "epidemic" of youth violence as well as the rising specter of the superpredator. Somewhat predictably, talk of solutions focusing on school discipline and security policies began to wane. Nonviolent conflict resolution programs also moved from the center of discourse, and what remained joined with emerging talk of a public health approach to solving this new problem. Consider this excerpt from CBS's *Face the Nation* in which Deborah Prothrow-Stith—of the Harvard School of Public Health—said, "What we really need to do is focus also on prevention, and the public health approach says, 'Let's look at ways to teach kids how to handle their anger, teach kids how to get along" (1/2/94). In one sense, we might read this public health approach as a repackaging of earlier solutions based on mediation and conflict resolution training, and in some ways it was. However, it included other elements, such as gun control. What was *most* notable about this new solutions talk was a shift from merely talking about solutions to talking about *debates or conflicts over solutions*. Increasingly, like what happened in talk of causal accounts, solutions were not so much offered as they were *contested*. These contests were constructed along a number of dimensions. The *New York Times* fifteen-part series "When Trouble Starts Young" (1994) contained several instances of this sort of talk. One installment of this series asked what we should do with youth when they are released from institutions. Suggesting that the recidivism rate for these youths was more than 75 percent, this story offered the following: "They must be assigned advocates to lead them along the path of a life in which money comes from work and insults are absorbed without a deadly counter-strike" (12/29/94). The story went on to suggest that this "aftercare" approach did not enjoy much popularity nationally in part because it was new, but mainly because we were already putting our scarce resources toward incarceration and "some critics regard aftercare as coddling." A CBS story (4/15/95), headlined "Violence in Schools Has Many Teachers Afraid," reported on a new federal law that required one-year suspensions for students caught with a gun on school grounds. School districts had until October to comply or lose federal funding. According to the story, some districts around the country were now placing these youths in alternative schools. Some lauded this new policy, but it was also noted that "Advocates for children fear the program will only serve to warehouse children, not rehabilitate them." The story concluded by suggesting, "The debate will only get louder as the government's deadline approaches and as the toll mounts from the front lines in our nation's schools." A *New York Times* story reported:

> The real debate is over solutions. Should the country punish violent youths as it does adults? Should it try to rehabilitate them in boot camps and with counseling or focus on punishment, stiffer sentences and more prisons? Should it punish the parents? Should it focus on prevention with things like anti-violence education or midnight basketball leagues? Should it try to tackle the root causes, the poverty and joblessness that propel some people to violence? Should it look to biology and try to regulate the hormones of violence-prone children? (5/16/94)

The first sentence in this excerpt implied that there was little debate over causal accounts. We all agreed, it appeared, on what was causing the problem. The "real debate" was over what to do about it. As some of these excerpts illustrate, much of this "debate" was actually more of a quandary. Our fear of violent youth led to talk of incarceration, but incarceration had its problems. Mediation had its advocates, but we didn't know if it worked. Aftercare programs seemed an improvement over simple incarceration, but were we being too soft on these kids? Talk of myriad possible causes of youth violence complicated the task of choosing from an equally complex set of potential solutions. How should we—or even could we—conduct our search for solutions to this problem?

In the midst of these changes, talk of the superpredator emerged in 1995. As I suggested in Chapter 2, the superpredator was perhaps the most troubling framing of the problem, and its emergence appeared to add to the fear and anxiety in this talk. The superpredator enjoyed only a short stay as a visible topic in the news, but it appeared to fundamentally shape our talk about solutions. A CBS story (9/22/95) had as its headline: "Epidemic of Youth Violence Continues to Explode; Expected to Worsen by 2005." More and more kids had guns. The murder rate for young black males had tripled and doubled for young whites—and it would not soon improve. The focus of this story was not "why" this was happening, but rather "What should we do about it?" There were two alternatives. According to a "criminal justice expert," "we needed, literally, hundreds of thousands—probably 500,000 new police officers," and "we should spend $30 billion to create an army of new . . . college-educated cops looking out for the good people of the inner city." In contrast, a "criminologist" suggested we take those "billions" and "invest in these kids"—spend the money on programs "to keep kids busy after school." Likewise, in November 1995, *USA Today* reported: "Anti-crime activists say time in 'kiddie jail' is no longer adequate for a nation on the brink of an unprecedented youth crime wave. The problem we're faced with now is that the age at which kids are capable of very serious crimes seems to be marching down" (11/28/95). That implies a reluctance to incarcerate very young kids—even those who commit "very serious crimes." Nonetheless, the specter of a coming "wave" of superpredators occasioned considerable talk of "getting tough" with violent youth—requiring stricter law enforcement, waiving or transferring cases from juvenile to adult court, and sending these kids to adult prisons. However, at the same time—often in the same stories—the practice of sending kids to adult prison was critiqued as a bad idea. As one story suggested, "society might feel better punishing the children who make egregious mistakes, but prison will only harden them and forge a new generation of criminals" (*USA Today* 12/28/95). In June 1996, the Subcommittee on Crime of the US House Judiciary Committee held its hearings on the *Violent Youth Predator Act of 1996*. As I suggested in Chapter 2, these hearings were held under the specter of the superpredator. In his opening statement, chair Bill McCollum of Florida offered his solution:

> When families fail to instill virtue in children, government must be prepared to immediately send a message to those children and their parents that lawbreaking will not be tolerated and that children will be held accountable. To do that will require a complete overhaul of the juvenile justice system. All juveniles who break the law must be subject to a certain punishment. Today, that's simply not the case. The juvenile justice system lacks credibility.

As this and earlier excerpts illustrate, talk of punitive solutions was often grounded in a critique of the juvenile justice system. According to this argument, this juvenile system was not punitive enough; it "coddled" kids; it did not hold them accountable for their behavior.

In the early years of the 1990s, there was considerable talk of prevention programs as an alternative to incarceration or punishment. However, by mid-decade the debate changed, reducing the talk of prevention. Incarceration was now pitted against rehabilitation; punishment was pitted against *treatment*. In a *New York Times* story at the end of 1994, we read of a medium-security facility in New Jersey that housed some of the state's "toughest" violent youth. According to the story, this sort of institution likely did not change the "outlook or behavior" of these youth. It was expensive and by necessity focused more on "confinement" than "therapy" or education. Like many stories during that year, solutions focusing on punishment or incarceration were portrayed as less desirable—that is, less effective and more expensive—than alternatives such as community-based treatment programs. However, it was unclear if these latter programs would be appropriate for these "tough" youth.

Several stories in early 1996 focused on the sentencing of two boys who, two years earlier, had killed a four-year-old by dropping him out of the fourteenth-story window of a Chicago public housing building. These stories linked the sentencing in this case to broader discussions of the causes of and solutions to urban violence. According to the *New York Times,* "How can a society protect itself from its own lost children? Should they be locked up as if they were tiny adults or should they be sent to secure residential treatment centers where they can get intensive counseling? In state after state, including Illinois, the answer has been harsher punishment" (1/31/96). These two boys, though not explicitly identified as such, were portrayed as if they were superpredators. Indeed, without saying so, early stories about them seemed to treat them as poster kids for this problem. As this excerpt illustrates, by 1996, talk had shifted from a debate over prevention versus intervention or punishment to a debate over alternative forms of intervention. Should we punish or rehabilitate? It was as if we had abandoned hope of preventing this violence. As many excerpts suggest, these debates were not simply so much academic talk. These kids were dangerous, and they scared us—gangs ruled the inner-city streets, teachers were afraid to do their jobs, and there was a coming wave of superpredators. We could not afford to simply continue debating solutions; we needed to do something *now.*

Debates over punishment versus rehabilitation or treatment continued into 1997. In a *New York Times* story, charging local teens with murder was said to "stir a debate" over "whether to treat young defendants as children or adults" (5/28/97). The implication seemed to be that treating them as children meant rehabilitating them, and, conversely, treating them as adults meant punishment. Indeed, a *Washington Post* story pitted the "need for deterrence" (implying adult prison) against "some kind of therapeutic service which would be far more available in the juvenile justice system" (10/8/97). We were, in part, debating when and how kids should be placed in the juvenile justice system, as opposed to the adult criminal justice system. In this context, the debate over punishment versus prevention reemerged. For example, early in the year, stories on President Clinton's "crime package" mentioned a debate over whether "to deter youth crime and punish it more severely" or to promote "social initiatives" such as after-school programs and "midnight basketball" (*Washington Post* 2/20/97). A *New York Times* story talked of "tougher laws" and "punishment" as a way to deal with kids who had "no respect for the rules of society." Positioned against this stance was an argument that we needed to "rehabilitate them." However, the same story stated "the real question that needs to be addressed is what conditions in society create these monster kids" (6/22/97), seemingly a nod at prevention programs. In addition to references to effectiveness and costs as criteria for debating these alternatives, increasingly "compassion" was used to advocate rehabilitation programs. Arguments for prevention programs began to suggest that "law enforcement efforts" didn't address the root causes of the problem. Although their prominence waxed and waned, these debates continued through the following year.

Toward the end of 1997, solutions talk again began to change. Recall that in the fall of that year, shootings occurred in Pearl, Mississippi, and West Paducah, Kentucky. Recall that stories cast these events as instances of a putative increase in school violence. At the same time, guns were once again being implicated in causal accounts, and thus gun control was added to the mix of proffered solutions. For example, *US News and World Report* reported that President Clinton had called for "schools to show 'zero tolerance' for guns" (12/15/97). This talk of gun control continued and garnered increasing attention throughout the next two years. Similarly, after-school programs began to assume a more prominent place in this talk. Then, in 1998, school-based nonviolent conflict resolution and security programs reemerged. Although they had been a staple of solutions talk during the early 1990s, they had all but disappeared for years. An NBC story on the Jonesboro school shootings in 1998—cast as yet another instance of the growing trend of school violence—suggested that lessons might be learned from a Los Angeles school that had controlled its gang and violence problem by making "mediation a priority" (NBC 3/26/98). The implication was clear: School violence was now a problem in small towns and suburbs, and solutions that worked in urban settings needed to be considered for this new problem. A series of back-to-school stories in August and September focused on "strict new security measures" (ABC 9/9/98), including how "many school districts are working closely with law enforcement authorities to make their buildings and schoolgrounds more secure" (NPR 9/2/98). As earlier, such talk did not go unchallenged. For example, a *Washington Post* editorial argued that media "hype" over school shootings had resulted in "misdirected public policy" that focused on school security and "get tough" laws rather than programs that "productively occupy our children after school hours and keep them away from handguns" (8/25/98). Punitive solutions such as adjudicating youths in adult court were now being linked with "security" solutions such as guards and metal detectors, and after-school programs were being linked to gun control.

Nonviolent conflict resolution programs became intertwined with, and in some ways gave way to, talk of counseling. That sometimes gave way to the more general ways that we raised our kids *as boys and girls*. We needed to teach our kids how to "think, how to act, how to deal with their anger" (*Washington Post* 5/23/98). According to this talk, because of the ways they were raised, boys and girls dealt with problems in different ways—girls turned inward and engaged in self-destructive behaviors, and boys turned outward with their violence. We were told the solution was that "we have to look at the way we raise boys and encourage them to be sensitive as well as strong" (NBC 3/28/98). NPR told us that "focusing on moral development is the only way to effectively deter this kind of erratic behavior" (3/30/98).

On April 20, 1999—the day of the Columbine school shootings—the landscape changed once again. Perhaps counterintuitively, talk of school security and after-school programs fell into the background, and the debate over "getting tough" versus "rehabilitation" virtually disappeared. Guns remained a visible topic. There was talk of gun control legislation in the nation's capital, including President Clinton's various gun control proposals, which "include charging parents of children who commit gun crimes" (*New York Times* 4/27/99). However, new solutions and new debates emerged. In the immediate aftermath of the shootings at Columbine, much of this talk focused on identifying students who might become violent. For example, a *Washington Post* story claimed that over the past year, more and more schools had installed "tip lines" and encouraged students to call these lines if they knew of classmates who threatened violence. NPR told us, "After Springfield, the Justice Department and the Department of Education put together a guide to help schools detect such children. The handbook lists a number of what it calls early warning signs, including being picked on, removing themselves from the rest of the student body, intolerance of those of other races" (4/21/99). A *Washington Post* editorial (4/22/99) suggested that "parents and teachers should be on the lookout for erratic behavior." There was considerable talk of "early warning signs," and schools were said to be implementing plans to "identify potentially violent students . . . and drafting detailed plans on how to deal with a student who threatens violence" (*Washington Post* 4/21/99). A *New York Times* story (4/22/99) suggested that since schools screen students for vision and hearing, they might as well screen for aggressive behavior. Parents and teachers should be trained to identify the early symptoms of potentially violent youth. Likewise, another *Washington Post* story in April reported more and more schools beginning to "identify potentially violent students, putting more emphasis on conflict resolution programs and drafting detailed plans on how to deal with a student who threatens violence" (4/21/99). Some of this talk went further, suggesting that prevention begin much earlier in life. The *New York Times* suggested that teenage alienation—by now widely identified as a factor in late-1990s school shootings—could be prevented with "early childhood education and careful nurturing" (5/4/99). Similarly, NPR told us "preventative measures need to be started at the kindergarten years" (4/21/99). By the end of the year, and decade, this talk grew into talk of *profiling*. A *New York Times* story in October reported that the Bureau of Alcohol, Tobacco, and Firearms (ATF) was working with a company to develop profiling software to "help administrators spot troubled students who might be near the brink of violence" (10/24/99). According to an ABC broadcast in December, some schools in Illinois had decided to adopt a profiling program in order to "identify violent students" (12/15/99).

Also new, or at least more visible than previously, was talk of how to mitigate the putative influence of media on youth. Although the media had long been a focus of causal accounts, relatively few methods of lessening its influence had been proffered. The *New York Times* (4/26/99) talked of controlling the media in much the same way that the tobacco industry had been controlled. NPR ran a story titled "Senate Commerce Committee Holds Hearings to Determine If Entertainment Industry Is Directing Violent Products to Young People" (5/4/99). Articles about the proposal to require all teens entering R-rated films to provide proof of age asserted that it would "protect children from violence" (ABC 6/9), but its effectiveness was questioned: Kids, we were told, were exposed to violence from a host of other media; once inside a multiplex, they could walk into any theater they wanted; they could (and likely would) use fake IDs; and some even suggested parents were buying tickets for their teenagers. School security, which had been absent as a topic for much of 1999, reappeared in the annual back-to-school stories in August and September. As in 1998, stories talked of "school safety and how schools across the country prepare for the return of students with new regulations regarding security" (NPR 8/16/99). Locally, schools near the nation's capital were "enhancing security" (*Washington Post* 8/25/99), and many were "enhancing ties with law enforcement" (*New York Times* 9/12/99).

The emergence of new solutions and the reemergence of old ones were signature features of solutions talk in the post-Columbine era. More importantly, a host of debates and critiques arose about solutions. So-called zero-tolerance policies were talked about and critiqued. They seemed to make sense as a preventive measure, but did they go too far? School officials proposed using metal detectors and armed guards, but kids told us they didn't work and made them feel even less safe. Early warning systems and profiling programs might help, but some argued *any* kid having a bad day might exhibit the "signs" of violence (they were, after all, *teenagers*); others argued profiling programs were, at best, a "technological Band-Aid driven by profiteering in parental fears" (*New York Times* 10/24/99).

As the year wore on, two debates dominated the landscape. One such debate was gun control versus media control. This debate was certainly not new—it had been a staple of solutions talk for two years. The *Washington Post* suggested that the three-year series of school shootings had "altered the nation's gun debate" (4/22/99), and in another *Washington Post* story, the headline read, "World Blames Shootings on Lax US Gun Laws" (4/22/99). However, the weight of scientific evidence appeared to suggest that exposure to violent media played some role in real world violence. Should we require proof of age for R-rated films? Should marketing of video games be regulated ? In short, according to the *New York Times* (5/9/99), should we be "censoring or restricting entertainment media" or "restricting the availability of guns"? This debate found its way into talk about what the federal government was going to do about the problem. In the aftermath of Columbine, there was considerable talk of debates in Congress—should there be legislation to control or limit mass media, or should there be stricter gun control? President Clinton himself was said to be offering proposals that contained elements of both solutions.

With all the talk of security, early warning systems, and prevention programs, it was perhaps inevitable that they would be measured against one another. This debate was similar to the earlier debate regarding punishment versus treatment. Security programs, we were told, had become an obligatory feature of the contemporary school landscape. Almost every school had one, but we were told "their effectiveness is another matter" (NPR 4/21/99). These programs seemed to be a necessary feature of providing "safe" schools, but they had not prevented the Columbine shootings. They were "quick fix" solutions in contrast to "long-term" solutions, such as counseling and proper socialization of our children. Like many other solutions proposed during the 1990s, those based on securing American schools became a popular topic, but just as quickly attracted criticism. There was a strong sense that metal detectors and emergency plans (like ideas for "getting tough" with kids in the mid-1990s) would not really provide much security in our schools, but they were installed anyway. We *had* to have them in place. "Prevention" strategies, however, had their own sets of problems. Profiling, we were told, wasn't necessarily accurate, and, besides, there were important issues of confidentiality and privacy at stake. Although we might agree that how we raised our boys made them more violent, how should we go about changing our child-rearing methods? No one seemed to seriously explore what it would mean to raise our boys to be more sensitive and caring. By decade's end, our search for solutions seemed mired in complexity and contradiction. Solutions were cast against one another in debates, and in the course of these debates, these solutions were critiqued and deconstructed in ways that seemed to label all of them ineffective or impractical.

Voices, Debates, and Culture Wars

In his book *Culture Wars,* James Hunter (1991) argues that the United States is, and indeed has long been, embroiled in cultural conflict. Unlike past conflicts, which tended to be based on religious doctrine or principles, in the contemporary United States, the major cleavages have more to do with moral visions of right and wrong, of "how we order our lives" (p. 42) as individuals, communities, and as a whole society. Hunter suggests that at the heart of the current culture war lies a conflict between two impulses—one toward "orthodoxy" and the other toward "progressivism." The former comprises a "commitment on the part of adherents to an external, definable, and transcendent authority" (p. 44), whereas the latter comprises a "tendency to resymbolize historic faiths according to the prevailing assumptions of contemporary life" (pp. 44–45). These two impulses have found their way into, and fundamentally shape, debates over the family, education, media, law, and politics. Indeed, Hunter observes that these two worldviews are closely associated with political dispositions:

> It nearly goes without saying that those who embrace the orthodox impulse are almost always cultural conservatives, while those who embrace progressivist moral assumptions tend toward liberal or libertarian social agendas. . . . For the practical purposes of naming the protagonists in the culture war, then, we can label those on one side cultural conservatives or moral traditionalists, and those on the other side liberals or cultural progressivists. (p. 46)

To explore this distinction further would divert me from my main task in this section, which is to examine how these two worldviews—and the "wars" themselves—were manifested in talk of causal accounts and solutions. I begin this exploration by examining the "voices" that were part of this talk.

Voices and Credibility

It should come as no surprise, given the myriad causal accounts and proffered solutions, that a seemingly countless number of voices engaged in talk about the problem of youth and violence. Sometimes, individuals were invited to this talk as guests on television or radio news shows. Similarly, others appeared by way of quotes or paraphrases in print stories. Still others contributed by way of letters to the editor, guest columns in the *Washington Post* or *New York Times,* or commentaries on NPR. In these ways, the news served as a vehicle for these voices—or to use Best's (1990) term, the news functioned as a secondary claims-maker. Of course, the news itself also served as a primary claims-maker in this talk and thus contributed its own voice. In many respects, how such voices found their way into this talk is much less important than to whom these voices belonged and the attributions made to them. Put another way, who spoke was more important than how they became part of the discourse.

One of the most prominent set of voices comprised individuals and groups associated with the criminal or juvenile justice systems, such as police or probation officers, judges, lawyers, and district attorneys. Child protection workers were also frequent participants, as were defense attorneys. Educators at all levels contributed to this talk—classroom teachers, principals and other sorts of school administrators, and even students. All these voices were associated with causal accounts and solutions. Even when they seemed incapable of offering explanations, their voices became part of the talk. For example, a *New York Times* story about the fatal stabbing at a Dartmouth, Massachusetts, high school—an early instance of violence in a suburban school—reported the following: "The principal had no more answers than his students did. There are no gangs at Dartmouth, he said, where most of the students are children of fishermen or of professors at the nearby University of Massachusetts campus" (4/14/93).

Professional associations of lawyers (e.g., the American Bar Association) or police or teachers (e.g., the National Education Association) also chimed in. For example, in 1993, an NPR story about the growing problem of school violence told us: "In an attempt to curb the violence, the National Education Association recently announced plans to pressure Congress to pass a bill that would provide schools with money to set up crime prevention programs" (1/23/93). Another NPR story from 1998 told us that the National School Boards Association had "called on all school boards not just to examine their school security policies, but to look closely at what they're doing for troubled kids—kids prone to violence" (12/20/98).

Members of the academy—usually social scientists—constituted another notable set of voices. A "professor of education" told us that the heart of the problem was a "deterioration of our morality" (NPR 12/29/98), whereas a "sociologist" told us the basic causes of violence included "broken families, teenagers with low self-esteem, and lack of after-school programs" (NPR 10/10/97). Alternatively, a "law professor" commented on "parental responsibility laws" (NPR 3/29/98), and a "research fellow at the Southern Poverty Law Center" lauded the merits of training in conflict resolution.

Psychologists and psychiatrists, as well as public health experts, occupied an interesting interstitial place between law enforcement or justice personnel and academics. Sometimes, these voices were located in academic settings. One notable example is Deborah Prothrow-Stith, who appeared as a guest on many news shows and was quoted in numerous stories. By the mid-1990s, she had become a spokesperson of sorts for a public health approach to the problem. She was always introduced as affiliated with the Harvard School of Public Health, which appeared to grant her the same kind of credibility as other academics, and she had conducted considerable research on the topic. Her association with antiviolence campaigns suggested she had "practical" experience as well. Psychologists and psychiatrists were typically not explicitly located in academic centers. Their routine appearance in this talk certainly suggests they were granted no small degree of credibility to offer insights on the problem. Although their titles might have granted them some "learned" experience, their authority appeared grounded in their *practical* experience. That said, they were generally not grouped together with the aforementioned "frontline" practitioners like police, teachers, and district attorneys.

Of course, victims and their relatives also made important contributions. They offered us their own lay theories of the origins of violence among youth. Likewise, residents of big-city neighborhoods told us how guns, gangs, and drugs had created the violence. Residents of small towns and suburbs searched, seemingly in vain, for explanations for the violence that had invaded their communities yet still offered solutions to the problem. Youth participated in this talk as well, but not just youthful victims or perpetrators of the violence. They were interviewed in stories, but just as often they were invitees to "summits" or congressional hearings to offer their own unique perspective on the problem and its solutions.

What was the significance of knowing that the voice that told us we needed to "get tough" on violent youth was that of a cop? Or that the person who wrote a letter to the editor urging us to address the mental health of our children was a psychologist? Or that some of the participants in this talk were members of the academy who had done research on children and violence? Put most simply, knowing these things established the *authority* of these voices. When a district attorney told us that the problem was caused by an antiquated juvenile justice system, her job lent some degree of credibility to that claim because we assumed she *knew* whereof she spoke. Likewise, when a sociologist told us that spending money on more police and jails didn't address the underlying causes of the problem, we might listen to him because, again, he knew what he was talking about. On what grounds, however, was this credibility based? Victims, teachers, cops, and social scientists might all know what they're talking about, but why? *How* did they know?

The credibility or authority of these voices derived principally from knowledge. Clearly, there were different forms of knowledge here, which in turn were based on different kinds of experience. The credibility of judges, police, teachers, and principals appeared to come from *direct experience* working with violent youth. These were people working on the "front lines." For example, CBS covered the debate over what to do about students expelled for carrying a gun on school grounds. According to the story, "the debate will be louder . . . as the toll mounts from the front lines in our nation's schools" (4/15/95). Likewise, according to a county district attorney, we needed "tougher laws" because "One only needs to spend a few days on the front lines to see what's happening. In many cases, there's no respect for the rules of society" (*New York Times* 6/22/97). A related sort of experience was attributed to victims and their families. Like district attorneys and teachers, their knowledge was gained from firsthand experience. For example, NBC described an "anti-crime" organization comprised of "police, prosecutors, and crime victims" that advocated after-school programs as a way of "reducing youth violence" (10/15/98). Note that in this excerpt, victims are grouped together with police and prosecutors, which might suggest they share similar experiences. However, beyond that similarity, victims' experience could *not* be the same as the others'. Police and prosecutors and teachers had had a continuing series of encounters with violent youth, often a career's worth of such encounters. That was what they did for a living; it was their job. The knowledge attributed to victims, however, appeared to be based on much more limited experience. Indeed, it was typically based on a single encounter. That said, their experience, as well as the knowledge it allowed, was of a special sort—personal rather than professional. Throughout the decade, atrocity tales were replete with the terror of the experience as told by either the victims or their relatives. In these tales, victims' talk of accounts and solutions provided a unique perspective—and credibility— that other voices did not, and could not, convey. For example, in a *Newsweek* story an eighteen-year-old "survivor of the massacre of Littleton" reflected on the horrors of the experience and of "her own campaign for reasonable gun control" (8/23/99). This was cast as a rather remarkable tale. Presumably, this young woman had little, if any, experience with politics, and it certainly could not have been assumed that she had conducted much research on guns and violence. However, her own personal experience seemed sufficient to grant her some credibility. In a similar way, we turned to the relatives (almost always parents or grandparents) of violent youth to find answers. Although we seldom asked them for accounts of the origins of the problem itself, it was common to invite them to speculate on why their own children or grandchildren had turned violent. Here again, as with the parents of victims,

Americans assumed that these adults knew their children better than anyone else and, thus, could provide some valuable insights. This same assumption seemed to underlie the incredulity expressed when parents of youth responsible for late-1990s school shootings claimed they were unaware of what their children were up to in the weeks and months leading up to the events. Perhaps these parents were fooling themselves. Perhaps they really didn't know their own kids. In any event, we still turned to them for insights.

Debates, Politics, and Culture Wars

The section above might suggest that most of the decade was a veritable free-for-all of voices offering up different causal accounts and solutions. Perhaps it was, and if so, it would seem to contradict how constructionists often think about problems talk. It is useful here to revisit the sociological concept of the social problems frame (Sasson 1995; Snow and Benford 1988; Gusfield 1981). According to conventional wisdom among constructionists who study social problems, frames constitute interpretive or rhetorical *packages*. In addition to other elements, these packages contain what can be called a diagnostic or analytic component as well as a policy or ameliorative component. In addition, because they are *packages,* the diagnostic and policy components are tightly interwoven or, to put it another way, logically interrelated into an interpretive whole. Thus, for example, to locate the origins of the drunk driving problem (Gusfield 1981) in the individual driver (as opposed to, for example, automobile or highway design) strongly suggests solutions that target drivers, such as stiff legal sanctions or perhaps counseling. In the first section of this chapter, I suggested that talk of the causes of and solutions to the problem of violence by youth appeared more complex and ambiguous than a focus on the individual would provide. The two searches—for explanations and for solutions—at times appeared connected and mutually aware of each other. However, at other times, it seemed as if they proceeded along two separate tracks. Solutions were often proffered without an accompanying suggestion of what causal factors they might ameliorate. For example, early in the 1990s solutions to the problem of big-city school violence were provided without talking about its causes. Causal accounts were often voiced without any suggestion as to what solutions might profitably be pursued to address them. In short, causal accounts did not always seem directly shaped by talk of solutions, and, in turn, solutions talk did not always seem directly, or singularly, shaped by causal accounts. I am not seriously suggesting the decade-long discussion was a free-for-all in which nothing was connected. However, I did not see much in the way of "interpretive wholes" at work either.

Nevertheless, two particular moments—and two sets of debates—were different. One took place at mid-decade and the other during the last third of the decade. At these two moments, debates and conflict most directly connected causal accounts with solutions. It was also during these moments that the voices participating in this talk connected most directly to the culture wars. The two main sets of voices involved those working on the "front lines" and academics. The former were typically associated with incarceration and punitive solutions. The latter were associated with prevention or rehabilitation. Just as incarceration was pitted against prevention, so were the voices of academics cast against those on the front lines. For example, a *Washington Post* headline declared that a local youth was sentenced to "5 Years in Gang Related Death." Appearing to support the sentence, a local prosecutor told us the judge "sent a message that if you do things like this in this city, you can expect a lot of punishment" (2/28/97). Likewise, in talk about the coming "epidemic of youth violence," criminal justice experts told us we needed more cops, whereas a sociologist told us we needed to "invest in these kids" (CBS 9/22/95). In a *New York Times* story, a county district attorney recommended "tougher laws" because violent youth had "no respect for the rules of society." This stance was positioned against that of a member of the state bar association committee on children and the law—and an adjunct instructor at the John Jay College of Criminal Justice—who said that "getting tougher is not necessarily the answer. The real question that needs to be addressed is what conditions in society create these monster kids" (6/22/97). The connection among these voices, stances on solutions, and ideological positions was established in other ways as well. Thus, *US News and World Report* told us that "conservatives" favored "tougher prison terms and law enforcement," whereas "liberals" advocated "massive new spending on prevention programs." Since we knew that criminal justice personnel advocated punitive solutions and that punitive solutions were favored by conservatives, then criminal justice personnel must be conservative. Likewise, academics—especially sociologists—must be liberals since they always seemed to advocate prevention-based solutions. This association became so entrenched it was often assumed. In an airing of *ABC This Week,* several reporters, commentators, and news analysts discussed the causes of youth violence (including family, media, and southern culture). After this wide-ranging consideration of possible causes, one participant suggested, "Well, we're right to be disturbed by those things, but there is a danger of committing sociology here and not holding people accountable for evil deeds." The implication of this statement was soon made evident. Sociologists (and perhaps by extension many other academics and researchers) concentrated so much on the underlying causes of the problem—on explaining it—that their efforts blinded them and us to a simple fact: "There will be some evil men in a society, and evil things will happen. Society can hold people accountable for those deeds, and I do think the problem is we do too much explaining of evil and not enough condemning of it" (3/29/98). In this exchange at least, "explaining" seemed incompatible with "condemning." To explain violence appeared to excuse it.

Other voices were implicated in this debate. Child advocates and teachers tended to be associated with the more "liberal" side. For example, a letter to the *New York Times* written by the director of the Children's Aid Society told us "youngsters who have productive alternatives do not commit violent crimes" (12/15/95). Likewise, a letter written by a "teacher" appearing on the same day claimed that "tougher laws won't curb youthful violence"; instead, we should "supply them with tools for self-expression and an environment where they feel valued." So-called anticrime activists were almost always said to advocate tougher laws, stricter law enforcement, and longer sentences. That said, teachers weren't *always* associated with "liberal solutions." For example, the *New York Times* (3/3/96) told us that "teachers' unions and some educational experts" were suggesting we "need to adopt tough standards to weed out "violent, disruptive students." It was cast as an unusual stance for teachers, but it was part of a story about the growing dangers facing teachers in schools. Perhaps when teachers started taking this position, we really *did* need to get tough. Similarly, not *all* researchers were liberals. On June 1, 1996, an NPR story brought in Deborah Prothrow-Stith and Patrick Fagan to discuss how "youth crime forces a look at causes, cures." (You may recall that Prothrow-Stith became the spokesperson for a public health approach to the problem.) In her NPR June 1996 appearance, she told us we needed to look at the causes of youth crime (including drug use by mothers and domestic abuse) and apply a "prevention mentality." Fagan, however, was described as a "researcher" at the Heritage Foundation and, according to him, the causes were "moral, cultural, family and neighborhood deficits." In turn, he suggested, government prevention programs didn't work. What *would* work, he suggested, was turning marriage around, restoring moral order, and increasing religious attendance.

Although we were not told as much, it was as if we were supposed to know that the Heritage Foundation was a *conservative* think tank.

Of course, not all those on the front lines proposed a tough approach, yet the association was so entrenched that whenever these folks advocated something different, it was newsworthy. Police sometimes occupied an ambiguous position in this talk. Most of the time, they were said to advocate "tough" stances on laws, enforcement, and sentencing. By the mid-1990s, however, they also came to be associated with prevention-related programs. For example, a CBS story was headlined "Police Officers in Chicago's Cabrini Green Area Form Rap Group to Spread Message of Non-violence to Youth." The story related how these tough cops had become "rap stars with badges, on a mission to save the world a child at a time" (10/30/95). In other stories, police were part of after-school programs, weekend programs for inner-city kids, and other prevention efforts. A *Washington Post* commentary talked about a program called "Fight Crime: Invest in Kids." It noted that

> the fight against crime needs to start in the highchair, not wait for the electric chair. What gives this message so much clout is that it comes from a group whose members include 500 police chiefs, sheriffs, district attorneys, violence prevention scholars, as well as parents who have lost children to violence. This is not the ivory tower liberal set. These are people who are on the bloody front lines. (7/28/99)

From roughly late 1994 to early 1997, voices in this debate became more visibly and strongly linked to political parties. Before then, causal accounts and solutions were certainly part of political or ideological talk but were rarely tied to specific political affiliations. For example, a *Newsweek* story (8/15/94) suggested that the violence of the 1990s could have been prevented through programs that helped parents at risk for neglect or abuse, if that idea had not lost favor in the 1980s "as the nation's mood grew more conservative and its crime agenda shifted to more prisons and stricter laws." Here, as we already knew, prisons and other get-tough approaches were associated with a conservative ideology. However, in stories like this, incarceration and other get-tough solutions were cast as outdated—as a sort of ideological relic of an unenlightened past. Yet this type of solution was said to enjoy increasing support among the general public, in large part because of growing anger and anxiety over the epidemic of youth violence. Politicians were said to be catering to this anxiety. The *Washington Post* (10/31/94) outlined the proposals for reducing local youth violence offered by two DC mayoral candidates.

One candidate offered a plan for tougher prosecution of gangs and construction of a new maximum-security facility for violent youthful offenders, whereas the other candidate preferred programs focusing on drug treatment, recreation, and education. The story went on to suggest, "Because public safety has become such a dominant and visceral issue among voters, candidates often cobble together grand plans for improving public safety without identifying viable funding sources. Around election time, there are a lot of promises that are just rhetoric" (10/31/94).

Conservatives wanted to get tough and liberals liked prevention and rehabilitation, and around mid-decade, these associations were tied to specific political parties. Predictably, perhaps, the associations between incarceration or getting tough and conservatives and between prevention or rehabilitation and liberals were linked with Republicans and Democrats, respectively. In 1996, a *Washington Post* story mentioned President Clinton's proposals for addressing "gang and youth violence" (5/14/96). Specifically, there was talk of "tougher prosecution." However, this solution seemed to be something not typically attributed to Clinton or perhaps Democrats more generally. Indeed, "the proposal represents part of the administration's strategy of preventing Republicans from taking the crime issue as their own in the campaign this year." The inference here was unmistakable. Although Democrats generally did not advocate such "tough" approaches, President Clinton was doing just that. However, as was common, this part of the proposal appeared to be a *political token*. Later that same month, NPR told us how Robert Dole—a Republican on the presidential stump in California—had suggested "the best crime prevention is welfare reform." The story went on to suggest he meant that making poor people work would prevent crime. This policy stance, it was said, "would draw the middle class to the polls." In response, a local Democratic councilperson was quoted as saying that the recent decline in local crime rates was "due to community-based policing" (which, we were told, was paid for by the Clinton administration). Through early 1997, there was more talk of the "Clinton crime package" designed to "deter youth crime and punish it more severely" (*Washington Post* 2/20/97). Although parts of this package were oriented toward prevention, the White House emphasized that the tougher parts of the package were a response to Republican criticisms of his 1994 crime bill, especially their "making sport of subsidies for midnight basketball." This conflict between Democrats and Republicans over the problem existed at the state level as well. In New York, for example, the two sides fought over a juvenile justice reform bill that would, among other things, expand the list of crimes for which juveniles could be transferred to the adult court.

Beginning in early 1997, debates over accounts and solutions began to change in ways that would eventually become firmly established until the end of the decade. It was during the last years of the 1990s that the debate shifted from getting tough versus rehabilitation or prevention to mass media versus guns. To be sure, there were causal accounts regarding teenage angst, mental illness, and how we raised our boys, as well as solutions tied these accounts such as early warning systems and changing the ways we raise these boys. However, the most visible talk about accounts centered on the causal roles played by the putative influence of the mass media versus access to guns, and talk about solutions concerned a debate over whether we should control the media or control guns. Debates over the causal role of guns and mass media in crime have a long, heated history in the United States. In the 1950s, the problem of middle-class delinquency was thought to be caused by, among other things, the influence of movies and especially comic books (Gilbert 1986). Popular music has been blamed for adolescent misconduct from the swing music of the 1940s to the rock and roll of the 1960s to the rap music of the 1980s. For their part, the causal role played by access to guns in youth violence had also been a visible topic of talk for much of the 1990s. It might be argued that this debate has been particularly heated since the late 1960s, with the passage of the Gun Control Act of 1968 and subsequent legislation designed to control access to firearms. In some ways, 1990s talk regarding media and guns can be seen as an extension of these more long-standing conflicts.

Recall that the appearance of guns and mass media in causal accounts and solutions did not *suddenly* appear in the late 1990s. As we have seen, "access to guns" and a "violent culture" were talked about as early as 1992 and were then part of a critique of school security measures. As the argument went, metal detectors and security guards could only do so much. The main causal factors, it was argued, were kids' access to guns and a culture that glamorized violence. Guns continued to be a topic of talk throughout the decade, although they were not always the subject of debate. Instead, guns were typically offered as a foil in debates regarding other accounts and solutions. Just as important, guns and media were not typically cast against each other, and more often than not they were mentioned together—as co-causal factors, in a way. What was different about the late 1990s was that they were pitted against each other, and that debate became a highly visible and salient element of our talk about the problem. Indeed, in many ways it might be argued that it became *the* debate at decade's end.

Rather explicit and forceful causal accounts accompanied this debate over solutions. According to liberals, the problem was that kids had far too easy access to guns. As the argument was cast in this talk, we had long known that teenagers were moody and that their cliques and status hierarchy resulted in teasing, bullying, and ostracism. However, what was new—what was causing this new problem—was that they had greater access to guns. As one NBC story put it, "a gun in the hand of a 13-year-old is a very deadly situation" (3/24/98). The solution seemed inescapable—we should make it harder for kids to get their hands on guns. Alternatively, according to this talk, conservatives located the problem in our culture. Ignoring conflicting research results, they claimed that Americans had long known that kids' exposure to media violence resulted in aggressive behavior. In some of this talk, media violence was said to be a symptom of a larger deterioration of our cultural fabric that also included the breakdown of the family and a decline in the influence of religious values. This argument was linked with a number of different solutions, including, for example, bringing religion back into public education. However, mostly we heard about controlling media violence, from making it harder for kids to get into R-rated films to controlling violent media in the same ways we had prevented the tobacco industry from marketing its product to children.

There were a number of voices in these debates. Academics and those on the "front lines" of the battle against youth violence were frequent participants. Indeed, they had been as early as 1994, when academics and cops and judges offered conflicting views on mass media. Academics and frontline personnel continued to be part of this debate late in the 1990s. Jack Levin, a sociologist, suggested "we really have to take a real hard look at ways to disarm our kids" (5/25/98). It should come as no surprise that the National Rifle Association (NRA) also had a major voice in this debate, apparently resisting *any* attempt to restrict or monitor gun ownership. Indeed, in the wake of the Columbine shootings, the *New York Times* (4/22/99) told us that Charlton Heston (then president-elect of the NRA) and Jesse Ventura (then governor of Minnesota) had both said the violence might have been averted if "someone else had been armed at the school."

However, the main participants in this late-decade debate were Democrats and Republicans. As other voices focused on early warning systems, counseling, and teaching nonviolent conflict resolution, these two parties were embroiled in the debate over guns versus mass media. The Democrats were almost always said to offer an account that focused on guns and, therefore, advocated gun control legislation. Republicans, by contrast, were said to offer accounts and solutions focusing on the mass media. According to a 1998 NBC story, "many Republicans say money and laws are not the answer. They call for more parental supervision and a reduction of violence on TV and in the movies" (4/12/98). When Gary Bauer—said to be a "religious conservative"—announced his candidacy for the Republican presidential nomination, he said, according to the *New York Times* (4/22/99), "the culture glorifies death in a thousand different ways. In the America I want, those Hollywood producers and directors, they wouldn't be able to show their faces in public, because you and every other American would point to them and say: 'Shame! Shame! Shame!'" The story went on to suggest that Bauer was unmovable on issues such as abortion and gun control and quoted him as saying, "It's not the availability of weapons but the hearts of those who use them." The story didn't suggest his stance was unusual. Instead, the story was about how Bauer might use this stance politically in his quest for the presidency by catering to the Republican conservative base.

In the wake of the Columbine shootings, talk about this political debate increased. In May, in an NPR commentary, Daniel Schoor offered his summary of Washington's attempts to find solutions. He suggested that Republicans, who receive money from the NRA, should hold hearings on the media, and Democrats, who receive money from the entertainment industry, should hold hearings on guns. Members of each party took predictable stances on the issue—save for President Clinton. For example, in 1998, a Clinton adviser told NBC that "if we want our schools to be safe, we need to do two things: hire more prosecutors to break up the gangs, and start more after-school programs to keep kids off the streets in the first place" (4/13/98). It was not the first nor the last time Clinton had offered a policy that seemed to defy conventional political logic. His policies were often said to contain elements associated with both political ideologies. His White House conference on guns and media in the wake of Columbine was a putative attempt to find a middle ground that did not point fingers at, or attribute blame to, either gun makers or Hollywood.

That was how the decade ended. Debates continued over guns versus mass media. There was talk of hearings and proposed legislation. Republicans and Democrats gave speeches and held press conferences. Pundits estimated the political points that the contestants on one side or the other might have scored with these speeches and conferences and hearings. In the midst of all this, there was little talk of what solutions might actually work, much less how we might implement such solutions.

Ambiguity and Culture Wars

What Hunter called "culture wars" was appropriated in the debates and, in the process, given specific meaning or form. In this talk, academics and Democrats were cast as liberals, whereas Republicans and those on the front lines of the fight against the violence were the conservatives. Casting the groups in these ways gave a "face" to each ideological position, but it also reinforced what would appear to be long-standing assumptions regarding ideologies associated with Democrats and Republicans as well as academics and criminal justice personnel. After all, we all "knew" that academics—especially social scientists—were the liberal "ivory tower" set and that folks who worked on the "front lines" were more conservative. In turn, the stances taken in these debates gave specific form to these ideological positions.

Take, for example, the debate over punishment versus rehabilitation. As constructed, the liberal argument—rehabilitation and prevention—appeared to focus on the youths themselves. Children and teenagers were not supposed to be violent, or at least not *this* violent. Liberals, like their Progressive Era counterparts of the late 1800s, argued that youth were troubled. They were victims. Kids were not naturally violent, so this behavior must result from abuse, neglect, gangs, bullying, or, perhaps, their own inner demons. According to this argument, we should try to ameliorate the problems themselves—that is, prevent violence. Barring this, we could at least fix the consequences of these problems as they were manifested in these kids—that is, rehabilitate them. Prevention and rehabilitation appeared to be motivated by a sense of sympathy or compassion for these kids. These youth were victims of forces and factors beyond their control. They needed our help.

The conservative argument for punishing violent youth appeared to focus more on their behavior. They were *violent* youth. Irrespective of the origins of this violence and irrespective of their age, there appeared to be a moral imperative to impose or restore justice or at least to protect us from these kids. The impulse to punish appeared motivated by different emotions: adults' fear of them and our pity for their victims. In short, liberals focused on who these youth were, conservatives focused on their behavior (Spencer and Muschert 2009). The two stances took on one or the other side of the paradox of youth violence—the innocence of youth versus the evil of their behavior. In so doing, this debate reinforced the image of the problem as a paradox. It seemed that both sides were right. However, it also seemed we could not actually implement policy based on both. Hence, we were in a quandary from which there was no escape.

In the process, however, liberalism and conservatism appeared to be reinvented in the debate over guns versus media. The conservative commitment to an external moral authority found form in the focus on the media. Violence in the media was, put simply, morally wrong. Further, it was symptomatic of a broader deterioration of American culture. However, the progressive commitment to the prevailing assumptions of modern society found form in the liberal stance on gun control. Guns may be part of a *southern* culture—or at least a rural culture—where hunting was said to be part of boys' upbringing. However, there seemed little need for them in our more modern, and perhaps enlightened, society. This stance was also expressed as an extension of the liberal stance on rehabilitation and prevention. When liberals talked about gun control, they always seemed to talk about "troubled" kids with guns.

More important, perhaps, was that as these debates appropriated culture wars, the stances in these debates often seemed to be reduced to ideological or political tokens. Certainly, that happened in late-decade debates between Democrats and Republicans, but also to a lesser extent any time politics were implicated in this talk. When the media reported on debates between Democrats and Republicans over guns versus media, their reports used language that rendered each argument somehow dishonest, or at least not very heartfelt. It didn't seem as if either side *really* believed what they were saying—instead, they wanted to win a political battle. So when Gary Bauer—the conservative candidate for president—said a cultural breakdown rather than guns was the problem, the story strongly implied that he took this stance to hold the party accountable to its conservative base. Similarly, President Clinton's stance on getting tough with violent youth was almost always cast as an attempt to wrest the issue away from his Republican adversaries. In this way, the problem of youth violence was as much a *political issue* as it was a social problem.

Politicians fighting it out in Washington, DC, or academics arguing with cops and district attorneys made for entertaining spectacle. No doubt that is one reason it became such a salient—and visible—part of talk about youth violence. However, this spectacle seemed to deter or sidetrack our collective search for causal accounts and solutions. Were we talking about the problem of youth violence or simply playing out old, traditional ideological conflicts and disagreements? Did gun control or media control make sense as solutions, or were the proponents of each solution simply trying to score political points? All those arguments were added to already complex and contradictory talk regarding what we supposedly knew of the causal effects of media violence and the efficacy of school security programs or nonviolent conflict resolution training. The cumulative effect of all this talk seemed to be that we didn't know much with any certainty, yet that didn't prevent us from taking strong stances for or against what we talked about.

Race, Place, and Class Revisited

Just as cultural assumptions and beliefs regarding race, place, and class shaped talk about the problem of youth violence, so did they shape talk about causes of—and solutions to—the problem. Early in the 1990s, the problem was primarily located in the big city and there seemed little debate that its causes lay in the big city itself. All the usual suspects were implicated: gangs, dysfunctional families, disorganized neighborhoods, poverty, racism, and a general acceptance of violence. In most respects, this talk was a contemporary manifestation of environmental accounts that are, it seems, always invoked to explain lower-class and working-class delinquency (Gilbert 1986). Likewise, there seemed little debate regarding a proper solution in these early years. Security programs were an accepted solution to the big-city school violence problem, and gangs were to be dealt with by a combination of strong law enforcement and prevention programs (such as job programs). Throughout, we also heard considerable talk of tougher penalties.

Later in the 1990s, talk turned to violence by middle-class children living in suburbs and small towns. As these images of violent youth changed, so did causal accounts for the problem. Why were *these* kids committing violence? Clear answers were not forthcoming. Sure, these kids might have adopted the Goth subculture, they might have been troubled by their parents' divorce, or they might have acted in response to bullying, but they didn't seem all *that* out of the ordinary. Weren't these things all normal teenagers experienced? Middle-class delinquency of the 1950s had prompted a serious examination of how adult society—middle-class society—had failed its kids (Gilbert 1986). There was no such examination in the 1990s. It seemed as if middle-class Americans could not question the stability of their families, communities, and institutions. Of course, middle-class parents supervised their children. Instead, talk focused on a host of other potential causes, including guns; media violence; teenage angst; adolescent biology, socialization, and gender roles; and high school social structures and teen subcultures.

There was also talk of how American culture had changed in recent years, becoming more crass, less civil, and more tolerant of violence. Mostly, however, there was talk of how violence by middle-class children was changing American life. The school shootings of the late 1990s were said to have fundamentally changed their communities and schools. Stories that followed how residents of these suburbs and small towns had dealt with the tragedy spoke of a collective loss of innocence. These communities were no longer safe havens. Now, their residents had to think about how their police would respond to future shootings. Schools were now implementing security systems and disciplinary programs, as their urban counterparts had been forced to do earlier in the 1990s.

Intertwined in talk of causes and solutions were conflicting emotions. The fear and horror accompanied images of random and senseless violence, but sympathy and compassion seemed to accompany images of young children growing up in the violent big city. Although there was a degree of pessimism that not much could really be done about urban lower-class violence, this ambivalence served as the basis for the debates over incarceration versus treatment in the early 1990s.

A new constellation of emotions emerged as talk turned to middle-class violence in the late 1990s. To be sure, this talk reverberated with fear of this new sort of violence, and anger was directed at the kids committing it. Compassion was expressed for the victims and their families as well as the communities that had lost their innocence. However, the sense of mystery that accompanied earlier talk of suburban and small-town violence was now expressed as confusion and anxiety. The middle-class school shootings called into question long-held beliefs that these communities were somehow safe havens from big-city problems. If these kids could commit these mass shootings, we were told, any kid in any community might be the next to wield a gun. In many ways, this new problem seemed to paralyze us. We seemed incapable of explaining this violence. We were equally incapable of developing solutions.

4

The Drama
of Iconic Narratives

In Chapter 2, I focused on how the news talked about the condition of youth violence and the person-categories that populated the problem. In Chapter 3, I examined the searches for causes of and solutions to this problem. As with other social problems talk, specific individuals or instances, cast as atrocity tales (Best 1990; Bromley, Shupe, and Ventimiglia 1979) or horror stories (Johnson 1995), illustrated the more general condition and its person-categories. Such examples were typically mentioned within the context of stories about the problem itself. Similarly, what might be called "model programs" were the topic of solutions talk—programs located in various places around the country that had enjoyed putative success in preventing or deterring or rehabilitating delinquency. However, sometimes individual instances appeared to serve as more than mere examples, and became iconic representations or enduring symbols of the larger problem of youth violence. I call the talk about these events *iconic narratives*. How did these narratives differ from atrocity tales?

We can begin understanding the differences between atrocity tales and iconic narratives by comparing a short story with a novel. Because the former is shorter, its plot is not as detailed, and its characters are much less developed. In this way, atrocity tales of youth violence might include a relatively brief description of the event itself and, sometimes, short biographical sketches of the victims and offender. These events might even be referred to multiple times across news outlets. A good example of such tales appeared in a *People* magazine cover story on June 23, 1997. The cover of that issue read: "Heartbreaking Crimes: Kids

115

Without a Conscience?" After a relatively brief introduction telling us that the number of murders by teenagers had recently increased dramatically, the story went on to provide tales of six such teenagers and what they had done. The youth themselves ran the gamut from middle-class suburban teens to inner-city kids. Each tale was short, roughly five or six paragraphs long, and provided sketches of what the youth had done, a few details about the victim, and one or two brief quotes from people familiar with the situation. Each tale served as an example of the various sorts of violent youth, their acts, and their victims that comprised this disturbing trend.

Novels, however, are longer, and the plot and characters are much more developed. Similarly, the discursive space created by iconic narratives was both considerably deeper and wider than that created by atrocity tales. The former comprised multiple stories across different news sources. I employed this approach because of the way I conceptualized the news: as talk that is intimately tied to its cultural context. Thus, rather than viewing each news source as a singular narrative, I see iconic narratives as more truly cultural narratives—shaped by and shaping broader discourses, understandings, and assumptions. Narratives also comprised multiple stories or plotlines. We learned about myriad aspects of the initial events, intimate details about the victims and offenders, how the event was affecting the local community, and why or how the event occurred. These narratives also followed the case in the justice system, detailing police investigations and arrests, charges and arraignments, defense strategies, and, ultimately, the resolution of the court case. Another signature characteristic of iconic narratives was that they combined both "hard" and "soft" news. According to Leslie Henderson and Jenny Kitzinger (1999, p. 568), "Put simply hard news is 'serious'; 'fact-based' coverage and soft news involved 'light' or 'human interest' stories. Both terms relate to the subject matter, the positioning of the story, the sources used, the journalist who covers it and the implied readership." Thus, "hard" news is talk about crime rates, the rise and fall of stock values, or daily casualty figures from the battlefield. "Soft" or human interest news might also be about war, the stock market, or crime, but the talk would focus on the "human face" of these topics. Thus, we might read about how wounded soldiers cope when they return home. We might see a story about how the recession is affecting how families get ready for the new school year. As useful as the distinction may be, Henderson and Kitzinger (1999) point out that "In recent years . . . several researchers have argued that the traditional divisions between hard and soft news had become blurred" (p. 568).

That suggests the media now often combine two formats or discursive styles. Altheide (2002) made a similar argument regarding the increasing use of the entertainment format in the news. Iconic narratives wove together hard and soft news in the same way. They combined the "serious" news of on-the-scene crime reporting, court cases, and police investigations with the "softer" news of the lives and backgrounds of the victims and how the local residents were coping in the aftermath of the tragedy. In this chapter, I examine these iconic narratives as dramas that symbolized the condition of youth violence—the offenders, their victims, the contexts of the violence, and how we might properly deal with it. Specifically, I examine how their structure and content manifest the uncertainty, ambivalence, and ambiguity that are the focus of this book.

Seven Exemplars

A number of iconic narratives appeared over the course of the 1990s, serving as symbols of the more specific frames of gangs or school violence or the superpredator. Some symbolized the more general, unmarked frame of youth violence. Some narratives symbolized the problem of big-city violence, whereas others signified the problem in small towns and suburbs. I have chosen seven of these narratives as the subject of this chapter. Before turning to my analysis, I provide short sketches of these exemplars. In a sense, each of these sketches represents a second-order narrative—that is, my own brief narrative of the more complete news narrative. That said, I present these exemplars to provide a sense of how each of the full narratives unfolded over time. The seven exemplars are

- Jefferson High School, February 1992–September 1993;
- Eric Smith and Derrick Robie, August 1993–September 1994;
- Robert "Yummy" Sandifer and Shavon Dean, September 1994;
- Eric Morse, October 1994–February 1996;
- Bermudez Infant, March 1996–July 1996;
- Sam Manzie and Eddie Werner, October 1997–April 1999; and
- West Paducah High School, December 1997–October 1998.

Figure 4.1 provides a view of these seven exemplars along a timeline. As the figure illustrates, some of these narratives were quite long—lasting several months or years. Others lasted a shorter time. As I discuss below, some narratives comprised dozens or even hundreds of individual

Figure 4.1   Timeline of the Seven Iconic Narrative Exemplars

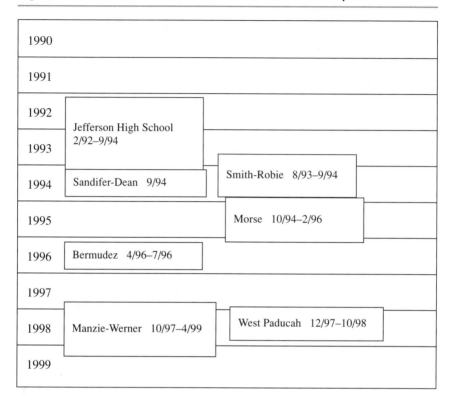

stories, whereas others comprised many fewer stories. Nevertheless, all these narratives came to symbolize the problem of youth violence.

Jefferson High School in the Bronx

This narrative—set in Jefferson High School in the Bronx, New York City—did not garner the same volume of interest in the news as most of the other events that follow below. It was the subject of five stories in the *New York Times* and a handful of stories on ABC, NPR, and CNN (including *Larry King Live*). However, its significance lay less in the volume of news talk and more in the content of the narrative and its relationship to talk about the larger problems of which it was part. According to this narrative, early in the morning of February 26, 1992, Kahlil Sumpter entered Jefferson High School and shot two other students—Ian Moore and

Tyrone Sinkler—with a .38 caliber revolver in one of the school's hall-ways. He was apprehended by police as he fled the school. Within forty-eight hours, NPR, CBS, and the *New York Times* ran stories on the shootings. According to a CBS story, it was the worst violent incident in the New York City school system's history.

In the days, weeks, and months that followed, there was considerable talk about the lives of the three principal actors—Kahlil, Ian, and Tyrone—and the events that led to their deadly encounter. NPR told us that the shooting was motivated by a grudge that Kahlil had held against the other two boys since December. We learned about their families. Mostly, however, we learned about Jefferson High School, its students, and the neighborhood that surrounded it. We learned what it was like to live in the Bronx and to attend Jefferson, a once proud school that had fallen on hard times. According to a CNN story, it was "a very famous high school and has sent a lot of people to positions of acclaim in this country" (3/18/92). A number of stories and letters to the editor recounted the noted alumni from that school. One letter noted that in the late 1920s and early 1930s, "a certain magic existed in those days between teach-ers, students and parents" (*New York Times* 6/28/93). However, that "magic" was now long gone, and more recently the school had become a place where "death is a reality for students" (NPR 2/27/92). Although some said the school had turned a corner on violence, a mere three months earlier a fourteen-year-old student had shot and killed another student and seriously wounded a teacher. Violence was so common at Jefferson High School that the school maintained its own burial fund and a grieving room for students.

The violence inside the school was inextricably tied to the neigh-borhood that surrounded it. The shootings were said to be the result of a "fatal vortex" that most recently appeared to concern a bracelet. In this way, this event symbolized how, "in the world of Jefferson and the sad, terrifying streets that surround it, adolescence includes the possibility that young people could be gunned down anywhere at anytime for any reason" (*New York Times* 2/27/92). According to one resident, "It has its beauties, but it's a sad neighborhood" (*New York Times* 3/1/92). Under-cover ATF teams were making buys of "high-powered weapons" a "block away from a school" (NPR 3/14/92). Predictably, this neighborhood had the highest homicide rate in New York City. The narrative treated us to an insider's look into this urban environment. We learned local slang terms for guns ("cronz"), power ("juice"), and friends who would back you up when threatened ("props"). Mostly, we learned what it was like to live here from the point of view of the kids who did. The *New York Times* ran a story headlined "Life at 'Jeff': Tough Students Wonder Where Childhood Went" (3/7/92). Based on transcripts from three hours of interviews with students at the school, the story chronicled the corrosion of the spirit that characterized both the neighborhood and its school. It was an environment that robbed youth of their childhood, a place where they learned how to deal with the violent deaths of family and friends at an early age. In such a context, the shooting was inevitable. Something like it was bound to happen as soon as the dispute arose among these three teenagers. More importantly, what happened seemed to serve as a microcosm of the big city where they lived. In a recurring theme in this narrative, local residents expressed concern and fear regarding the shootings. Perhaps more importantly, they harbored little hope that anything of substance would or could be done to fundamentally change the conditions around the school. Jefferson High School students also expressed similar resignation. Some students blamed the school's chancellor for the latest shootings, suggesting he had failed to sufficiently tighten security at the school after a previous shooting. Kahlil, Ian, and Tyrone were typical teens in this neighborhood. They liked to play basketball, football, and video games. Ian tinkered with cars and aspired to be an electrician. Tyrone's father had hoped his son might become a professional athlete or, if not, join the army to escape east New York.

In this narrative, the trial revolved almost entirely around whether the attack was premeditated and, to a lesser extent, whether it was motivated by self-defense. Leading up to his trial, talk about Kahlil produced an ambiguous account of the teenager. At times he was cast as a cold-blooded killer intent on settling a score, whereas at other times he was cast as a skinny teenage boy scared for his life. Ian and Tyrone were cast as somewhat less than innocent. Each one had had his share of trouble with the police. The trial began on June 24, 1993, occasioning stories that provided new details of the events leading up to that fateful day, as well as updates on what had happened at Jefferson in the intervening year. There was little talk about the trial itself, and ultimately, this narrative ended two months later—a little less than eighteen months after it began—when the *New York Times* ran a story on the verdict in the case:

> The killings admitted by Kahlil Sumpter became symbols of the violence that has invaded many New York high schools and of the often deadly consequences of teen-age disputes in an age of easily accessible guns. And while the verdict indicated that the jury did not accept Mr. Sumpter's claims that he had fired his gun in self-defense, one juror

said afterward that she believed that he had been in fear of his life because of bad blood between himself and the victims. (9/8/93)

Eric Smith and Derrick Robie: A Double Tragedy in Upstate New York

The narrative of Eric Smith and Derrick Robie began with a *New York Times* story on August 15, 1993. The lead paragraph told us that "residents of this picturesque village tucked in the hills of the Southern Tier say they've lost two children: a 4-year-old boy and the teen-ager charged with killing him." According to police, two weeks earlier Eric Smith had lured four-year-old Derrick Robie to a wooded area, where he was beaten and choked. Derrick was on his way to a village recreation program. Local residents gathered at the elementary school for a prayer service. There was apparently nothing to indicate that Eric—"a slightly built, freckle-faced 13-year-old"—was capable of this act. He was to be tried as an adult, and the case would soon go to a grand jury. A second *New York Times* story on August 22, headlined "A Big-City Horror in a Small Town," told us that village residents had overcome their "shock and horror to behave with all the virtues that are associated with small towns." Ministers consoled Derrick's parents, and neighbors and friends brought food to the Robies' house. Arrangements were made for Derrick's funeral, and there were plans for a Labor Day country and western concert to help pay its costs. There was talk of naming a new baseball field in Derrick's memory. The townspeople searched for answers as to why Eric Smith might have killed Derrick. Eric watched television and liked Garth Brooks, but he also seemed to have a fascination with books on the macabre side. Police told us that Eric had confessed to the killing and that the deadly encounter was by chance—"any child could have been the victim. Derrick just happened to come along."

Except for a single *New York Times* story on September 3 comparing the maximum sentences facing Eric in juvenile court versus those he would face in adult criminal court, the narrative would not continue for another eleven months. A *New York Times* story on August 2, 1994, was occasioned by the start of Eric's trial. According to this story, Eric still did not look like a sadistic killer: He was a "baby-faced teen-ager" with "aviator glasses perched atop his freckled nose." Although he had "grown taller and gained weight since his arrest last August, he was still lost in the shadow of the burly deputy who escorted him." The district attorney opened the trial with vivid details of the attack, while the defense promised to present evidence that Eric suffered from "diminished capacity." Two subsequent *New York Times* stories provided us with courtroom testimony by Eric's mother that she had taken prescription drugs while pregnant with Eric, and a psychiatrist for the defense testified that these drugs caused "intermittent explosive disorder" that resulted in episodes of uncontrollable rage. The psychiatrist also suggested that Eric's stepfather used extreme methods of discipline that contributed to his disorder. A CBS story on August 11 set the killing in a broader context: "Murders happen every day, in big cities and small towns. And one day, the town was in upstate New York. The victim was a child; so is the killer." The story went on to describe how the town was struggling to comprehend this killing and continued with details of the attack. On the one hand, the local minister told us, "Until the perpetrator of the crime can really repent of what he did, then there is no forgiveness possible." On the other hand, "in Eric Smith's long, blank stare, there appears to be no repentance, so Savona is waiting for the trial to end, the media to leave, so life, maybe, can move on."

Less than a week later, on August 17, Eric's conviction on the murder charge occasioned a host of stories. CBS alone ran multiple stories in both its morning and evening news slots. Several stories noted how after nine hours of deliberation, "the jury rejected the defense claim the boy suffered fits of rage" (CNN 8/17/94), bringing an end to "an exceptionally emotional and troubling case" (CBS 8/17/94). Eric's mother and grandfather were shaken, and the defense team was shocked. Derrick's parents "expressed relief that their yearlong ordeal seemed, in part, over" (*New York Times* 8/17/94). That evening, the CBS newsmagazine *48 Hours* featured the case with the headline: "Why Did Eric Kill?" The show had been following the case since its beginning, and the August 17 episode brought us the story "from those who lived it: the parents, friends, and loved ones, still struggling to try to understand what went so horribly wrong." We watched family videos of Eric swimming and Derrick playing T-ball and fishing. We relived the hours from when Derrick's mother was told he never arrived at camp until his body was found in the woods. Until Eric confessed to the murder, Savona assumed the killer was a "stranger from out of town," and everyone kept their children inside. We learned how the police had questioned Eric and how he confessed. We learned that Eric had sexually abused Derrick after he killed him—a fact never before released to the public. We relived the trial, remembering what the defense and the prosecution presented to the jury.

We learned of Eric's speech problems and how other kids teased and picked on him. We learned of his sister's molestation at the hand of their stepfather and his possible molestation of Eric. We learned again of Eric's "intermittent explosive disorder." The story ended, "And so, for one small town, the healing can begin. Tonight, as the parents of Savona put their children to bed, many hold this hope: that by trying to understand why this tragedy happened, perhaps they can stop it from happening again." A *New York Times* story ran on August 19 with the headline, "When the Face of Evil Is 13: A Small Town's Pain." It described the town of Savona: "The timeless tree-covered ridges that shelter this village and its 970 inhabitants still seem like bulwarks against the outside world. Residents continue to stop by the small post office to pick up mail and exchange gossip. They buy groceries or a six-pack at a general store, or drop in at the Savona Diner for a cheeseburger or the daily special, which today was baked lasagna at $4.95 a plate." But, the story continues, change was "inevitable" in this town in the wake of this murder of a child by another child. The good citizens of Savona now shut their doors to reporters. They had tried to organize a neighborhood watch committee but ultimately did not. A sense of suspicion had descended on the town. Townspeople suggested parents needed to find better ways to teach their children how to deal with anger. Some criticized laws that meddled in how parents disciplined their kids. This narrative ended with a *New York Times* story on September 8, 1994, headlined "Youth, 14, Draws 9 Years to Life in Killing of 4-year-old." Eric would spend the first four years of his sentence in a juvenile institution, and when he turned eighteen, he would be transferred to a state adult prison. At the sentencing Derrick's father read a prepared statement that "listed many things Derrick had done by age 4, including his ability to make peanut butter cookies and meat loaf, as well as his love of sports, especially fishing and baseball."

Robert "Yummy" Sandifer and Shavon Dean: Chicago's Guns

The narrative of Chicago's Yummy Sandifer and Shavon Dean is the shortest of these seven exemplars—for all intents and purposes lasting only a week. However, during that short time the narrative gathered dozens of stories in all the major national news outlets. It began on September 1, 1994, with no less than seven stories in the *New York Times* and on NPR, CBS, and CNN. The earliest stories related the death of Shavon Dean:

> Someone stepped out of the shadows between two storefront churches
> on the city's far South Side the other night and started shooting wildly
> at a knot of teen-agers playing football. When the gunfire stopped, a
> 14-year-old girl lay dead by a bullet apparently meant for someone
> else. At first, the shooting appeared to be another senseless, though in-
> creasingly common, story of an innocent slaughtered in the street. But
> the slaying of Shavon Dean has become more than that. It has shaken
> this city and made many fear for the future, not because of the victim's
> tender years, but because of the even younger age of her suspected
> killer, an 11-year-old boy. (*New York Times* 9/1/94)

According to early stories, the suspect was a sixth-grader who belonged
to a gang. Later that same morning, we were told that the suspect in the
shooting—Robert Sandifer—had been found shot to death. Police did
not name a suspect, but apparently had solid leads. Later that day, NPR
told us that Yummy had been shot through the back of his head, suggesting "a gangster execution" (9/1/94).

In the days that followed, we learned more about Yummy, about
Shavon, and about how the neighborhood and, indeed, Chicago were re-
acting. Shavon, who was to start high school the following week, aspired
to own a beauty shop. An impromptu memorial was erected for her in the
neighborhood. However, most of the talk was about Yummy—a nick-
name given him because he liked cookies so much. He was small—just
under 5 feet tall and 66 pounds. Records showed he was an abused
child—taken from his mother at age three and placed with his grandmother "after investigators found his body covered with cigarette burns,
rope marks, scratches and bruises" (CBS 9/1/94). We also learned he had
"been prosecuted numerous times for a variety of felonies" (CBS
9/1/94)—including robbery, auto theft, arson, and burglary.

The neighborhood was "stunned by the loss of two of its children,
one an innocent bystander, the other a child robbed of his innocence a
long time ago" (*New York Times* 9/2/94). Although some local residents
weren't surprised by Yummy's death and suggested it provided some
measure of retribution, most were sympathetic. Shavon and Yummy lived
in the same neighborhood and knew each other. Shavon's father and
cousins had tried to talk him out of the gang. There was talk that the
neighborhood—and indeed the city of Chicago—should come together
to do something about the gang violence that was killing so many black
youth. A few days later, city church leaders led "a rally for peace" (CBS
9/4/94) in the wake of the killings. On September 2, the day that Shavon
was buried, we learned that Chicago police had arrested "two gangsters"

for Yummy's murder—one sixteen and the other fourteen years old—one of whom had confessed to being the shooter. We were told that the bullets that had left Shavon dead were meant for someone else and the shooting had been ordered by Yummy's gang. In the days that followed the shooting, gang members apparently decided that Yummy knew too much to allow him to be taken into custody and, thus, ordered him killed. Some who knew the two boys described them as "normal kids living in a tough neighborhood," whereas others described them as "bad kids," as "vicious" (*New York Times* 9/3/94). Prosecutors planned to charge them as adults. After that, these two boys disappeared from the narrative.

As for Yummy, there was much talk about how local social services had "failed" him. How, it was asked, could such a troubled—and troubling—young boy fall through the cracks? "In the aftermath of his death, Sandifer's brief life is being closely examined; in particular, how, with a record of more than 20 arrests, he managed to spend so little time in juvenile custody. Last fall, he was placed in a low-security detention center but escaped in March" (ABC 9/2/94). There was much talk about the dangers of the streets and the gangs that ruled them. The consensus seemed to be that these gangs filled a gaping hole in Yummy's life, providing acceptance, kinship, and protection. His funeral occasioned more talk of Yummy's life and death. Parents and grandparents took young children to view his body at the wake to show them what can happen on those mean streets. In ironic fashion, we were told how the gang, the closest thing Yummy had to a family, turned out to be his executioner. That, according to a *New York Times* editorial, "is where gangs will take you. Beware." Yummy was "neglected and abused by his family, bounced from group homes to squad cars and killed, the police say, by his own street gang. Robert was buried today, a symbol of the nation's most troubled children" (9/8/94). CNN's *Larry King Live* and *Both Sides with Jesse Jackson* featured this narrative in discussions about the growing problem of youth violence. We learned that the good people of Chicago—and for that matter around the country—were "tired of juvenile criminals," that they were "outraged" over the "killings of and by children" (CBS 9/6/94). Robert's death was yet another in a long list of examples of "an epidemic of violence" that was "sweeping American children out of homes and classrooms and onto our meanest streets" (CNN 9/7/94). President Clinton mentioned the deaths of Shavon and Yummy in an address to the National Baptist Convention as an example of the need for community values, and Yummy's name came up in several testimonies before congressional committees. Afterward, the deaths of Shavon and Yummy appeared in stories and editorials about the big-city problem of gangs, in political speeches, and in a December NPR retrospective of the top stories of the year. Perhaps their story was overshadowed by another instance of Chicago kids killing other kids. Stephen Hilgartner and Charles Bosk (1988) have argued that social problems appear and disappear from our radar because, among other factors, the news has a limited carrying capacity. In short, there is only so much space—and time—to cover the news, so events compete for space. Here, it seems, the media was limited in how many iconic narratives it could carry at one time.

The Fourteen Stories of Eric Morse: Death in a Chicago Housing Project

The narrative of Eric Morse began on October 14, 1994, with stories on CBS and CNN. Both stories told us of the tragic death of Eric Morse the previous day, when he was pushed to his death by two other boys—ten and eleven years old—from the fourteenth floor of the Ida B. Wells public housing high-rise on the South Side of Chicago. His brother Derrick had frantically tried to save his life, even running down the stairs in a vain attempt to catch Eric before he hit the concrete. We were told that Eric was killed because he refused to steal candy for the two other boys. On the heels of the Yummy Sandifer narrative just a month earlier, here was another instance of children killing other children. The *New York Times* and *Washington Post,* ABC, and CNN featured the story in the following days, including a report on a speech given by President Clinton to a conference of police chiefs in which he referred to Eric's death. As in the Yummy Sandifer narrative, we never learned much about Eric's two killers. In fact we never learned much about Eric himself. A single *New York Times* story told us that "Eric and his brother lived in a dilapidated apartment house separated from the public housing building by a dirt courtyard strewn with hypodermic needles and other litter." In the same story, we learned that the two boys charged in Eric's murder had been in trouble with the law before and both their fathers were in prison. Their mothers attended a hearing at which the two boys were charged as juveniles.

Eric's funeral occasioned an October 18 CNN story in which his grandmother and other residents of the housing project spoke about the tragedy of Eric's death and the poverty that "is claiming lives in their community." Two days later, CNN reported that the two boys "may never really pay for the crime" because Illinois law prevented the incarceration of offenders under age thirteen. After a five-month hiatus, the narrative reappeared on March 31, 1995, in a CNN story headlined "Two Teens Make Public Radio Documentary About Violence." The documentary was produced by LeAlan Jones and Lloyd Newman, who lived in the housing complex where Eric died. We learned that LeAlan and Lloyd were conducting interviews about Eric's life and death. This documentary, we would later learn, was titled *The 14 Stories of Eric Morse* and received a number of awards, including a Peabody award for journalistic excellence.

A CNN story on November 28, reporting on the conviction of the two boys who killed Eric, asked, "What do you do with a pair of 12-year-old convicted killers?" Since Illinois had no secure facilities for inmates so young, there was speculation they would have to be sent out of state. No one, it seemed, really wanted to lock up boys so young, but the increasing murder rate for children under the age of eighteen was forcing the legal community to consider such a practice. On January 29, 1996, the sentencing of the two boys occasioned a series of stories. Were the boys to be "treated as troubled youth and sent to a residential treatment facility," or were they to be "treated as murderers and remanded to the Department of Corrections"? The judge ruled that they would be sent to the Department of Corrections under a new state law—passed largely in reaction to the incident. A flurry of stories followed, all addressing this "Juvenile Justice Debate" (NPR 2/6/96) of what to do with such young violent offenders. A *New York Times* editorial by Alex Kotlowitz—author of several books about children in the inner city, including *There Are No Children Here* (1992)—titled "It Takes a Village to Destroy a Child," examined the backgrounds of the two boys. He suggested that they had "come to symbolize the so-called super-predators, children accused of maiming and killing without a second thought" (2/8/96).

After that, the narrative came to an end except for stories on NPR and CBS featuring the Jones and Newman documentary. Yet Eric's death had considerable staying power. For years, it was mentioned in congressional testimony and conference speeches and was referenced as late as 1999 in an NPR story headlined "History and Current Status of America's Juvenile Justice System."

The Bermudez Infant in Richmond: Three Young Boys, a Baby, and a Tricycle

Like the Sandifer-Dean narrative, the narrative of the Bermudez infant was short-lived—lasting less than three months—yet became a visible symbol of the problem of youth violence. It began on April 23, 1996, with a CNN story headlined "California Kids Suspected in Infant Beating Incident." Within four days, other stories quickly followed in the *Washington Post* and *New York Times,* as well as on ABC, CNBC, and, again, CNN. Two local papers—the *San Francisco Chronicle* and *San Jose Mercury News*—gave extended coverage to the attack and its aftermath. As the narrative unfolded, we learned that a six-year-old boy and twin eight-year-old friends entered the Bermudez family's house in Richmond, California, to steal a Big Wheels tricycle. In the house were four-week-old Ignacio Bermudez, Jr., and his babysitter. The rest of the family was on a shopping trip. While in the house, the three boys "went on a rampage, dumping the sleeping baby from his bassinet, then kicking and beating him with such ferocity that they fractured his skull in two places and caused severe internal bleeding" (*San Francisco Chronicle* 4/25/96). The three boys then left with the tricycle. The babysitter, who had been in the bathroom during the event, found the infant and called the police.

The three boys and the Bermudez family lived in a neighborhood called the Iron Triangle, located in Richmond, California, a northeast suburb of San Francisco. It was a name that connoted "the hardships of this depressed area" (NPR 4/27/96). Indeed, the area was "rundown" (*New York Times* 4/26/96) and was "a rough, working-class neighborhood" (*Washington Post* 4/27/96). The area was "no stranger to juvenile crime and violence against children" (*San Francisco Chronicle* 4/25/96). Recently, however, conditions had been improving. The *New York Times* reported that "crime has been dropping lately and things are looking up" (4/26/96). According to Reverend Lawson of the Easter Hill Community Church, "This tragedy has assaulted the sensibility and the feeling of the community" (*San Francisco Chronicle* 5/3/96). Because the family had no money to pay the escalating medical bills, "residents of Richmond's Iron Triangle neighborhood have rallied in support of the family and the children accused of assaulting him" (*San Francisco Chronicle* 5/3/96). Toward this end, a collection hat was passed in the Easter Hill church.

On April 26, the story continued when the county prosecutor brought burglary charges against all three boys and, more importantly, attempted murder charges against the six-year-old. This announcement occasioned talk about a number of topics related to the case. These stories provided updates on the infant's condition—he was still in critical condition and might never fully recover—and background on his family. His father Ignacio Bermudez, Sr., had moved from Mexico in 1974, and his wife and three children had joined him in 1994. Ignacio, Sr., worked for a company that made fiberglass pipes, but he was spending nearly every waking hour at his son's side. Both parents were understandably inconsolable. They had lived in their neighborhood without fear for years. Now they wanted to move "but can't afford to" (*San Jose Mercury News* 4/26/96). We learned that the six-year-old was "overly aggressive, often wandering the streets unsupervised" (ABC 4/24/96). In fact, all three boys were aggressive and "obsessed with firing make-believe guns," although no one in the neighborhood expected such "brutality" from them (*New York Times* 4/26/96). We also learned that the six-year-old had been involved in a dispute with the Bermudez family and had previously threatened the infant.

The narrative quickly turned to how the case should be handled. We learned that the justice system was in uncharted territory. As far as anyone could tell, the six-year-old was the youngest ever to be charged with a crime of this magnitude. Experts opined that neither the adult nor the juvenile systems were equipped to deal with this sort of case. Local residents were not sure what to do with the boy. Even the infant's father wasn't sure. At first he seemed to reject a punitive response, suggesting if anything happened to him, his mother would suffer as he and his wife were. Later he said a psychologist should see the child and determine if "he is clear about what he did" (NPR 4/27/96) before proceeding; perhaps suggesting that if he was "clear," a punitive response might be appropriate. In the face of this ambiguity, however, the prosecutor stood firm. He argued the crime was so serious and brutal that "I don't think we can look the other way. When you're talking about another person's death, society must assign legal responsibility if the law permits it to" (*Washington Post* 4/27/96).

The next month, stories provided more details and updates. There was still considerable talk of the infant's condition following the attack. How was he doing? Would he survive? If he did survive, would there be permanent damage? Would he be blinded or suffer cerebral palsy? Nearly every story provided an update on his condition. Ultimately, after weeks of being in a coma and on life support, we were told that the infant would "never function normally" (*San Francisco Chronicle* 5/3/96) and that he would likely need to be on antiseizure medication for the rest of his life.

New details about the six-year-old emerged. His father was shot to death in 1994, his grandmother had a history of drug abuse, and his mother had been arrested in 1995 on a charge of drunk and disorderly conduct after a drunken brawl. For their part, the twins' father had dropped dead a few years earlier from unknown causes. Their house had been shot up during an apparent drive-by shooting. Their mother had a history with the police and courts and was now dying of cancer. There was still talk, however, that the six-year-old had committed a most horrible act with premeditation. In a *Washington Post* editorial, William Raspberry queried, "What do you do with children who appear to be, well, evil? That's a hard word, I know. But there's a difference between children whose violations of parental rules and (presumably) their own consciences sometimes lead to tragedy and those who seem not to have consciences" (5/10/96). The narrative came to an end with a handful of stories about the court case against the six-year-old. On June 28, 1996, a *San Francisco Chronicle* story told us the boy had been released from juvenile hall and sent to a "structured care program." The charges had been reduced to "assault with great bodily injury" due to "severe psychological problems" that limited his ability to understand events around him. Eventually, the boy could "face a seven year sentence as a ward of the court." On July 14, the *New York Times* reported that criminal charges against the six-year-old had been suspended and that he would remain in a group home for the time being. The infant had returned home, and although things looked promising for his recovery, it was too early to tell for sure.

Sam Manzie and Eddie Werner: Death in Suburban New Jersey

The narrative of Sam Manzie and Eddie Werner comprised more than thirty-seven stories in all the major print and broadcast media as well as newsmagazines like *20/20, Dateline,* and *Rivera Live.* It began on Wednesday, October 1, 1997, with several stories telling us that an "11-year-old boy" had been found dead in a wooded area in suburban New Jersey and that police were searching for his killer. The dead boy, Eddie Werner, had last been seen the previous Saturday, "selling candy door to door as part of a school fund raiser" (CBS 10/1/97). We quickly learned that the police were questioning a suspect—a local fifteen-year-old boy named Sam Manzie. The local area—variously identified as Jackson Township or Toms River, New Jersey—was a "quiet community" that had been considered safe by local residents. Now, however, this community was "shaken" (CBS 10/1/97), "reeling" (CNN 10/2/97), and "scared, petrified" (CBS 10/1/97). We learned that a makeshift memorial for Eddie Werner had been erected across the street from Sam Manzie's house. We were told that when "friends and neighbors formally said goodbye to Edward Werner, they also mourned their lost innocence" (CBS 10/4/97).

NBC ran a story the following day in which we learned that the fifteen-year-old suspect had been arrested. The local prosecutor described the crime in a public statement that would be quoted in many subsequent stories: "The door-to-door sales resulted in a chance encounter between the victim and the accused. During the course of the encounter, the victim was sexually assaulted and strangled with a ligature" (10/5/97). The narrative quickly turned to the implications—and causes—of Eddie's death. Questions were raised about the practice of kids selling candy for fund-raisers—a hallowed tradition practiced around the country every year. Kids were warned not to sell to strangers, but rather to "Raise money only from family, friends and neighbors you know" (CBS 10/1/97). That such a thing could happen in this sort of community was a "sad commentary on our times" (CBS 10/1/97). A New Jersey lawmaker even suggested we might consider restricting such fund-raising by kids. On October 2, CBS and ABC ran stories asking if such fund-raisers should still be practiced. The ABC story described their "dangers" and asked if the incentives might encourage kids to put themselves in dangerous situations. Two months later—in December—we learned New Jersey was considering a ban on door-to-door fund-raisers for public schools. CBS aired stories in which putative experts—such as a former police detective, a "crime consultant," and the director of the National Center for Missing and Abused Children—told parents how to keep their kids "out of harm's way."

On October 3 the narrative became more complex—and dramatic—as we learned that just three days before the killing, the teenage suspect's parents asked to have him committed to a psychiatric center. A judge rejected the request. There was speculation that the boy had been "the victim of sexual abuse by an older man he met through an on-line chatroom" (NBC 10/3/97) and that the police might have used the suspect as an informant to gather evidence against the older man. That same evening, CNBC's *Rivera Live* asked, Who was to blame for this "tragedy"? Was it the teenage suspect himself? Was it the judge who refused the parents' commitment request or the New Jersey commitment statutes? Was it the police who used the boy as an informant in a sting operation? Stories— many occasioned by Eddie Werner's funeral—related how the town was coping with the tragedy. It was a place where this sort of thing was not supposed to happen. Some residents suggested the killing made them rethink how well they knew their neighbors. Once again, there was talk about who or what was to blame. Someone blamed the judge who rejected the commitment request. Someone asked why the boy's parents left him alone in the house that day. Some criticized the press for portraying the killer as a victim: Perhaps he should be dragged into the woods like his victim or raped in prison. In a CNN story on October 6, we learned the suspect's name was Sam Manzie. That same story asked, "Is juvenile crime on the rise? And what can be done to stop it?" The Eddie Werner killing was coupled with the Pearl, Mississippi, school shootings to suggest that, despite FBI statistics that violent crime was down in the previous two years, something was amiss. Why did some kids commit these heinous crimes? Was it abuse? Was it violence on television? Was it guns? Was it that we no longer held kids responsible for their behavior?

Talk about the court case returned on October 7 when we learned that

> By law, prosecutors had 30 days to decide whether they wanted the 15-year-old suspect tried as an adult. He's charged with a crime so horrific they say they didn't need much time at all to make that determination. And one week to the day that he was first questioned in the disappearance of 11-year-old Eddie Werner, authorities announced that they have filed a motion to have the juvenile charged with the boy's murder waived to adult status. (CNBC 10/7/97)

A spokesperson for the township said the motion was justified "'cause it just seems like he knew what he was doing," and the prosecutor argued that the "heinous" nature of the crime demanded such an action. There was considerable talk about possible sentences for the boy. If he was convicted as an adult under a new state law, his sentence would be life without parole. The defense attorney, however, was "upset" by this decision, arguing that the juvenile statutes allowed for a twenty-year sentence— "anyone's definition of punishment"—and, besides, his client had been under psychiatric care and on medication at the time of the murder. He reiterated that Sam's parents had tried to have him committed because of his behavioral problems resulting from his "sexual liaisons" with a man we now knew as Stephen Simmons—a Long Island man who was facing charges of his own. His client's behavior was a "cry for help."

In the following weeks, two television newsmagazine shows—ABC's *20/20* and NBC's *Dateline*—each ran full stories on the case: the former titled "Sam's Story" and the latter about Eddie Werner. "Sam's Story" related the details of his life through an interview with his parents. According to the story, he was a "loving and loved child." However, he was confused about his sexual identity and was teased by schoolmates as

"Manzie the Pansy." Thus, Sam was the "perfect target for sexual pred-ators," and we learned how he was lured by Simmons into several sex-ual encounters. *Dateline* featured an interview with Eddie Werner's mother and father. They told us of his love of performing and dreams of being in show business—dreams that he "would never get to live out." They told of the day he went missing and the agonizing days waiting of news of his whereabouts. We learned how they always told him to be careful when selling door-to-door. When asked what they thought of the "legal strategy" of portraying Sam Manzie as a victim, Eddie's mother replied, "There is one victim here." Later that month, we learned that the Werners had filed notification of their intent to sue "law enforcement, court, and mental health officials who had dealings with" Sam prior to their son's death.

For all intents and purposes, the narrative fell off the cultural radar for almost sixteen months until, on March 20, 1999, we learned that Sam Manzie had pled guilty—against his attorney's and parents' advice—to murdering Eddie Werner. We learned of a "split over defense strategies," with Sam on one side and his parents and attorney on the other. His par-ents and attorneys wanted the case to be tried on grounds of mental ill-ness, a case they were convinced they would win. Instead, Sam would be sentenced in a few short weeks. On April 15, 1999, NBC ran this head-line: "Seventeen-year-old Former Honor Student Sentenced to 70 Years in Prison for the Brutal Murder of Little Boy Selling Gifts Door to Door."

West Paducah: Bloodshed in a Schoolyard

A string of shootings from 1997 to 1999—Pearl, Mississippi; West Pad-ucah, Kentucky; Jonesboro, Arkansas; Springfield, Oregon; and, of course, Littleton, Colorado—served as the basis for iconic narratives of school violence. All these narratives were set in small towns or suburbs, and all received sustained coverage in all the major national sources. The shooting at Columbine High School in Littleton was almost assuredly the most visible of these narratives. It was the subject of considerably more talk than any other narrative considered in this chapter or, for that matter, any single act of youth violence of the decade. However, I did not select Columbine as an exemplar for several reasons. First, there is already considerable scholarly work on Columbine—indeed, scholars themselves seem to have treated it as an iconic event. Second, the sheer volume of news stories on Columbine makes it difficult to do the sort of close analysis done in this chapter with other exemplars. Indeed, the same can be said of the Jonesboro shooting. For these reasons, I chose the narrative of the shooting in West Paducah, Kentucky. It was near the beginning of this string of shootings, so this sort of narrative was still relatively new. With each successive school violence narrative, the news progressively packaged them together as part of a "terrifying" or "horrifying" trend of similar events. Over time, the news developed templates that provided a structure for these narratives. In a way, the West Paducah narrative was positioned early enough to still be "fresh" while being treated as an instance of the "new" problem of school violence.

This narrative began on December 1, 1997, in stories about a four-teen-year-old freshman at a "suburban Paducah high school in Kentucky" (NBC 12/1/97) who opened fire into a group of fellow students gathered for an early morning informal prayer service. There were conflicting reports about the number of dead and wounded. Eyewitnesses spoke of hearing the gunfire and thinking someone was setting off fireworks as a prank. Others told us that the shooter had warned them not to go to the prayer group that morning, but he would not say why. Some stories reported the fourteen-year-old—who was arrested immediately after the shooting—had confessed but gave no motive. The following day we learned that at least three were dead and five wounded. We learned the name of the gunman—Michael Carneal. CNN told us of a "hero," a senior at the school who grabbed the gunman and prevented him from firing more shots. The community of West Paducah was "grieving" and "in shock" but was "healing" and "recovering." Members of the community were gathering and praying at local churches. Grief counselors met with students and parents. There was talk of instituting "big-city" precautions such as metal detectors and security guards at the school. Many were asking, "How did this happen in this community of small farms and unpretentious homes on spacious properties?" (CNN 12/2/97). ABC (12/2/97) asked, "What makes a teenager kill?" How could it be *this* young teenager, whom many thought they knew? There were no easy answers to these questions.

In the following days, we learned more about Michael. He was a "normal" child—a member of the school band and a "B" student. He was smaller than other kids, which brought him more than his share of teasing by other students. Some of his fellow students described it as the "usual teen-age banter" (*New York Times* 12/4/97), and some adults talked of Michael's anger about being teased. His family was ordinary for this community. His father was a respected attorney. The family was well-off and attended the local Lutheran church where Michael had been baptized. Police talked about their investigation: They suspected Michael had accomplices and were interviewing other students. Although much early talk speculated about cults or religious hatred as possible motives, police had ruled them out. There was talk that Michael had been "influenced by *The Basketball Diaries*" (CNN 12/4/09), in which a character shoots some high school classmates. On Friday—four days after the shooting—the funerals of the three slain victims occasioned more talk about religion, the details of the ongoing police investigation, and *The Basketball Diaries*. We learned that West Paducah was a "community of churches" (CNN 12/8/97). In fact, there was much talk of the community forgiving Michael—as much because of its religious faith as for its own collective mental health.

On December 10, the narrative turned to the court case—occasioned by a hearing at which we were told Michael would be charged as an adult. Police still suspected accomplices—the sheriff had a "gut feeling" (CBS 12/10/97) but could not yet prove it. Two days later, a host of stories reported that a grand jury had indicted Michael as an adult on eight felony counts. Five days later—on December 17—Michael attended his arraignment, where he pled not guilty. Talk now began to turn to his mental status and the possibility that his attorney might be working on an insanity defense. The narrative went on hiatus until the following March. Here, we heard again that the defense was to be based on Michael's mental health, although the prosecutors said they would not accept anything less than the maximum sentence of twenty-five years without parole. The trial date was set for October. That month, the shooting in Jonesboro, Arkansas, renewed talk of West Paducah, especially how these two events were linked to the broader problem of school violence. NBC told us that the town "was forever changed." One of the victims of the West Paducah shooting—Missy Jenkins—was being released from the hospital to go home. She was paralyzed from the waist down.

The final chapter in this narrative began on October 4, with talk of jury selection for Michael's trial. The defense had filed a motion asking the court to allow Michael to plead guilty but mentally ill, and the prosecution opposed the request. There was considerable talk of the possible sentences: At stake was a sentence of twenty-five years without parole, versus the possibility of parole after twelve years. The following day, a series of stories reported that Michael had been allowed to plead guilty but mentally ill. The judge imposed the maximum sentence—twenty-five years without the possibility of parole.

The Structure of Iconic Narratives

Like all stories, iconic narratives have a beginning and an ending. The beginning of these iconic narratives was easy to identify and comprised what I call "first stories." In some narratives, first stories presented an instance of youth violence (West Paducah and Jefferson High School). In other instances, first stories told us of a child gone missing (Manzie–Werner). In a way, the Yummy Sandifer–Shavon Dean narrative combined both beginnings: It told us of Shavon's death and the search for her killer, which was quickly followed by news of Yummy's death. Endings, however, were sometimes more difficult to discern. I was tempted to define the ending of a narrative as the last story that mentions an event. However, events might be referred to for years after they first occurred, and in this way an iconic narrative might be open-ended. It is always possible that a future story might refer to an event. Instead, I took a different—and more practical—tack: I defined the end of a narrative as the last story or stories that made a substantive contribution. Most often, that happened in stories that reported on the disposition of the trial.

Stories have a narrative arc (Fine and White 2002)—that is, between the beginning and the end, a story develops. In the case of iconic narratives, there were multiple story lines and thus several narrative arcs. These narratives covered considerable ground, often ranging far and wide. As we saw above, stories in the Manzie-Werner narrative discussed state laws banning door-to-door sales for public school fund-raising. In the Smith-Robie and West Paducah narratives, there was talk of how the media was "hyping" and exploiting youth violence for its own purposes. There were four recurring topics that I consider basic elements or plot-lines in these iconic narratives: (1) the originating event, (2) the local community or neighborhood, (3) the principal characters (always the offenders and the victims, but at times parents and other adults close to the offender or victims), and (4) the trial. We might call them chapters, but these four basic elements did not always appear in succession. All narratives began with first stories about an event (an attack, a killing, or a missing child) and most times ended with the disposition of the legal case. However, in between there might be talk of the local residents, stories about the victims, and finally stories revisiting the local residents and the victims. Sometimes elements were intertwined so that, for example, the development of the legal case might also include details about the victims' or the offenders' lives before the event.

These narratives were not isolated from the broader talk of the problem of youth violence. Remember, they are *iconic* narratives, so they served as symbols of the larger problem of youth violence—principally the condition, violent youth and their victims, and debates over its origins and solutions. Narratives comprised much talk that explicitly linked the specific instance of youth violence to the broader problem. Also, and more importantly, these narratives were imbued with the same uncertainty, ambivalence, and ambiguity that characterized talk about the problem itself. Further, in symbolizing the problem of youth violence, iconic narratives also provide a view of the broader cultural assumptions and beliefs I discussed in Chapter 2—discourses that were appropriated in talk about the problem of youth violence—but in these narratives, cultural discourses appeared considerably more clear and available for close inspection.

First Stories

In her book *Deciphering Violence,* Karen Cerulo (1998) offers a framework for studying narratives of acts of violence. Finding examples from the news, the arts and literature, comics, and photography, she argues that different moral assessments of virtually identical acts of violence are possible, depending on their *narrative structure.* Central to her framework are three types of violence—deviant, normal, and ambiguous—that vary in terms of conventional moral assessments. Deviant violence is assessed as wrong, but normal violence is morally accountable or defensible. Ambiguous violence, however, may be "distasteful and unpleasant, but nevertheless defined as justifiable" (p. 47). Ambiguous violence, as the term implies, refers to acts that are difficult to classify simply as right or wrong. Each of these types of violence is associated with a particular sequence of five narrative elements: (1) the violent actor or performer, (2) the victim, (3) the act, (4) the context, and (5) the consequences of the act. The *victim sequence* unfolds as follows:

Victim > Act > Performer > Context

Since this sequence begins with the victim—who becomes its central character—the audience is encouraged to identify with him or her, rendering the performer and his or her acts wrong or bad. This sequence is, thus, associated with deviant violence. Alternatively, the *performer sequence* follows a different format:

Performer > Act > Victim > Context

Here, the actor or performer is introduced first, encouraging the audience to identify with him or her. Because that tends to render the performer's actions justifiable, this sequence is associated with normal violence. In narratives of ambiguous violence, Cerulo found two narrative sequences: contextual and doublecasting. *Contextual sequences* highlighted the context that provides possible reasons or explanations for the performer's act. Not surprisingly, then, the narrative structure of that type of sequence is:

Performer or Context > Act > Victim

In *doublecasting sequences,* context is important, but in that type of narrative it functions in a different way than in contextual sequences—it casts the central character as both victim and performer. In one of its most basic forms, that structure would be:

Victim > Context/Performer > Act > Context

Cerulo's framework was useful in examining first stories for several reasons. First, it was in these stories that the five central narrative elements in Cerulo's framework—performer, victim, act and its consequences, and context—were all introduced. Dramatic characters (victim and performer), context (the local community or neighborhood), and the legal case (act and its consequences) constituted the major plotlines of iconic narratives. The content and sequencing of elements in first stories set the stage for—and in some ways foreshadowed—how these plotlines would eventually develop in iconic narratives. Thus, first stories help make visible some of the ways that these narratives served as symbols—or icons—of the problem of youth violence.

However, it is important to keep in mind that it was *not* moral readings of acts of youth violence that were at issue in these first stories— or, for that matter, in the narratives themselves. As I argued in Chapter 2, the acts committed by these youth were roundly condemned in large part because instances of this problem were always of the most extreme or serious sort. That was especially true in iconic narratives, which all told of "kids killing kids." Such malevolence was a central aspect of the paradox of youth violence, in which violent actions stood in contrast to the youthful status of the offenders. Thus, it might seem at first glance that Cerulo's framework—developed as it was to examine moral readings of violence narratives—would not be the most useful analytic tool. However, using Cerulo's framework to examine these first stories provides an opportunity to examine the deployment of these narrative elements in a different discursive space and to address a different question: how the paradox of youth violence was constructed.

In examining the headlines and lead paragraphs (in print news) or highlights (in broadcast news) of first stories, we find an eclectic mix of narrative sequences. We find the *victim sequence* in the narratives of Eric Morse, Jefferson High School, and the Bermudez infant.

> Eric Morse: "A 5-year-old fell 14 floors to his death after two older boys shoved him out a window" (*Washington Post* 10/15/94)
> Jefferson High School: "Teen-Agers shot to death in a Brooklyn school" (*New York Times* 2/27/92)
> Bermudez infant: "Baby hurt in theft" (*New York Times* 4/25/96)

On the other hand, we find instances of the *performer sequence* in the Sandifer-Dean, Bermudez, and Morse narratives.

> Sandifer-Dean: "Chicago police hunt for 11-year-old murder suspect" (CBS 9/1/94)
> Bermudez infant: "Children involved in beating of infant" (ABC 4/24/96)
> Eric Morse: "Chicago youths drop five-year-old to his death" (CNN 10/14/94)

The appearance of the victim sequence in first stories makes sense. The victims in all three of these narratives—indeed, in *all* these examples—were young, and in the Bermudez infant and Eric Morse narratives, they were portrayed as *particularly* young. As constructed in these narratives, the youth of the victims was part of what rendered these acts so tragic. At first glance, then, the performer sequence seems out of place, since according to Cerulo, this type of sequence is typically associated with normal violence, and these events were decidedly *not* treated as normal violence. Instead, in first stories the performer sequence served to highlight the youthful status of the offender. That was done in a variety of ways (Spencer 2005). Sometimes, stories simply mentioned their chronological ages. However, just as often it was accomplished through the use of terms that served as proxies for age. In one of the Morse excerpts above, Eric's age is mentioned, but the term "boys" is used to refer to the performers. In the Bermudez excerpts, we see the terms "baby" and "infant" used to describe the victim and "children" to describe the performers. The mix of victim and performer sequences—sometimes in the same narrative—seems to suggest that the performers and the victims assumed somewhat equal salience in these narratives. Further, establishing the youthful status of both often served to construct these acts as *double tragedies,* as in a *New York Times* headline from a first story from the Smith-Robie narrative: "Grief over a Dead Child, and over the Child Accused" (8/15/93). Thus the problem of youth violence was constructed as a paradox in which the youthful status of the offenders was contrasted with the violence they committed.

Although performer and victim sequences were common in first stories more generally, the doublecasting sequence dominated the first stories in the Sandifer-Dean narrative. The earliest stories mentioned only Yummy's age and his status as performer, but after his body was found, stories quickly turned to doublecasting Yummy as both performer *and* victim, as in this CBS story: "Eleven-Year-Old Murder Suspect Found Shot to Death." Similarly, an NPR story told us: "An 11-year-old wanted by police for the murder of a 14-year-old girl was himself found dead this morning." Such doublecasting—at least in first stories—was unique among these narratives and was likely shaped partly by Yummy's death shortly after the stories of Shavon's death. Later in the narrative, story after story recounted a life that was so short but so full of abuse and neglect. Doublecasting also rears its head in the Manzie-Werner narrative. First stories began to hint that something was amiss with Sam. For example, we were told that "just days before the murder, the parents of the suspect cried out to a judge for help, but they were rebuffed" (CNN 10/3/97). It was only later, when the narrative turned to the biographies of both Sam and Eddie, that we learned exactly why Sam's parents asked for help.

We find victim, performer, and doublecasting sequences throughout these first stories, but the contextual sequence was by far the most common. Let's begin by examining two excerpts from first stories in the West Paducah narrative:

> In West Paducah, Kentucky, today, a 14-year-old boy took out a gun and opened fire on students at his high school. The victims were *gathered in an informal prayer circle in the high school's lobby,* when the shooting began. At least two students are dead, and six others were wounded. (NPR 9/1/97)
> Student at *Paducah High School* opens fire on *prayer circle,* killing two. (NBC 9/1/97)

Both these excerpts begin by mentioning the performer—a "14-year-old boy" or a "student"—and then describe his act before mentioning the victims. It does not seem to be an example of a victim sequence. However, I would argue it is also not an example of a performer sequence. It is the mention of "prayer circle" that is salient here. Almost every first story in this narrative included this reference. The same can be said of references to "high school." First stories in the Jefferson High School shooting narrative also named the high school: "Officials are calling it the worst violent incident *in the New York City school system's history,* two students shot dead in a *second-floor hallway of Brooklyn's Thomas Jefferson High School,* 17-year-old Ian Moore and 16-year-old Tyrone Sinkler" (CBS 2/28/92). These excerpts illustrate the two kinds of contexts that appeared in these sequences—those of *place* and *activity*. Here, "high school" referred to the context of place—as both a physical and social location—whereas "prayer circle" referenced the context of activity. In the West Paducah narrative, we find both contexts being used. Of course, the context of place did not always comprise schools. Consider the following excerpts from the Manzie-Werner narrative:

> *Jackson Township, New Jersey, is another town in mourning.* The victim here is an 11-year-old boy. . . . The suspect, a 15-year-old. (NBC 10/2/97)
>
> Residents of *Jackson County, New Jersey,* shocked by the murder of an 11-year-old boy. (CBS 10/4/97)

In these excerpts, the context of place was highlighted. Before we learned anything else, we were told this murder took place in "Jackson Township, New Jersey." It may seem like a mundane reference, merely placing the violent act in a particular place. However, note that in the first excerpt we are told that it is "another town in mourning." There were two kinds of context in play here. First, we learned that Jackson Township is a *town*—not a big city. We see this same kind of reference in a headline from the Smith-Robie narrative: "A Big-City Horror in a Small Town" (*New York Times* 8/22/93). Second, we learned that this was *another* town—that other towns had experienced similar incidents. We can contrast these references to small towns with a *New York Times* headline from the Sandifer-Dean narrative: "Boy Sought in Teen-Ager's Death Is Latest Victim of Chicago Guns." Here we learned that this incident occurred in *Chicago,* so another instance of big-city violence. We learn the same thing from the Jefferson High School shooting excerpt above: It was a school in *New York.* As I argued in Chapter 2, news talk oriented to big-city violence and small-town violence in rather different ways. Through these contextual sequences, first stories partially established the grounds for the development of *narratives* of big-city versus small-town or suburban youth violence.

Context sequences also established the activities that surrounded the acts. What were the victims or the performers doing at the time of the violence? In the West Paducah excerpts above, the answer to this question was that the victims were part of a prayer circle. However, much more common were references to what I call "routine childhood activities." Consider the following excerpts from the Manzie-Werner narrative:

> Young New Jersey boy *selling school products* found strangled in woods near his home. (CBS 10/1/97)
>
> It's a parent's worst fear: their child *selling candy door-to-door* is raped and murdered. The suspect a troubled teenage neighbor. (NBC 12/2/97)

Once again, even before we learned that a child was murdered, we knew the context, what he was doing at the time of his death. He was *selling door-to-door.* We see something similar in other narratives. Consider two additional excerpts—the first from the Bermudez narrative and the second from the narrative of Eric Morse:

> Three boys—two 8-year-olds and a 6-year-old—were booked for investigation of attempted murder after they knocked a 4-week-old baby out of its crib and kicked him, critically injuring the infant *while breaking into a house to steal a tricycle.* (Washington Post 4/24/96)
>
> From this open window at a *public housing high-rise,* a little four-year-old boy was shoved 14 stories to his death, police say, by two other boys who told investigators he had *refused to steal candy for them.* (CBS 10/14/94)

In the first excerpt, we were told that the performers—"three boys—two 8-year-olds and a 6-year-old" attacked the baby while in the house to steal a tricycle. In the next excerpt, we read that the victim was shoved out the window because he refused to steal candy for two other boys. The second excerpt also serves as an example of a double-context sequence: It provided us with both place and activity, a "public housing high-rise" that strongly suggests this took place in the big city.

Again, each quote might be read as providing mundane details of instances of youth violence. However, they seem more usefully read as reinforcing the youthful status of the performers and their victims. In the Manzie-Werner narrative, the activity—selling door-to-door for a school fund-raiser—reinforced the youthful status of Eddie Werner. In the narratives of the Bermudez infant and Eric Morse, context seems to have served two interrelated purposes. It certainly established the youthful status of the performers. However, it also seems to have cast the performers' putative motivations as trivial, certainly not sufficiently serious as to warrant the killing of a child. In this way, the appearance of routine childhood activities served to mark these narratives as symbols of the paradox of the larger problem of youth violence. It is worth mentioning that these context sequences often established the signature or moniker of each narrative. Thus, the narrative of Eric Morse *became* the narrative of the little boy who died because he would not steal candy. Indeed, in a 1994 speech, President Clinton described Eric's death in specifically that way. Eddie Werner became known as the little boy who died selling door-to-door for his school fund-raiser. Yummy Sandifer was the little gang member who killed for his gang, only to be killed by that gang.

Whether it was of place or of activity, context often served to mark a narrative as symbolic of a specific frame of youth violence. For example, first stories in the Sandifer-Dean narrative identified it as a symbol of the problem of "gang violence," whereas context sequences in the West Paducah and Jefferson narratives marked each as a symbol of "school violence." Indeed, as instances of school violence began to accumulate between 1997 and 1999, talk increasingly focused on this context. Consider, for example, the partial headlines from the narratives of Jonesboro, Springfield, and Columbine, respectively: "Bloodshed in a Schoolyard," "Shootings in a School," and "Terror in Littleton." These soundbites became standard parts of the headline for any story about these shootings. Thus, for example, a headline might read: "Shootings in a Schoolyard: The Victims" or "Terror in Littleton: The President; Clinton, 'Shocked and Saddened,' Hopes for Prevention." Not only did these headlines establish the context of place, but they highlighted the ironic juxtaposition between the sort of place—school—and the acts of violence. In short, school was supposed to be a haven from violence. It is important to note that in the third headline above, it was unnecessary to use the word "school." The reference to "Littleton" seemed to suffice as an identifier: a story about "Littleton" was about "school violence."

The sequencing of first stories, then, performed several kinds of work. It highlighted the youthful status of both victims and performers. Almost by definition, this emphasis marked these narratives as symbols of the larger problem. By doing so with victims, it established their innocence and their deaths as tragic. By doing so with performers, it marked them as children whose lives had somehow gone terribly wrong. By doing so with both, it marked these events as double tragedies. Contextual sequences highlighting childhood activities reinforced the youthful status of the two major types of characters. Place defined these acts as gang violence or school violence, but place also made these narratives symbolic of big-city or small-town violence. In later stories, narratives progressively backgrounded the originating acts of youth violence and increasingly focused on the other three main plotlines. Even though we might learn new details of the originating acts, most of the talk centered on the major characters and their lives, the local community or neighborhood, and the legal case. Each plotline developed along its own narrative arc.

Narratives of Communities and Neighborhoods: Place, Race, and Class Revisited

As narratives unfolded in the days, weeks, and months after the shootings, other plotlines developed, and the language of "hard news" progressively gave way to that of human interest. That is, the first stories developed into narratives about the *lives* of these people: their tragedies, struggles, and emotional travails (Fine and White 2002). What could the lives of these violent youth tell us about how they came to commit these horrible acts? We knew the victims were all children, but who *were* they? How was all this affecting the local residents? How were they coping with this tragedy? Much of the story line of the legal case was offered in the language of hard news, but there was still considerable human interest even here. Indeed, it was in and through stories about the legal case that we learned much about these characters.

These narrative arcs provided dramatic, and personal, meanings to the uncertainty, ambivalence, and ambiguity that surrounded the problem of youth violence. The story line of a violent youth would eventually flesh out a character who symbolized the person-category that populated the problem of youth violence: that is, someone whose life and actions presented a paradox of brutal and deadly violence committed by someone so young. These "characters" were, of course, children, and in some of these narratives, they were *young* children. As in first stories, descriptions often focused on their youthful appearance and their small stature, although these descriptions appeared in stories about the legal case or local residents or about the offender himself. Eric Smith was barely tall enough to see over the defense table in the courtroom. Yummy

Sandifer looked so small in his coffin. Their putative motives were also childlike. Eric Morse's attackers wanted him to *steal candy* for them. The boys that attacked the Bermudez infant entered the home to steal a *tricycle*. In these ways, these youth embodied the paradox of youth violence.

The victims in these narratives were children themselves and, almost by definition, innocents. These deaths were, therefore, tragic. The victims did not always die—Ignacio Bermudez survived his attack, and Missy Jenkins lived to tell her tale of Michael Carneal's attack on her prayer group in the West Paducah narrative. However, these plotlines were no less tragic: Little Ignacio may have suffered permanent brain damage, and Missy is confined to a wheelchair for the rest of her life. As it developed, this story line provided the details of the tragedy beyond the chronological ages of the victims. We did not learn much about Ignacio Bermudez beyond his age, but the fact that he was a four-week-old infant seemed sufficient grounds for this being a tragedy. Similarly, Derrick Robie was only four years old, and Eric Morse was only five. In the other narratives, the victims were teenagers and perhaps not quite as innocent. However, as stories informed us about their personalities and future plans, their deaths came to seem no less tragic. We learned that Shavon Dean was a "friendly girl with a smile that could chase a tear." In a neighborhood fraught with poverty and violence, she had planned to open her own beauty shop some day. The victims in the West Paducah narrative were all members of a prayer group. Even the two victims in the Jefferson High School narrative, who had criminal records (Ian and Tyrone), were cast as typical Bronx kids who played sports and video games and (like Shavon Dean) had plans for their futures. Their innocence—and the tragedy of their deaths—was reinforced in other ways as well. Eddie Werner, Eric Morse, and the victims of West Paducah were *good* kids: Eddie died while selling door-to-door for a school fund-raiser, Eric Morse was killed because he refused to steal candy, and the victims of Michael Carneal's shooting rampage were praying. These markers of innocence were so salient that they not only came to define the victims but became monikers of the narratives themselves. Ultimately, Eddie, Ian and Tyrone, Eric, Shavon, and the other victims in these narratives came to symbolize the entire category of victims of youth violence. They became poster children of sorts for its tragic consequences.

The story line of the legal case had its own dramatic arc. In his book *Manufacturing the News,* Mark Fishman (1980) argues that events in the criminal justice system (arrests, arraignments, plea bargains, sentencings, and so on) provide journalists with schemes of interpretation for producing crime news. Each event is a phase, and taken together, the entire sequence of phases comprises a phase structure that portrays activities as a single object moving through a career. In this way, events help structure or format what is otherwise a continuous and ongoing flow of information about a "case." In iconic narratives, such events structured the telling of the legal case, or put another way, occasioned talk of initial "facts" and "new developments" in the case. Such developments always furthered the dramatic arc of this story line. Thus, early stories of police searches, investigations, and arrests told us about the youthful offenders and their victims. Stories on arraignments often contained new information that, it was speculated, might help us understand the offenders' motivations. Press conferences in which police provided updates on their investigation might occasion talk of how the community was coping. Of course, much of the remainder of this story line concerned the outcome of the trial. Since we almost always knew the identity of the suspects early on, these were rarely "whodunit" narratives. The guilt of the accused was rarely challenged. Thus, the drama of these narratives usually addressed different questions: Would this child be tried in juvenile or criminal court? Would he be convicted? What kind of sentence would he receive? Here, too, stories about developments in the trial and its disposition occasioned talk about other story lines in these narratives. For example, stories detailing the daily events in a trial would certainly involve talk about the strategies employed by the defense and prosecution. Just as often, however, these stories provided a vehicle for talk about the suspects and their lives. Stories reporting on convictions and sentencing often included reactions of the parents of the violent youth as well as their victims.

The story line of the local area and its residents had its own dramatic arc, almost always an *emotional journey* filled with complex and often ambivalent emotions: shock and disbelief, fear and anger and bitterness but also often sympathy and forgiveness, hope as well as resignation. In many respects this story line provided a context that shaped—and was shaped by—the other story lines. It might be argued that it was the *master* story line. As first stories established the setting for a narrative, they also established the grounds for one of two different iconic narratives: those of communities and those of neighborhoods. These two terms are both empirical and cultural referents. In these narratives, communities and neighborhoods were different sorts of places—physically, socially, economically, and culturally. Each seemed populated with different sorts of people who lived different lives and had their own concerns. In each set of narratives, the major plots developed along different lines, and thus youth violence was presented as a different kind of mystery or paradox in each. The local residents traveled different emotional paths. Even the story lines of the legal cases differed from one community or neighborhood to another.

I've argued above that talk about the problem of youth violence conflated race, place, and class. That is, talk about violence in suburbs and small towns was almost always about middle-class whites, whereas talk about big-city violence was typically about lower-class and working-class minorities (almost always African Americans, though sometimes Latinos). Narratives of communities and of neighborhoods appropriated—and symbolized—this kind of talk. Thus, the narratives of Eric Smith and Derrick Robie, Sam Manzie and Eddie Werner, and West Paducah presented violence in communities. They were narratives set in small town or suburbs. The narratives of Jefferson High School, Yummy Sandifer and Shavon Dean, Eric Morse, and the Bermudez infant were about violence in neighborhoods. They were narratives set in the big city.

Community Narratives

The Smith-Robie, West Paducah, and Manzie-Werner narratives were cast as symbols of the growing problem of youth violence in the suburbs and small towns. West Paducah itself was also linked to Columbine, Jonesboro, and Springfield as symbols of the problem of *school* violence in these sorts of places—a frame that dominated talk of the problem during the late 1990s. In these narratives, communities were tranquil and often serene places. They were sometimes, though not always, places where religion was the bedrock of social and cultural life. They had nice houses with well-kept lawns. Parents cared about their children and protected them from harm. They were the last sort of place where youth violence was supposed to occur. Residents were shocked and confused by the killings because their communities were no longer insulated from the violence that plagued the inner city. Things would never be the same. *They had lost their innocence.* As a result of the death of Eddie Werner, New Jersey seriously considered banning the timeless childhood ritual of door-to-door fund-raising. There was talk of metal detectors and armed guards in the school where Michael Carneal fired into a prayer group. Savona—the tranquil little town in upstate New York where Derrick Robie was killed—was no longer a place where strangers were welcome.

This story line of the community took us on an emotional journey that symbolized the range of emotions associated with the broader problem of youth violence. Initially, there was shock and disbelief. These emotions intensified when it was discovered the violence had been committed by one of their own children. Thus, this violence presented not just a paradox but a mystery. Children and adults alike in Toms River—the setting for the Manzie-Werner narrative—were "shaken," but their shock and disbelief soon changed to grief and sorrow. In Savona, according to a *New York Times* headline, there was "grief over a dead child and over a child accused." In West Paducah, there was considerable talk of "forgiveness" for Michael Carneal. Perhaps because these communities had lost their innocence, much of the dramatic arc of this story line focused on their recovery. Story after story asked how West Paducah was "healing." Could Savona ever be the close-knit community it had been? Could Toms River regain the sense of safety it had enjoyed before Eddie Werner's death?

The story lines of Sam Manzie, Eric Smith, and Michael Carneal began as tales of unremarkable and seemingly normal kids. Like all kids from these communities, they came from ordinary, sometimes exemplary families. They did all the usual things. They were always good students; sometimes they were honor students. Their parents were respected members of the community. However, as the narratives developed, additional biographical details (Spencer 2005) came to light, which quickly led to questions about their mental status. Eric Smith was said to have few friends and spent much of his time reading Stephen King novels. Later we learned he had strangled a neighbor's cat, and there were suggestions that he had been physically if not also sexually abused. Michael Carneal had been teased by members of the prayer group he fired on. Police suggested that he preferred playing video games with his friends to physical sports. Sam Manzie was confused about his sexuality and had been teased about it. He had been lured into a relationship with a pedophile in New York. He was so troubled that his parents tried, unsuccessfully, to have a judge commit him to a psychiatric facility.

When stitched together, these particulars became stories of troubled young boys. As I suggested in Chapter 3, causal accounts of violence in the suburbs and small towns tended to focus on the youths themselves and their putative mental status. The boys in these community narratives served as symbols of those accounts. For the most part, we did not—or perhaps could not—take seriously the notion that their family lives or their community environments could have contributed in any significant way to their actions. However, as always, the story was not so simple. Just as talk of the broader problem included contests and debates, so did these narratives. As the story of the legal case began and developed, prosecutors painted a different image of these violent youth, one that tended toward an image of youth who killed with premeditation. Michael Carneal had brought a total of five guns to school that day and even brought earplugs that he put in his ears before opening fire. After he killed Eddie Werner, Sam Manzie had taken his body to a nearby field to hide it. Eddie's father talked of the "injustice" in the effort of Sam's defense attorney to "paint" him as a victim. Eric Smith had lured Derrick Robie to a vacant lot and then choked him and smashed his head with a rock; then he stuffed part of the contents of Derrick's lunch bag into his mouth, dumping the remainder on his body. In the West Paducah narrative, the parents of one of his victims were glad Michael Carneal had received the maximum sentence but were also frustrated. The plea agreement accepted by the judge left the question of Michael's sanity unresolved. During his trial, Eric Smith's "blank stare" was said to exhibit little remorse or any other emotion. After Eric Smith's conviction for murder, Derrick Robie's parents were relieved; something had to be done with Eric.

Perhaps predictably, the legal cases developed into a contest between the defense and the prosecution over whether the actions of these children stemmed from mental illness. There was considerable talk about the "strategies" that were to be employed by each side. The boys' attorney might be said to be pursuing an "insanity defense," while the prosecutors were steadfast in their pursuit of a more clear, and serious, charge of murder. The parents of these boys and their victims testified in court or offered their opinions outside court. We were treated to frequent updates on what the defense was planning or of disagreements over how the defense should proceed. The outcome of the legal case could have served as a resolution to the contest over the boys. The jury rejected Eric Smith's claims of mental illness and convicted him of murder. Sam Manzie ultimately pled guilty to murder over the objections of his attorney and parents. Michael Carneal, however, made a plea deal that resulted in a conviction of guilty but mentally ill. Did the adjudication of these cases finally resolve the debate over the perpetrators' culpability? Did we now "know" whether these three kids were evil killers or troubled kids driven to murder by their personal demons?

Such simple resolutions rarely presented themselves in these narratives. The last words in the Sam Manzie narrative seemed to be those of Sam's parents, who expressed outrage and dismay over his seventy-year sentence. Despite the verdict, in their minds their son was a deeply disturbed boy and was deserving of a different disposition. In the wake of the court's acceptance of Michael Carneal's plea of guilty but mentally ill, the parents of two of his victims were asked what they thought of the outcome. All claimed the plea agreement left "many unresolved issues" (NBC 10/7/98) that would have been clarified if there had been a trial. They believed the verdict absolved him of responsibility for his crime. One of the last stories in the wake of the verdict in the Eric Smith narrative was a CBS report (8/17/94) in which parents and other town residents were interviewed. How did they feel? Was justice served? There were conflicting opinions: Some felt he got what he deserved, while others were saddened. This ambiguity was reinforced as we watched family videos of Eric swimming and Derrick playing T-ball and fishing.

Neighborhood Narratives

In contrast to communities, neighborhoods were sad, dirty, and dangerous places. The streets surrounding Jefferson High School were "terrifying." The neighborhood that served as the setting for the Sandifer-Dean narrative appeared to be ruled by "gangsters." Eric Morse was dropped to his death from the fourteenth floor of a high-rise public housing project littered with trash and drug needles. In all these neighborhoods, poverty and drugs prevailed. The Iron Triangle area of Richmond where the Bermudez infant and his attackers lived was "rough" and "depressed." There was violence everywhere, and it could strike at any time for the most trivial of provocations. Kids here hardly ever lived with both parents, and they often lived with their grandmothers. As a result, they were often left unsupervised to roam the streets on their own. No wonder these kids were in trouble all the time. In these narratives, these were *youth who had been robbed of their innocence.* The judge who sentenced Eric Morse's killers asked "how the boys who caused his death had become so indifferent to human life" (*New York Times* 2/6/96). The world of that housing project was compared to the landscape of *Lord of the Flies.* Indeed, in a *New York Times* editorial, this narrative became a symbol of the superpredator:

> His killers displayed no remorse. In court, the younger of the two, who could barely see the judge above the partition, mouthed obscenities at reporters covering the trial. Last week, they became the youngest offenders ever sent to prison in Illinois. And they have come to symbolize the so-called super-predators, children accused of maiming or killing without a second thought. (2/8/96)

Recall that causal accounts of big-city violence often appeared to be taken for granted and, thus, explanations were often left implicit. The causes of big-city violence were assumed to lie in the nature of the big city itself. As a result, these narratives of neighborhood violence were as much—or more—about the neighborhoods that had robbed them of their innocence as they were about the individuals themselves.

In part because violence was such a commonplace, albeit unwelcome, occurrence, residents of these neighborhoods were sad and angry about the death of yet another of their children, but they were not terribly surprised. With the exception of the Jefferson High School shootings—in which the major characters were teenagers—what shock there was appeared linked to the young age of the killers. There were always calls that something must be done to stop the killing. There was talk in Chicago of marches to bring attention to the violence. The mayor of New York was scheduled to talk at Jefferson High School the day of the shootings. Young children were taken to view the tiny body of Yummy Sandifer as a lesson on the dangers of gangs. Some said these killings were evidence of the moral decay of these neighborhoods, if not American society itself. However, in spite of the initial shock over each tragedy, for the most part, neighborhood residents expressed no hope that the killing would stop anytime soon. There was a heavy feeling of resignation hanging over these narratives. These violent youth had been robbed of their innocence by their big-city surroundings, but their neighborhoods seemed to have lost their own a long time ago.

In these narratives, the youthful victim of the violence garnered at least as much attention as his or her killer. In the Jefferson High School narrative, each of the three main characters—Kahlil, Ian, and Tyrone—filled the same role. These were typical teens in this neighborhood—yes, they got into trouble, but they also had goals to someday make something of themselves. Killers and victims alike, these three kids were products of their neighborhood. Yummy Sandifer occupied both roles—he killed Shavon Dean, only to be killed himself. His killing of Shavon Dean was cast as paradoxical, but his own death was almost *ironic:* He had mistakenly killed Shavon while carrying out a shooting for his gang, only to be killed by that same gang. Perhaps because of the "irony," the story of Yummy's life was full of talk of physical abuse, foster homes, and the failure of the local human services system to protect him from what seemed in retrospect as an inevitable fate. The same sense of inevitability could be found in the Jefferson High School narrative—something like that was bound to happen eventually.

For their part, Eric Morse and the Bermudez infant garnered considerably more talk than did their assailants. Why might this be? The violent youth in these narratives were cast as both violent criminals and as victims of their urban environments. This kind of paradox was the stuff of considerable talk about the broader problem of youth violence, perhaps because we took for granted that this sort of environment would produce such kids. The violence remained a paradox in these narratives, but it was not a mystery. It was tragic, but it was not surprising. As a result, these narratives never developed a serious debate over how to best characterize these kids. They appeared to remain unfortunate victims of the big city and all its problems. Even Yummy Sandifer was, at the end of the day, allowed to stand as both victimizer and victim. There seemed little sense that this paradox had to be resolved.

Instead of comprising a contest over how to portray the violent youth in these narratives, the story of the legal case focused almost exclusively on how, or whether, justice would be served. At first, there was uncertainty about whether the case would end up in the juvenile or adult system, but that was quickly settled. Ultimately, what little we learned about these violent youth became part of their demonization, which led to a story line that asked: What was to be done with these kids? While Yummy Sandifer had already met his fate, what would happen to the others? Surely, they were victims of the myriad problems that beset their big-city neighborhoods, but they appeared so ruthless and so indifferent to human life—their crimes were so heinous—that something *had* to be done with them. We understood how they turned out the way they did and even held some pity for them, but our fear appeared to overwhelm other emotions. In the absence of a drama of competing visions of these kids being presented in court, their actual trials did not garner much attention. In the Eric Morse narrative, most of the talk centered on whether Illinois had an institution adequate or appropriate for his killers. Likewise, much of the story line of the legal case in the Bermudez narrative was what we might do with a six-year-old who so brutally attacked an infant. As a result, most of the stories about the legal case occurred at the beginning of the trials and at the conviction and sentencing of these youth.

Conclusion

The foregoing analysis brings us to three important questions:

- What made these narratives iconic?
- How were these narratives to be read in relation to talk of the broader problem of youth violence?
- From whose, or what, perspective were these narratives told?

First, what makes a narrative *iconic*? We might begin to answer this question by referencing the events that these narratives were putatively about. According to this point of view, there are characteristics of events that render them iconic, or at least potentially iconic. Some events might make for more dramatic and compelling and thus iconic narratives. The narratives discussed in this chapter—Sam Manzie and Eddie Werner; Eric Morse; Eric Smith and Derrick Robie; Yummy Sandifer and Shavon Dean; and Jefferson High School and West Paducah—provide some clues as to these qualities of such events. In most of these events, we might point to the especially young ages of the offenders and their victims. In the Jefferson and West Paducah shootings, we might emphasize the number of victims. In the Eric Morse narrative, the main point was that he was killed because he would not steal candy for his killers. Likewise, in the Bermudez infant case, the offenders entered the house to steal a Big Wheels tricycle. Eric Smith supposedly tortured Derrick Robie. Undoubtedly, these "concrete" or "objective" characteristics of events might play a role in understanding why an event rises to the level of "iconic."

However, I argue that these events only provide the raw materials out of which iconic narratives were constructed. The important or main "action" resides in the discourse or language. In short, iconic narratives are not so much *about* events as about events *existing in and through* their narrative telling. The storytelling draws our attention to the features of the narratives themselves; three such features are important in answering our question. First, as I have argued throughout this chapter, iconic narratives comprised talk with considerable depth and breadth. That is, these narratives involved a large number of stories across a wide range of news outlets. Further, these narratives comprised multiple plotlines that were introduced and developed during the course of their telling. In literary terms, for example, we might say that there was considerable character development in the talk about the offenders, their victims, and even the local residents.

Second, iconic narratives were constructed as *symbols* of the problem of youth violence. That may seem intuitively obvious, and it is almost by definition, but it is an important point. Narrative symbols of youth violence were constructed in ways that symbolized more than the youthful status of the offenders and their violent acts. One signature feature of these narratives was that they made visible the *paradox of youth violence*. For example, the youthful status of both the offenders and victims was always highlighted. It was reinforced by highlighting the context of childhood activities, as in the narratives of Eric Morse and the

Bermudez infant, or the context of place, as in the Jefferson and West Paducah school shootings. In turn, iconic narratives sometimes symbolized a particular kind—or frame—of youth violence. Thus, the Jefferson and West Paducah narratives symbolized school violence, and the Sandifer-Dean narrative symbolized the problem of urban gangs. The narrative of Eric Morse symbolized the problem of the superpredator.

Relatedly, the main plotlines developed in ways that articulated closely with other signature features of the problem of youth violence. Thus, talk about the local community or neighborhood brought into specific relief the conflation of place, race, and class that characterized how the problem was constructed. As we have seen, residents of "communities" and residents of "neighborhoods" reacted in different ways to the violence. In turn, this distinction was tied to talk that explored the reasons for the violence. As we saw in the narratives of Eric Morse, the Bermudez infant, and the Jefferson High School shooting, in "neighborhoods" youth violence was tied to and explained by abuse and neglect, street violence, and absent parents. Alternatively, as we saw in the narratives of Sam Manzie–Eddie Werner and Michael Carneal, this sort of explanation was missing, resulting in a "mystery" that was potentially solved by focusing on the violent youth himself and his putative mental illness. Finally, talk about the legal case focused on the sentence that would be or was imposed on the violent youth. In turn, this plotline typically progressed to talk about the justice system more generally, which often meant speculating about the sentence the youth might receive from the juvenile system versus adult criminal court. That, in turn, often rekindled the debate over the use of each justice system in handling violent youth.

Third, iconic narratives were characterized by their "carrying power." By this I mean, while serving as symbols of youth violence, they were often constructed as symbols of a number of other problems. For example, the narrative of Yummy Sandifer and Shavon Dean partially constituted a symbol of the failures of the child welfare system in the United States, as well as a cautionary tale about urban gangs. The narratives of Eric Morse and the Bermudez infant served to reinforce familiar assumptions about street violence and family breakdown in the big-city ghetto. In these narratives, such problems were constructed as origins of youth violence. In a different way, consider the narrative of Sam Manzie and Eddie Werner. Recall that in this narrative Eddie was the innocent victim—killed while going door-to-door for a school fundraiser. In addition to being the victimizer in this narrative, Sam was himself cast as a victim in at least three respects. First, he was lured into a sexual liaison by a male pedophile through the Internet. Second, he had been used by police as an informant against this man. Third, his parents' attempts to have him committed to a treatment program were rebuffed by a juvenile court judge. Cast in these ways, Sam and Eddie became characters in a cautionary tale of the dangers facing our children in the modern world that reads like this: "The Manzie case has become a vexing metaphor for the complexities of juvenile justice and for the dark potential of the Internet to damage the lives of some vulnerable adolescents" (*Washington Post* 10/8/97). Stories offered up talk about the dangers of the Internet. *Newsweek* asked "whether we're doing enough to protect our kids online" (10/13/97), and CBS felt compelled to "discuss the dangers for children on the Internet" (10/13/97). A number of experts offered up recipe knowledge on how to protect our children from online dangers. The coeditor of *Home PC Magazine* spoke on CBS about "ways that parents can protect your children from dangers of the Internet" (10/13/97); joining him was "a mother who used the Internet to track down her son's molester."

The narrative of Jeremy Strohmeyer serves to illustrate my argument that the iconic nature of narratives resides in their telling. According to this tale, Jeremy and his friend—David Cash—were at a Nevada casino one evening in 1997. At some point, they followed seven-year-old Sherrice Iverson into the women's bathroom, where Jeremy raped and killed her. Cash did nothing to stop the attack and left without reporting it. Strohmeyer was identified on a security video and was quickly arrested. A little more than a year after the attack, Strohmeyer pled guilty to four felony counts, including first-degree murder—and was sentenced to three life prison terms without parole. This event garnered more than its share of media attention—at least seventy-five stories across the spectrum of national news outlets, including television newsmagazines. There was certainly as much discursive space afforded this narrative as the ones that comprise the focus of this chapter. In addition, this narrative was linked in several stories—including *Rivera Live* and *People* magazine—to the problem of youth violence. Consider an ABC *20/20* report around the time of his sentencing: "Tonight, you are going to meet a young man who is loved by his family. He was an honor student, accomplished in many ways. But the tale he tells is so chilling, it turns our blood cold. He committed a crime so horrible that it captured headlines around the country" (10/30/98). In this excerpt, Jeremy's act is characterized as "chilling" and "horrible"—reminiscent of language in narratives that symbolized youth violence. Talk about being "loved by his family" and being an "honor student" seems to speak to the paradox of youth violence. However, in most other ways this narrative did not serve as a symbol of the general problem of youth violence. Here, Jeremy was not a "boy" or even "teenager," but rather a "young man." Further, little of this talk had the feel of a human interest narrative that characterized the other narratives in this book.

Regarding the main characters, consider how this narrative *could* have developed. There was some talk in a few stories—including a *60 Minutes* broadcast—that Jeremy was adopted and that his biological father was in prison and his mother in a drug rehabilitation program. His adoptive parents were well-to-do. At the time of the killing, Jeremy was in a "drunken haze" and did not remember the attack. Surely, all that was potential grist for a narrative full of ambiguity and complexity. Talk about his victim—Sherrice—could have developed in a way that emphasized her innocence. But it did not. There was talk that Sherrice's father liked to play the slots and was in the habit of taking his daughter with him to the casino while he gambled. Otherwise, we learned little of her character, and she remained a mystery. There was little talk of how Sherrice's family was coping with the tragedy. This tale could have developed in a way that cast Jeremy and David as symbols of the egocentric indifference of the rich, white, suburban teenager. However, at no time was there talk about how suburban culture might produce such kids. It might have developed as a narrative that problematized the actions of Sherrice's father who, in this tale, left her unsupervised while he gambled, which could have resulted in a narrative of parental indifference or neglect. There are a number of ways this narrative could have developed. However, the narrative plotlines discussed in this chapter—the tragedy of an innocent life cut short, a community left grieving, a legal case comprising a character contest over the offender or how justice might be best served—were left undeveloped.

In short, although this *could* have developed into a narrative symbol of the problem of youth violence, this potential did not seem to materialize. What did develop was a narrative that focused on the actions—or rather inactions—of Jeremy's friend. Remember that in this narrative, David Cash was with Jeremy and witnessed the early part of the attack, but he did nothing to stop it. Nor did he report the attack to the police. He, like Jeremy, was identified on security video and ultimately testified for the prosecution at Jeremy's trial. He ultimately came to be called the "bad Samaritan." Talk about David asked who he was, why he didn't stop the crime, and why he didn't report it. NPR and CBS's *60 Minutes* both ran rather lengthy stories addressing these questions. There was much talk about David's putative lack of remorse for his inaction and protests at the University of California at Berkeley campus, where he was a student. Indeed, in this narrative he became a kind of poster child for movements in both Nevada and California for the passage of Good Samaritan laws that would require witnesses to report cases of child abuse. As a CNN headline put it: "Strohmeyer Trial Overshadowed by Criticism Against Witness of Assault" (8/31/98). In this way, this narrative developed into a symbol of bystander indifference rather than of the problem of youth violence. What I am suggesting is that the iconic character of the narratives in this chapter depended on the ways they were told. In the process of this telling, certain raw materials of events were emphasized or highlighted, ignored or backgrounded, brought together or kept apart.

Finally, iconic narratives were rife with drama. There was the drama of good versus evil: the innocence of the victims pitched against the evil and malevolence of their attackers. But there was also the drama of paradox that juxtaposed the youthful status of violent youth against their terrible acts. There was the drama of tragedy—young kids gone bad and the lives of other kids cut short. There was also the drama of heroism: Eric Morse's brother who ran down fourteen flights of stairs to try to save him, and the student who stopped Michael Carneal from firing more shots. There was the emotional drama of communities and neighborhoods burying—and mourning—their dead. Would these neighborhoods ever find peace from the violence? Would these communities ever heal? Finally, there was the drama of conflict. Prosecutors and defense attorneys battled in the courtroom, and their battles symbolized the broader debates and contests regarding the problem itself. In narratives of neighborhoods, where there was little debate over *why* the violence occurred, prosecutors argued for justice and accountability, and defense attorneys argued for compassion and rehabilitation. In narratives of communities, however, these foes were embroiled in victim contests (Holstein and Miller 1990) in which the legal fates of Eric Smith, Sam Manzie, and Michael Carneal were at stake. Were these boys monsters who deserved the full wrath of the criminal justice system? Or were they themselves victims worthy of sympathy?

Consider our second question: how were these narratives to be read vis-à-vis talk of the broader problem of youth violence? To be sure, *neighborhood* narratives appropriated and reinforced broader cultural assumptions and images of the big city. We "knew" that the big city was dirty, dangerous; rife with gangs, drugs, and violence. And we associated these qualities with images of the urban poor and ethnic minorities. These narratives brought such assumptions into sharp relief. Although these narratives shocked us, they were not telling us anything we didn't already know. What these narratives simply did is symbolize images of big-city violence that was now getting worse and violent youth who were getting younger. The Jefferson narrative reinforced images of violence in big-city schools that was a product of big-city streets. The narratives of Eric Morse—and to some extent the Bermudez infant—served as icons of the superpredator problem and in this way gave specific form—and reinforced—our more abstract sense of anxiety and fear over images of hordes of young, cold-blooded killers in the coming decade.

What of narratives of *communities*? They were places of nice houses with well-kept lawns and well-to-do families. Here, parents cared about their children and took care to protect them from harm. They were always and consistently the last place where this sort of violence was supposed to occur, so these communities were no longer insulated from the violence that plagued the inner city. They were changed forever. Narratives of communities served as symbols of our broader, collective concern with the problem of youth violence. If there was any doubt that the problem had grown well beyond its inner-city boundaries, these narratives made clear that violence could now happen anywhere and to anyone. In a sense, the loss of innocence experienced by these communities symbolized the loss of innocence we felt as a nation.

Relatedly, the emotional journey traveled by these communities paralleled—and symbolized—the emotional ambivalence and complexity associated with the broader problem. These communities began this journey shocked and confused. The conclusion of the court case established legal guilt but not questions about justice. Likewise, the communities still had no answers to their most pressing questions: Why? Why here? They probably never would. They were afraid—could it happen again here? They were angry, but not necessarily at Eric or Sam or Michael. Sometimes they were angry at the injustice of the legal outcome. Sometimes they were angry at the changes that violence had brought to their doorsteps. Sometimes they felt compassion for these violent youth who had lived among them, and sometimes they pitied their parents. However, if they allowed themselves these emotions for these violent youth and their parents, what did it mean for how they felt about their victims? It was as if feeling compassion for their victims precluded reserving the same emotions for their killers and their parents. To paraphrase a CBS story (8/11/94) in the Smith-Robie narrative: Can we feel sorry for Eric's mom without being unfair to Derrick's parents?

My third and last question concerns the matter of perspective. From what—or whose—point of view were these narratives told? Were they told from the perspective of those living in communities or from the perspective of residents of neighborhoods? Or were they told from a more neutral, or removed, point of view? The answer to this question holds true not only for these narratives, but ostensibly for *all* the talk about the problem of youth violence. It is not an easy question to answer because we were rarely told the answer in the context of the narratives themselves. However, my readings of these narratives suggest to me that they were told from the standpoint of communities. Several clues led me to this conclusion. The first clue is provided by the narrative of Jefferson High School. In some of the stories that comprised this narrative, we were provided an in-depth view of the neighborhood surrounding the school from the perspective of its residents. What we learned appeared commonplace to those residents. The people who lived there seemed to know all this. Thus, it appeared to be provided for the benefit of those who did *not* live there. The same appeared to hold true for the documentary *The 14 Stories of Eric Morse*—the Peabody Award–winning film produced by LeAlan Jones and Lloyd Newman—two young residents of Chicago's South Side housing projects. This documentary provided an up-close-and-personal look at the neighborhood where Eric Morse and his killers lived. Time and again we were told this documentary was set in *their* world, a world that America rarely glimpsed. In other words, this world of big-city neighborhoods was not *our* world. The people that populated neighborhoods were someone else—not *us*. Other clues can be found. The ways in which the condition of youth violence was constructed strongly suggest a growing sense of concern as it was transformed from a big-city to a suburban or small-town phenomenon. It was as if *our* concern grew as it encroached upon *us*. Talk about big-city violence seemed to address a problem at some remove, whereas talk about small-town violence seemed to contain a greater sense of immediacy and urgency. The search for causal accounts and solutions to this problem also reinforced this conclusion. From a *community* perspective, the causes of big-city violence made sense at the same time that the causes of suburban violence remained such a mystery.

Thus, as appropriated in these narratives, broader assumptions and beliefs about place, class, and race form a set of discourses that can be called hegemonic. Those discourses represent the middle class and dominate the

American cultural landscape. As appropriated here, the discourses largely absolved white, middle-class lifestyles and culture from responsibility for the problem of youth violence. They did so by focusing on the psychology of middle-class, white youth or on considerably broader issues such as guns or the media. At the same time in this discourse, causal accounts of neighborhood violence focused almost exclusively on the lifestyle and culture of lower-class and working-class urban minorities. What was contested was what to do about the problem, not its causes. This talk did reserve some sympathy for neighborhood youth as victims of urban problems, but it still demonized them as it focused on their acts. Alternatively, despite some legal outcomes to the contrary, there was still considerable sympathy for the violent kids of middle-class families as "troubled" and an apparent empathy for the loss of innocence in places like West Paducah, Toms River, and Savona. Such did not appear to be the case for the South Side of Chicago, Oakland, or Brooklyn. They had lost their innocence long ago.

5

Lessons Learned

What lessons can we draw from this study? In this chapter, I discuss three sets of lessons. The first set pertains to constructionist theory and research. The second set is less academic and more "practical" in a sense and concerns matters of public policy. The final set of lessons concerns American civic discourse regarding youth violence and related issues.

Lessons for Constructionists

I propose that constructionist social problems theorists and researchers—those of us who study public discourse about social problems—can take three lessons from this book. The first lesson speaks to the benefits of searching for the ambiguous in talk about social problems. The second lesson concerns the staying power of youth violence as a problem. Third, this study provides some lessons on the role of place in the construction of social problems.

Lesson One: The Complexity of Social Problems Talk

Constructionists typically see social problems talk as simplifying problems. That was not the case with the problem of youth violence. I hope to have demonstrated that talk about the problem was anything but simple. At its core, this complexity comprised a paradox in which the assumed innocence of youth magnified the malevolence of their violence.

The problem of suburban and small-town violence took this paradox to the level of mystery. But there were other layers to this complexity and ambiguity.

Rather than constructing monocausal accounts and simple framings, talk about the problem comprised multiple and often competing causal accounts and solutions. According to constructionists, talk about other violence problems often decontextualizes the violence and in the process appears to hold offenders—especially men—unambiguously culpable for their acts. Rather than decontextualizing the problem, much of the talk about youth violence centered on the contexts of these acts and the youth that committed them. Focusing on the contexts performed important discursive and interpretive work: It helped establish not only the putative motivations of these youth but also cast the acts as instances of either big-city or suburban violence. It helped address the question that arose from this paradox: How could youth, who were supposed to be innocent, come to commit these heinous acts? In American culture it would be difficult to hold youth—even teenagers—fully and unambiguously culpable, since they are by definition not adults. They have not yet fully developed or matured. Put simply, if children are supposed to be innocent, there must be something that *made* them or *shaped* them into killers. Although there was some talk of biology, these accounts were almost always environmental. Far from decontextualizing the problem, Americans explored almost every conceivable social, cultural, and economic aspect of the problem's context. The violence of these youth seemed to *demand* some sort of causal accounting, and these accounts often seemed to mitigate their culpability. At the same time, these kids were often roundly demonized. They were called monsters and their acts evil. Throughout the 1990s there were constant calls to hold these kids accountable by taking a more punitive stance toward the problem. In short, the question of their culpability was, and remained, ambiguous.

A veritable cacophony of voices offered causal accounts and solutions. From news stories to editorials and letters to the editor to newsmagazine shows, it seemed everyone had something to say about why our children were turning into killers and what should be done about it. As one *New York Times* article put it: "As with other issues involving children, the gap between what one feels and what one knows tends to be filled by assumptions, surmises and hot air. Evidence on who is being damaged by what and how goes uninspected amid the jeremiads of religious groups, legislators, psychologists and the ever-growing profession of advocates for the young" (3/22/94). Of course, this list of "experts" could have been considerably longer, if the reporter had included criminal and juvenile justice officials, victims and their advocacy groups, educators, celebrities, and even the president of Nike, to name but a few. Americans profess to value children. Also, it appears, Americans claim some knowledge of how to properly protect and raise them. It was quite common for television news programs to invite experts to provide recipe knowledge on how to keep our kids "out of harm's way." We were told how to keep children safe on the Internet, in school, and while fundraising door-to-door. I have never been an expert on child development, yet even I was interviewed many times during the 1990s for local television and newspaper stories about how parents might better talk and relate to their children.

The debates and contests over causes and solutions were shaped, in part, by the ways in which the problem was constructed. They also added additional complexity and ambiguity. This was especially true in the case of talk that treated solutions as so many tokens in high-stakes political games. Here, it seemed, solutions were offered not because someone thought they might work but rather to garner votes or score political points. In such talk, it seemed we not only had to question the efficacy of solutions but also the sincerity of those offering them. Enmeshed in this complexity of images of violent youth and of causal accounts and solutions, we became ambivalent. Indeed, talk about the problem appropriated broader cultural understandings or beliefs about youth that are, themselves, ambiguous or ambivalent. In Chapter 1, I cited what Hine (1999, p. 11) had to say on this matter. Some of his observations bear repeating:

> Our beliefs about teenagers are deeply contradictory: They should be free to become themselves. They need many years of training and study. They know more about the future than adults do. They know hardly anything at all. They ought to know the value of a dollar. They should be protected from the world of work. They are frail, vulnerable creatures. They are children, they are sex fiends. They are the death of culture. They are the hope of us all.

I suggest that constructionist theorists and researchers take a lesson from what we've learned here and look for ambiguity and ambivalence in other social problems. We might begin by looking at the talk that comprises other problems associated with children, such as teenage drug use or teen pregnancy. Debates over proper solutions to these problems—such as abstinence versus education—might be examined for the ways they are shaped by our ambivalence regarding youth. We might extend our efforts to other categories of persons who share the same level of innocence or powerlessness typically associated with youth. In this way, social problems populated by women—especially mothers—might also be associated with ambiguity and ambivalence. Conventional wisdom seems to be that "welfare queens" or "crack moms" have been summarily demonized in the news. I believe that these two problems are primarily set in the big city and are populated by minority women. If so, then how might our cultural assumptions regarding women and the big city shape how we talk about these problems? Much like our cultural assumptions regarding children prevent us from unambiguously demonizing violent youth, so might our assumptions about women prevent the same thing with "welfare queens" and "crack moms." I am not suggesting that these person-categories are constructed as wholly sympathetic, but rather that our talk about them should be full of contradictions and ambivalence. I would challenge constructionists to take a more nuanced look at this talk. Finally, I suspect we would find ambiguity in our talk about problems such as mental illness and alcoholism. For much of the nineteenth and twentieth centuries, both these forms of deviance were blamed on the moral failings of individuals. In historical terms, only relatively recently have they been designated—at least by medical professionals and social elites—as illnesses. However, as Peter Conrad and Joseph Schneider (1980) have suggested, acceptance of this designation by the general public has lagged. As a result, I suspect we would find considerable ambiguity in talk about the culpability of individuals who populate these two conditions and, thus, some degree of ambivalence. Specifically, if we were to look at talk about mental illness, we might find a complex combination of both illness and individual moral failing, which might result in an ambiguous image of culpability.

Lesson Two: The Staying Power of the Problem of Youth Violence

Youthful misbehavior is a recurring social problem. The violence of the 1990s was not the first, nor will it be the last time that youth and their behavior have become objects of widespread concern and intense talk. In this way, youth violence may simply be a recent manifestation or expression of a more general problem that from time to time is rediscovered. This sort of recurrence certainly speaks to the importance of youth in relation to any number of cultural concerns or issues, such as anxiety about social or technological change or apprehension over an uncertain future. This particular manifestation, despite ebbs and flows of public attention, remained an object of concern for most of the decade. Why might that be?

We might begin by considering the nature of this talk as *news*. When we examine this talk, it manifested many well-known and understood characteristics of the news as an institution and as an industry. Altheide (2002) suggests that news-as-entertainment employs the problem frame, which implies that: (1) there is an undesirable state of affairs, (2) its effects are widespread, (3) its elements can be unambiguously identified, (4) it can be fixed and there is a mechanism for doing so, and (5) the agent for this change is known. The problem of youth violence articulated closely with some, but not all, aspects of this frame. Youth violence was universally cast as undesirable, and it was spreading across the country. Of course, most social problems are constructed that way. However, as I've argued consistently in this book, what youth violence brought to the table was ambiguity and ambivalence, *not* clarity and certainty. To be sure, there was much talk about its causes and solutions, but there was little agreement regarding what, precisely, the causes were and how we might mitigate the problem. I argue that it was this very uncertainty, ambivalence, and ambiguity that *provided* for greater entertainment—and news—value, and thus longevity. For example, debates and contests over causal accounts and solutions articulated with the news value of balanced reporting. However, these debates also provided for good drama—the drama of conflict—especially when these solutions became tokens in political warfare. Thus our talk about youth violence was also talk about politics, about strategy and votes and power. These battles were an integral part of the ambiguity of this problem, and in this way ambiguity made for good entertainment. In short, I disagree with Altheide (2002) that the entertainment value of news lies in its simplicity and clarity— at least in this case. Instead, I argue that the problem had such staying power precisely because of its uncertainty, ambivalence, and ambiguity.

Iconic narratives—especially as they were constructed in the language of the human interest story—also contributed to the staying power of the problem. As Gary Alan Fine and Ryan White (2002) suggest about human interest narratives more generally, the narratives of Yummy Sandifer and Shavon Dean, Sam Manzie and Eddie Werner, and others were *dramatic* narratives. I think we can safely assume that the public closely followed and presumably talked about these narratives. Indeed, some narratives, such as Columbine, were the biggest news stories of the decade. As they unfolded over time, we can imagine the public interest that accompanied uncertainty over the legal outcomes or stories about the victims. Although they often had predictable narrative arcs, stories about communities or neighborhoods still captured attention because they were emotional stories. Contests over how to imagine these youth or what to feel about them created dramatic tension—an important element of human interest narratives as well as entertaining news more generally. Finally, the multiple story lines of these narratives all but guaranteed that there would be "updates" to report—something new or "fresh" (Altheide 2002; Fishman 1980). Had an arrest been made yet? Would this case be tried in adult or juvenile court? What new information do we have regarding the violent youth's motivations? How are the wounded recovering? How are the local residents coping, and what can *they* tell us about the background of the killer? The victims?

The seriousness of the problem—as constructed in rising rates of violent crime and the heinous nature of the violence itself—certainly demanded attention. However, that alone might not have carried the problem for so long, especially when news of falling violent crime rates among youth began to fill stories in the mid-1990s. Most importantly, youth violence was a paradox, and the problem was complex. Yet our talk about the problem demanded clarity. Americans assumed the search for causal accounts and solutions would provide answers to our pressing questions, but the more answers that were proffered, the less clear things seemed to become. Voices that seemed to speak with some authority— law enforcement and district attorneys, social workers and teachers, victims and their advocates—all seemed to know what they were talking about. However, they all disagreed. Their answers were always contested, and their disagreements never appeared to be resolved. We may have agreed on the causes of big-city violence but could never agree on what do to about it. We could not even agree on the causes of, much less the solutions to, small-town school violence.

Of course, there was a great deal of variety in the particular ways in which the "why" question was phrased and, more importantly, the answers that were offered. As I argued above, although the problem of big-city violence was constructed as a paradox, it was not a wholly unexpected one. Indeed, talk about this problem often appeared drawn from a time-worn template that comprised young, lower-class, minority kids living in the dirty and dangerous big city. There were only two contests here. One involved our emotions—should we feel fear or anger or compassion for these young victims of the big city? The second, and related, contest was over solutions to this problem. Should we focus on prevention or incarceration? Was the answer rehabilitation or punishment?

The appearance of youth violence in communities helped extend the lifespan of the problem. The string of suburban and small-town school shootings that began in 1997 provided what seemed like never-ending instances of this troubling new problem. Yet violence in these places had been mentioned years earlier. As early as 1992, we were told that middle-class kids were joining gangs. In 1994, school violence appeared in the suburbs. Eric Smith was evidence that youth violence had found its way into small-town America. Despite all this talk, the school shootings of 1997 and beyond were cast as something new and troubling. With it emerged new causal accounts and new solutions and, no less important, new debates. They were waged with a renewed energy because the problem was on *our* doorsteps, in *our* communities. The media frenzy that followed Columbine was, in some ways, only quantitatively different from the attention that school shootings garnered over the previous three years. In effect, this "new" problem reenergized, reanimated, and in some ways transformed concern about youth violence.

The staying power of this problem was also a product of how closely it resonated with—and appropriated—a number of broader cultural discourses. Most obviously, the paradox of violent youth was partially predicated on the assumption of the innocence of children. But there is more to the matter than that. Best (1990), Gilbert (1986), and other constructionists have argued that concern for children often manifests our cultural fears and anxiety over broader social issues. Times of rapid social change often fuel such anxiety, which in turn finds expression in talk about youth and their behavior. The twentieth and early twenty-first centuries have been times of almost continuous political, economic, cultural, and technological change, so it makes sense that youth violence would from time to time find its way into social problems talk. For example, the public handwringing over mass media—especially the Internet and video games—might be read as manifesting anxiety over what were then relatively new technologies. I strongly suspect our feelings about these new technologies are full of ambivalence. The Internet could open the world to us, but are our children safe there? Video games are certainly fun, but are they teaching our kids violence?

Talk about the problems of violence in small towns and the suburbs, especially the explosion of discourse about school violence in the late 1990s, seems to suggest a particular concern about middle-class youth. In some ways, this talk is reminiscent of talk about the delinquency problem of the 1950s (Gilbert 1986)—in both instances it seems we confronted middle-class teens as a kind of strange and alien race among us, more strange than teenagers usually appear to adults. There was some talk of a putative change in the nature of communities and how that might have led to school shootings like Springfield and West Paducah, suggesting a degree of anxiety about change in the middle-class social landscape. The talk of a "loss of innocence" in those social and cultural places seems to evidence such anxiety. In a real sense, we seemed concerned that white, middle-class communities were becoming like the big city and that change was bringing with it all the problems that attended the big city— including youth violence. Comparisons with the "good old days," when kids were much less violent and we could trust the kids next door, served to reinforce claims about the seriousness of the present problem, but they also served to highlight anxiety about social and cultural change. In these ways, talk about the problem appropriated cultural understandings and images of the city (Hadden and Barton 1973). In doing so, it reinforced images of the big city while serving both to challenge and perhaps reinforce images of the suburbs and countryside.

As discourse about youth violence and its causes and solutions drew on, or appropriated, broader debates and issues—such as guns, violence in the media, religion in the schools, and a host of other issues—the problem got caught up in a number of long-standing culture wars. In fact, I think it's reasonable to suggest that youth violence was a site on which these culture wars were manifested or played out. To be sure, culture wars play out in other venues. For example, the "gun control debate" recurs in talk about adult violence or whenever Congress considers a "crime bill." The debate over solutions to poverty manifests in talk about welfare reform. Certainly, youth violence appears to have been a particularly fertile place to wage these culture wars. And wage them we did. As I argued in Chapter 3, although news items may have begun with an atrocity tale of youth violence, they often quickly moved to talk about causes and solutions. This talk was often couched in the language of culture wars. Conservatives advocated getting tough, whereas liberals talked of compassion and prevention. These culture wars are long-standing and, in many ways, not easily resolvable. Hunter (1991) suggests they are, in fact, irresolvable since they are founded on deep and almost intrinsically incompatible ideals about the nature of American society. Since youth violence was a site where these wars played out, in a sense these wars carried youth violence along for the ride. If these culture wars are indeed irresolvable, then so were debates over the causes of and solutions to youth violence. All this suggests that youth violence had the staying power it did because—to put it simply—the way it was constructed created a cultural space in which there was always room for another causal account. More importantly, the ways the debates were waged seemed to all but guarantee they would not be resolved.

I would encourage other constructionists to investigate how ambiguity and ambivalence contribute to the longevity of other social problems talk. A useful place to begin this sort of exploration would be problems that are easily implicated in culture wars—such as debates over abortion. How has the viability of this debate appropriated (and been appropriated by) the language of culture wars and, thus, been shaped in ways that preclude easy resolution? The same might be asked of drug problems. I would suggest revisiting Craig Reinarman and Harry Levine's (1995) readings of 1980s discourse on crack. Here we might find the same sort of debates and contestations over causal accounts and solutions that I found regarding youth violence, and much of this debate might well be couched in the language of culture wars. If so, that might partially explain its longevity as a social problem. If we go one step further, it might partially explain why we can't seem to find resolution to the more inclusive "drug problem," of which crack was only one manifestation.

Lesson Three: Race, Place, Class, and Social Problems

Sasson (1995) has observed that public talk about crime generally tends to attribute the problem to individual choices. Reinarman and Levine (1995) make the same argument regarding the crack scare of the 1980s. In both instances, such talk appropriates and reinforces what we typically identify as a conservative ideology as it attributes these—and any number of other problems (e.g., poverty, teenage pregnancy)—to individual moral failure. Race is implicated here. Constructionists have long argued that our cultural images of crime are intimately linked to race. As Gamson observes in the foreword to Sasson's (1995) book *Crime Talk,* the violent criminal provides a symbolic enemy against which the public can be rallied. However, "the image of the enemy—the violent criminal—has the additional advantage of providing a hidden image of the 'black' violent criminal whose content can be decoded in this way by the intended audience while providing the users of the image with plausible deniability of any racial intent" (p. xi). In talk about youth violence, the conflation of place, race, and class may be one way in which "plausible deniability" had been achieved. Sasson's (1995) focus-group discussions were dominated by a "social breakdown" frame—a causal frame that attributed crime to "moral decline, poor parenting, and community disintegration" (p. 161). This frame articulates closely with the causal accounts associated with big-city violence. Although those accounts partially hid race from view, they did not unambiguously attribute the problem to the moral failures of these youth per se. At the same time it cast them as remorseless predators, it also set them and their acts in the context of the pathology of their big-city environments. Once again, it appeared difficult to unambiguously attribute violence to a simple choice by these youth.

However, the other part of this conflation of place, race, and class concerns youth violence among white, middle-class, suburban youth. At the risk of simplifying what I hope to have shown was considerable ambiguity and uncertainty, I suggest that to a significant degree this sort of violence was attributed to *anything but* individual moral failure. Further, it was not attributed to social breakdown—at least not a breakdown of middle-class communities. Although there was talk of how the social and cultural lives of communities might be changing for the worse, such changes were typically cast as *consequences* of the violence rather than *causes* of it. Instead, causal accounts of middle-class violence focused on psychology or broad social and cultural issues such as media and guns. In so doing, this talk reinforced images of poor, minority, urban neighborhoods as breeding grounds for crime and violence and absolved white, middle-class, suburban communities of their roles in the problem.

In both instances—of neighborhood violence and community violence—talk appeared to be about place, while at the same being about class and race. Of course, class and race were typically not explicitly mentioned, but it seems clear that both were consistent subtexts in all of this. Race was always there without being mentioned. How might race, class, and place be implicated in other social problems talk? More to the point, how are class and place used to partially hide—or act as a code for—race? Reinarman and Levine (1995) provide a hint about where to start looking when they contrast the crack scare of the 1980s with the cocaine problem of the 1970s. The former appeared to be linked to lower-class minorities, whereas the latter was closely identified with the white middle class. How were these two problems constructed? What sorts of causal accounts and solutions were proffered for each?

Lessons Regarding Policy

Michael Schudson (1992, p. 221)—in reference to his study of "versions of Watergate"—talks of a moral imperative to contest memories of the past:

If a moral imperative to remember is to make any sense, it is necessary to accept a view of memory as a constructive act, not a neurological or documentary reflex. Yet it also requires acknowledging that there are limits to the pasts that can be reconstructed, that there is an integrity to the past that deserves respect. Only then is an imperative to study the past, to think and rethink it, to debate it, coherent. Only then is there a foundation for urging people to care about and care for fallible human truths, no matter how fragile or contestable. It is, indeed, the fragility of human truths that makes the duty of remembering so vital.

Of course, in this book I have been talking about the problem of youth violence rather than history per se. However, there is a lived reality to the problem of youth violence that has to do with the youth and their families, their victims and *their* families, and all the rest of us who are touched directly and indirectly by it and who contribute to civic discourse about it. It behooves us—all of us—to care about the "fallible human truths" that surround and are part of youth violence. Part of what this means to me is that the study of youth violence as a social construction must also concern the "real world" of policy and its effects. Regarding policy, Loseke (1992, p. 151) argued, "At the level of social policy, for example, there is a tendency for policy to reflect constructed images of problems rather than the underlying heterogeneity of lived realities . . . such policies will not be sensible for all potentially similar human troubles." Her point, like Schudson's, is well taken. What she argues is that *social images* of problems are simplified compared to their *lived realities*—which are more heterogeneous and complex. Even though I have argued that talk about youth violence is anything but simplified, I do argue that how this problem was constructed has shaped the search for solutions in fundamental ways. These lessons have to do with what we talked about and what we did *not* talk about.

Lesson Four: Doing Things "to" or "for" Kids Rather Than "with" Them

Talk about solutions to the problem of youth violence was almost always about doing something "to" or "for" kids. There was considerable talk about offering after-school activities and midnight basketball or about tougher punishments. There was talk about saving kids from physical abuse and drugs or controlling access to guns or protecting them from media violence or putting them away for the sake of public safety. As I discussed in Chapter 1, the second half of the 1990s saw a tidal wave of legislation that made it easier to try violent youth in adult criminal courts. We already know from a host of studies that using adult criminal courts to punish kids has little deterrent effect and may actually increase recidivism (see, e.g., Kupchik 2006). It seems clear that this revamping of the waiver/transfer provisions was not the result of careful study. Rather, it was a response to public fear and resulting calls to do something. It may have temporarily removed some dangerous kids from our streets, but it certainly did not make us safer in the medium term, much less in the long term. Given that most indicators of youth violence were declining by mid-decade, it seems clear that this punitive turn had little, if any, effect on the problem.

These ways of talking about solutions are easy to understand, given the way we talk about violent youth as either demons or victims. Thus, it's easy to talk about providing help or safety "for" kids while at the same time talk about providing stiffer legal sanctions "to" kids. That is a product of the paradox of youth violence. Based on cultural images of youth that are by now several centuries old, we appear inclined to protect them when they behave or perhaps even when their indiscretions are minor. When they commit serious violent crime, however, we often give in to our fear and anger and act on our inclination to punish. This bifurcation of solutions also makes sense given what Penelope Leach (1994), Hine (1999), and others have suggested: that youth are generally regarded as an out-group in our culture. Whether considered inferior and less worthy of respect (Leach 1994) or as strange and alien beings (Hine 1999), youth—and especially teenagers—are often kept at arm's length. William Corsaro (1997) argues that as a result, adults tend to ignore or discount young people's perspectives on their lives, and that, in turn, makes it easier to talk about doing things "to" or "for" our kids.

This is not to say there was an absence of talk of other sorts of solutions. For example, there was considerable talk about nonviolent conflict resolution, mostly in the first half of the decade. From time to time, people mentioned mediation programs, as in a 1992 NPR interview with the assistant dean of the Harvard School of Public Health, Deborah Prothrow-Stith (3/1/92). Although she talked about gun control, she spent much of the interview promoting programs based on anger management, student mediation groups, and "community parent and community agency–centered activities." Such programs offer solutions centered on definitions of violence, solutions that engage youth with each other and with adults. That said, such solutions did not dominate our talk.

To be sure, many, perhaps most, seriously violent youth may need treatment of some sort, and sometimes we need to institutionalize youth for the sake of their own, and public, safety. All that appeared to make it hard to talk about working "with" kids to solve the problem. Admittedly, sometimes we did. We periodically heard about "summits" or "conferences" in which government, community, or school officials met with groups of youth. We read about President Clinton urging parents to talk with kids about violence. We read interviews that journalists conducted with youth in which they described living in contemporary society in their own words. It should be noted that the documentaries made by Jones and Newman about "their" neighborhood (Chicago's South Side) garnered considerable attention. However, it is not at all clear that we— as adults—took all this talk very seriously. It doesn't seem we took what kids told us and did anything significant with it. Ellen Galinsky says as much in her book *Ask the Children* (2000) and in an interview with NPR:

> We talk a great deal about children, but we don't spend that much time talking to them in a systematic way, measuring their responses, understanding the conclusion they make about the world adults have made for them. So the arguments adults have about what children really need often take on an abstract quality that might need some real information from some actual children. What do they want? What do they value? How do they think their own parents are responding to their needs and providing for them materially and emotionally? Do they yearn for more time with their mothers and fathers? When their parents are around, are the adults really paying attention? Or do they seem distracted or rushed?

To be sure, it is naïve to imagine that youth would always be able to articulate their lives any more adequately than adults can. However, simply listening to them helps engage them with the adult world, and in fact we may learn something important from them. Ignoring their perspective appears to have prevented us from seriously exploring adult connections with youth and forging solutions based on those connections. There are a host of such programs, which are based on connecting youth with the adult world rather than treating these youth as passive recipients of our retribution, treatment, or protection. Such programs actively engage youth with their victims, the justice system, and the community. There has been considerable talk about these programs in the world of juvenile justice over the course of the past fifteen to twenty years, and there are numerous studies that explore how they work and how well they work.

One group of programs falls under the general rubric of mentoring. For example, the Juvenile Mentoring Program (JUMP) provides one-on-one mentoring of youth by adults. An evaluation by the Office of Juvenile Justice and Delinquency Prevention (Novotney et al., 2000) suggested that youth in JUMP projects may earn better grades, avoid violence, and get along better with their families. Big Brothers Big Sisters works on similar principles, and studies of this program also suggest that kids who participate benefit in a variety of ways (see, e.g., Tierney, Grossman, and Resch 2000).

Other programs, called victim-offender mediation, restorative justice, and nonviolent conflict resolution programs, bring together offenders, victims, professionals, and local residents or peers for the benefit of the victim and the community as well as to hold the offender accountable. Rather than focusing on punishment or rehabilitation in the strict sense, such programs connect offenders and victims. They are based on offenders taking responsibility for the consequences of their acts and seek to reintegrate offenders into their communities. Mediation is not a panacea, and such programs do not have 100 percent success rates. However, they appear to have recidivism rates that rival or better those of more traditional intervention programs and have the added benefit of being considerably more humane.

Likewise, restorative justice programs appear to have benefits. According to one study (Bonta, Wallace-Capretta, and Rooney 1998), youth participants in a restorative justice project had lower recidivism rates than those placed on probation or incarcerated. Like any program, restorative justice does not work equally well with all kids. According to Nancy Rodriguez (2007), juvenile participants in restorative justice programs have lower recidivism rates than comparable kids, but those programs work best with girls and minor offenders.

Lesson Five:
The Benign Neglect of Structural Solutions

The proposals for doing something about youth violence rarely addressed its structural origins. Although we partially understood youth violence in structural terms—at least in the case of big-city violence—we rarely talked about *doing something* about those structural factors. In this regard, conventional wisdom among constructionists—that the mass media ignores structural factors in framing crime, violence, and other problems—is correct when it comes to youth violence. Structure was often an integral part of causal accounts, but it was typically *not* a part of talk about solutions. Although Americans lamented the notion of the big-city neighborhood as a sort of factory that produced a seemingly endless supply of violent youth, there was little serious talk of doing something about the structural conditions that produced this kind of place. In the case of talk about suburban violence, structure was virtually absent, as it was in the debate over the juvenile justice system. There the focus was solely on the individual.

This neglect of structural matters showed in talk about the family. Again, we lamented the causal role played by broken or dysfunctional families and domestic violence but rarely talked of the broader conditions that produced these states of affairs. I'm not necessarily talking about how our "free" market economic system helps produce crime and violence (although one could indeed argue the point), but rather about conditions such as an increasingly polarized class structure and a host of other factors that impinge on families across the country. The same might be said of schooling. School violence in neighborhoods was typically attributed to the streets that surrounded schools, whereas school violence in communities was attributed to bullying and teasing, marginalized youth, and the like. Here there was a virtual absence of talk concerning how the structure of schooling in the contemporary United States—funding formulas, school size, student-teacher ratios, routinization of curriculum, and teaching to mandated standardized tests—might play a role in the problem. We did not examine how school size exacerbates the problems caused by school clique structures or how the routinization of curriculum helps produce alienated youth. Perhaps we talked about them in discourse about other problems, but they were not part of our talk about solutions to youth violence. Of course, structural conditions are difficult to comprehend and assess, much less change. It's much easier to pass gun laws, mandate tougher sentencing or psychological screenings, and build new prisons than it is to change the ways we fund our schools or systematically provide families with the resources they need to properly nurture their children.

Lessons About a Broader Civic Discourse

Anyone who lived through the 1990s can attest that talk about the problem of youth violence was not limited to the mass media. Indeed, it seems clear that this problem was a visible, salient part of a broader public discourse. As people read and watched news reports about the problem, they almost certainly also talked about it among themselves. The news engages civic discourse in complex ways. It certainly shapes the way the public thinks and talks about a problem or issue (Edelman 1988; Branton and

Dunaway 2009). However, it also partially reflects that broader discourse, providing a window on the ways we try to make sense of our world. The iconic narratives of Eric Smith, Yummy Sandifer, Michael Carneal, and others provided a focus for public discourse. However, public attention to youth violence was not limited to these "nomic events" (Fine and White 2002). The debates over punishment versus rehabilitation and gun control versus media control were also topics of intense public debate. My last set of lessons concerns implications for understanding this civic discourse. I cannot, of course, speak with certainty about how civic discourse was shaped by our talk about youth violence, but I will offer some observations.

Lesson Six: Public Cynicism and Disengagement

I suspect the complexity and ambiguity in news talk about the youth violence problem was shaped by, and shaped, similar ambiguity in civic discourse about the problem. However, there is likely more to this story. As I hope to have shown in this book, talk of solutions and causes were often treated as so many tokens in larger political contests. I have suggested that such talk might have resonated closely with America's culture wars and might have made for good theater. Thomas Patterson (1993) calls that a game schema and suggests that this form of reporting diverts attention away from and limits involvement in the political process. In the same vein, I've suggested that this talk diverted attention from talking about and pursuing other solutions. In similar fashion, civic discourse would have been diverted from talk about solving the problem to the role it played in the political game. Further, Patterson (1993) and Joseph Cappella and Kathleen Jamieson (1997) suggest that this sort of reporting often leads to public cynicism and mistrust. In the midst of this political maneuvering, how would—or could—we believe that politicians were sincerely interested in addressing the problem? *Was* there a solution? Although I cannot directly assess how this sort of talk shaped our civic discourse regarding the political process here, I would argue that the continuous barrage of talk that cast debates over solutions as political battles could only have served to inhibit serious, systematic public discourse. Iconic narratives may have engaged the public and, thus, provided a forum for collective talk about the problem of youth violence. However, like the broader debates over causes and solutions, these narratives did not lend themselves to political action (Fine and White 2002). Like talk of political conflict, these narratives provided for great drama, but they may have discouraged us from finding solutions to the problem. I'm not sure what the news would have to look like in order to encourage such systematic, serious civic discourse. However, I suspect it might look more like NPR than Fox News, although even NPR exhibited its share of hyperbole and sensationalism.

Lesson Seven: Race and Gender

I hope this book has shown that the conflation of place, race, and class rendered race opaque—if not invisible. I have already discussed how this process might speak to constructionist research and theory. It also speaks to civic discourse. It has been suggested that one of the reasons that race remains a problem in the United States is that we are reluctant to directly address or confront it. It is always there but rarely mentioned. What we've seen with youth violence is one way in which this happens. If the news avoids direct and frank talk about the role of race in the problem of youth violence, it is not surprising that we avoid directly confronting the issue in our talk across the dinner table and in the coffee shop.

I have suggested iconic narratives—and perhaps all talk about the problem of youth violence—were told from a hegemonic perspective: the point of view of suburban, white, middle-class Americans. This cuts a number of ways. The conflation of race, place, and class hides from view the idea that neighborhoods are not wholly populated with lower-class or working-class minorities. Nor are communities entirely white or middle class. To hide this from view not only reinforces age-old stereotypes but also discourages us from appreciating the diversity of both sorts of places. Further, this conflation almost certainly marginalized the perspectives of those who call neighborhoods their home. From a middle-class perspective, these were not *their* stories; they were stories of someone, and somewhere, else. Such talk served to reinforce—as Roland Barthes (1972) would say, to naturalize—long-standing notions of the inner city as an "unnatural" place. Historically, the countryside symbolized the natural order of things—nowadays, it seems suburbs and small towns have taken on that role. In either case, inner-city residents ended up being cast as "outsiders," which reduces the empathy and compassion "insiders" may feel. We may feel pity for Yummy Sandifer or the Bermudez infant, but that feeling is lessened by the social and cultural distance that we've created between these two boys and Michael Carneal and Eddie Werner.

Like race, gender was also partially hidden from this talk. There was some talk during the last third of the 1990s that sought to explain suburban school violence as a gendered phenomenon, that asked: Why are our boys shooting up our suburban schools? It appears the only consistent talk that addressed violent *girls* was within the gangs frame: From time to time there was talk of girls in gangs, and these stories suggested it was a new and disturbing phenomenon. Gangs were spreading not only from the big city to small towns but now from boys to girls. In her examination of media constructions of girls and women, Meda Chesney-Lind (1999, p. 131) asked, "How then to construct a femininity that dares to access aggression and other elements of 'hegemonic masculinity'?" In other words, how do the media construct violent girls in a culture in which males are supposed to be violent and females are not? Chesney-Lind suggests that the media cast violent girls and women as somehow emancipated. That may well be. In my reading of the news, violent girls were cast as doubly paradoxical: Not only were these youth in violent gangs, but they were young *girls* in violent gangs. In most respects, however, this sort of talk was an anomaly. If the news was any indication, as a public we spent precious little time talking about gender in any systematic way. It would seem we simply did not acknowledge that the vast majority of youth violence was being committed by boys and young men. In the same ways we neglected structural factors in our causal accounts, we engaged in a sort of cultural denial that the ways in which we raise and relate to boys might have been a significant factor in all of this. By failing to problematize these practices, they went unchallenged.

Lesson Eight: Public Discourse and Hegemony

It would be tempting to conceptualize talk about youth violence— especially about causal accounts and solutions—as coming from a kind of pluralist perspective. Here, the myriad causes and solutions found in the news would reflect the heterogeneity of interests and cultural attitudes toward youth and their misbehavior. The concept of culture wars reinforces this perspective. However, there is more to this story than a simple plurality of voices. The white, middle-class perspective from which much of this talk seemed to emanate represents a dominant or hegemonic perspective. As Barker (2003), Stuart Hall et al. (1978), and a host of others have argued, from this perspective crime, particularly violent crime, is attributed to young, lower-class, minority males. The news reproduces and reinforces this dominant assumption as it reports on incidents of violent crime and of more general problems of violence— all the while making its view appear to be "natural" or "common sense." Further, in doing so it justifies a punitive response to violent crime. We witnessed this in the 1990s—during a time when the problem was primarily located in the big city—as state after state reworked their statutes to make it easier to deal with violent youth in adult criminal courts.

Causal accounts for youth violence in the big city often failed to challenge and thus served to reinforce these hegemonic assumptions. However, these accounts did not locate the problem in individual choice. Rather, prevailing wisdom framed it as a problem with the environment of the inner city—in combination with guns and a violent mass media. In most respects, even causal accounts of suburban violence supported these assumptions as well by failing to implicate structural or cultural aspects of these places in the problem. That said, talk about youth violence at times problematized these dominant assumptions. Certainly, the debates over punishment versus rehabilitation seemed to challenge the view of violence as simply the choices of immoral youth. Likewise, the mystery that was white, middle-class violence suggested fissures in a hegemonic ideology. As it did in the 1950s (Gilbert 1986), such a mystery produced a flurry of attempts to explain the unexpected or mysterious. Although these attempts did not seem to seriously challenge broader structural and social arrangements, they did result in some talk about the nature of these arrangements. In other words, even though we never seemed to seriously question the middle-class way of life, there was a vague sense that something was wrong.

At the end of the day, I suggest that our understandings of hegemony as based on race, class, and even gender need to be expanded in civic discourse. First, I propose that they be expanded to include *place*. The conflation of place, race, and class in talk about youth violence did not so much challenge hegemonic assumptions as provide a foundation in another set of cultural assumptions regarding age. It may be that public discourse about *adult* violence unambiguously attributes the problem to the immoral choices of lower-class minority males and in the process demonizes them in rather simple and straightforward ways. However, it appears that talk about *youth* violence is more complex. To understand the difference, we need to appreciate that our cultural assumptions about adults and youth are different. We may view adult men as responsible for their actions, but we are most reluctant to do so with boys. We may debate whether or not to view them as demons and thus punish them more harshly, but those are *debates*. Of course, the debates suggest limits to these cultural assumptions regarding youth. We seem willing to assume innocence and vulnerability as long as youth behave. We're even willing to maintain this assumption as long as their transgressions remain mundane

and ordinary. However, when they are armed and join violent, drug-deal-
ing gangs, when they kill women and other children, when they shoot
up schools, this assumption is challenged. That may be a good thing—
problematizing cultural assumptions is one way to change how we look
at the world. However, it seems that as we questioned their innocence
and vulnerability, our approach to violent youth was to simply talk about
punishing them. I've suggested above that we seriously consider another
way of orienting to youth in our civic discourse—that of connecting with
our kids.

6

Confronting
Today's Challenges

One of the questions on my PhD preliminary exams went something like this: "You have just completed a job talk, and one of the senior members of the faculty raises his hand and asks: 'That's all very interesting, but what makes it sociological?'" This question was, of course, designed to get me to think (and write) about how my dissertation related to central sociological issues. In the same spirit, a related question might be asked of this book. Up to this point, this book can be read, in large part, as a period piece that focuses on the 1990s. I hope to have exposed some aspects of our public discourse about the problem of youth violence during this period. Further, I have tried to present some implications of this project for academics, policy, and civic discourse. That is all well and good, but in this final chapter I want to address a different question: "How does all this help us understand how we talk about (and make sense of) youth violence in our contemporary world?" In other words, how does this book help us understand how we are confronting *today's* challenges of youth and violence?

Addressing this question necessarily means engaging recent talk about youth and violence. I spent some time searching the LexisNexis database using search terms such as "youth violence," "youth and gangs," and "school violence" or "school shootings." I also searched for the term "bullying." In addition, I used my knowledge of high-profile events during the previous decade to search for news stories on, for example, the shootings at Red Lake, Minnesota, and on college campuses such as Virginia Tech. A good place to start this discussion is to present four iconic narratives that appear to capture the gist of our current concerns about youth and violence.

Iconic Narratives over the Past Decade

As you will recall, iconic narratives comprise multiple stories on an event across multiple news sources over a period of time. More important, they serve to symbolize some more-general problem. I want to briefly discuss four iconic narratives that appeared during the first decade of the twenty-first century:

- Red Lake, Minnesota: School shooting on the reservation;
- Virginia Tech: Columbine on a college campus;
- Derrion Albert: Chicago's gangs, again; and
- Phoebe Prince: The bullying epidemic.

Each of these narratives gives us important insights into the ways we talk about contemporary problems of youth and violence. In some respects, our current talk bears a striking resemblance to talk in the 1990s. However, in other ways this current talk suggests some discontinuities and, thus, new ways of appreciating how we understand and confront problems of youth and violence.

The first narrative was that of the shooting on the Red Lake Reservation in Minnesota in spring 2005. First stories—beginning March 22, 2005, on NBC, CBS, and NPR, and in the *New York Times*—told us that a sixteen-year-old boy had shot and killed his grandfather and his grandfather's companion before proceeding to his high school, where he killed eight others, including five students, a teacher, a security guard, and, finally, himself. The boy's name was Jeff Weise. The reservation was said to be shocked and in grief. We learned how students and teachers at the school hid from the boy while they called 911 on their cell phones. Eyewitnesses talked of how the boy grinned and waved as he fired his weapon while fellow students pleaded for him to stop. These first stories immediately began asking, "Why?" Why would a young person like this become so violent? The answers to this question were largely sought in the boy's motivations, and as with earlier school shooters, such answers were hard to determine. We discovered that he had led a "troubled life" (NBC 3/23/05) and was quiet and a loner. His father had committed suicide, and his mother was confined to a nursing home due to injuries suffered in a car accident. Subsequent stories provided more details about Jeff as well as the reservation—what sort of place it was and how it was coping with the tragedy. As the police investigation developed, we learned that authorities had arrested a second youth in connection with the shootings. His name was Louis Jourdain and he was the son of the tribal leader, which seemed to deepen what was already the darkest time in the tribe's history. Several months later, we learned that Louis would be tried in juvenile court and that the trial would be closed to the public. On November 30, stories told us that Louis had pled guilty to sending "threatening interstate communications" but that charges of conspiracy to commit murder and conspiracy to commit offenses against the United States had been dropped. The narrative concluded two months later—around January 14, 2006—with stories that Louis had been sentenced, but the details were not made public and participants at the hearing left without comment. Attorneys for some of the victims' families were said to be displeased with the secrecy, while Louis's father released a statement saying his son accepted no responsibility for the shootings.

The second iconic narrative comprised the shootings on the campus of Virginia Tech University that took place in April 2007. That narrative may well comprise the largest number of stories of the four narratives. For example, a LexisNexis search of "broadcast transcripts" (that includes television, radio, and Internet news) using "Virginia Tech" during the two weeks following the shootings produced over 3,000 news items. The same search of the *New York Times* and the *Washington Post* produced more than 112 and 249 items, respectively. My searches during the next two weeks suggest that the shootings remained a salient topic of talk. As constructed in this narrative, on April 16, a young man named Seung-hui Cho shot and killed two people in a dorm room around 7:30 AM. Two hours later, he shot and killed thirty other students and faculty in a classroom building across campus. First stories addressed several questions. Almost immediately, the media wanted to hear from university and police officials about "What they knew, when they knew it, what they did, and what they did not do" (NPR 4/17/07). Why had they not notified the campus and locked it down after the first shootings were discovered? Many stories addressed the "why" question: What led this young man to do this? What were his motivations? Did he know (and thus target) his victims? Through interviews with students, we learned about the victims and their lives and how this "tight-knit community" (CBS 4/17/07) was recovering from its shock and horror and coping with its grief. This event was linked to other shootings, including Columbine and the 1966 shootings at the University of Texas at Austin campus, and it became known as the deadliest campus shooting in US history. As the weeks drew on, several salient plotlines developed. The shootings were tied to the larger issue of gun control. What role, if any, could this tragedy play in the gun control wars? Would this event lead to more stringent laws or would it, like Columbine, simply result in partisan debate between Democrats and Republicans; between advocates of gun control and the NRA? The media also turned its gaze on itself. Numerous stories critically examined how news organizations were covering the story. Some said the news—and the rest of us—had become immune to the horror, and other stories accused organizations—notably NBC—of exploitation.

In a third narrative, Derrion Albert, a sixteen-year-old high school sophomore living on the South Side of Chicago, was on his way to a bus stop after school on September 24, 2009, when he unintentionally walked into a fight between two rival groups of students. He was hit with a wooden two-by-four and, after falling to the street, was repeatedly punched and stomped. He later died from the injuries. The beating was captured on cell phone video. Soon thereafter, the video was obtained by WFLD, a Fox television affiliate in Chicago, and ultimately made its way to newscasts and the Internet. This narrative comprised several hundred stories across all the mainstream news sources. The narrative itself did not begin immediately—as if the death of another inner-city Chicago teenager was not sufficiently newsworthy. It wasn't until three days later, presumably when the video was distributed, that the mainstream national news picked up the story. First stories related the details of the beating. We did not learn much about Derrion himself, other than that he was an honor student and loved computers, Bible study, and church. Friends said he was headed to college—a rarity in his neighborhood. And we learned of the arrest of three teenage suspects (a fourth was later arrested but subsequently released). This narrative quickly became a symbol of the mean streets of the South Side of Chicago. Stories routinely related the numbers of school kids killed during each of the past few school years. Derrion may have been in the wrong place at the wrong time, but in some ways that made it all the more tragic. His death occasioned cries to stop the violence that resulted from a mixture of poverty, gangs, and grudges.

Finally, we have the iconic narrative of Phoebe Prince, which began in fall of 2009 and continues as I write this chapter in September 2010. This narrative seems to have struck a chord, as it has already run almost a year and comprises stories in all of the major national media outlets. First stories told us that the fifteen-year-old student at South Hadley High School in Massachusetts had hung herself after months of relentless bullying and taunting by classmates. We learned of her last day and of the circumstances of the bullying. There were stories about a meeting of parents at the school two weeks after her death demanding answers—and action. The narrative—like all such narratives—comprises multiple plotlines. NBC told us of four "'mean girls' who reportedly saw Phoebe as a romantic rival" (4/21/10). Six children have been charged with various felonies, including statutory rape, violation of civil rights with bodily injury, harassment, and stalking. They have all pleaded not guilty. Opinions regarding the case have been offered by legal experts and, it seems, just about everyone else. Many questions have been raised. Although Phoebe's death was obviously a tragedy and the accused behaved badly, was the legal system the best way to deal with this? What did school officials know about the bullying, and what should they have done? We were told the state of Massachusetts was working on an antibullying statute in response to this case. Indeed, this narrative has occasioned numerous stories about similar legislation in other states. And, of course, much of the narrative has focused on Phoebe herself. NBC ran a story in which essays she wrote for her English class were used to paint "a vivid new picture of her emotional anguish and dark final days" (4/21/10). We are told she had been a happy girl in a "quaint Irish village," but after moving to the United States, things changed. Her parents had recently separated, and, of course, the bullying had started. To date, according to the narrative, the case is still in court, and we are still learning details of Phoebe's life and the events leading up to her death. In most of these stories, Phoebe is cast as an innocent victim. However, at least two recent stories have introduced some measure of ambiguity and ambivalence. According to an NBC story (8/17/10), Phoebe had herself bullied other kids while living in Ireland. According to the story, "What causes kids to be bullies or victims are literally the same things. They have issues with anxiety, with depression, with frustration, with anger." The story goes on to tell us that "Phoebe Prince battled all of this" both before and after moving to the United States. Defense attorneys for the youth accused in the case are planning to use this information in the trial. Such details seem to add additional complexity and uncertainty to how we confront this narrative. An article on July 21, 2010, in *Slate*—a self-described "general interest" online magazine—increased the complexity. Among other questions, this story asked, "Should we send teenagers to prison for being nasty to one another?" "Is it really fair to lay the burden of Phoebe's suicide on these kids?" Further, the article suggests "the uncomfortable fact that Phoebe helped set in motion the conflicts with other students that ended in them turning on her. Her death was tragic, and she shouldn't have been bullied. But she was deeply troubled long before she ever met the six defendants. And her own behavior made other students understandably upset."

As presented in this story, Phoebe was a troubled girl. Further, the story suggests she was not necessarily the innocent victim presented in mainstream media reports. The details are complicated, but there seem to have been romantic triangles, accusations of backstabbing, and unsuccessful suicide attempts. In short, the story suggests that much of what has been reported in the media is, simply put, one-sided and that criminalizing the behavior of the accused kids is both shortsighted and counterproductive. To date, the narrative continues to develop the plotline of the legal case. Pretrial conferences are being held, and there is much talk about defense strategies. We have also learned that in addition to their legal troubles, the accused teenagers are in an academic limbo. They remain suspended from school and may face problems being accepted into other schools in order to finish their degrees.

Contemporary Problems

The narrative of Derrion Albert has been constructed as a symbol of big-city violence. In most respects this narrative, and talk of the larger problem, is strikingly similar to talk in the 1990s. However, there have also been significant differences. The *Washington Post* and *New York Times* both talk of local problems involving gangs on the streets and violence in the schools. Although these problems aren't as bad as they were fifteen years ago, they are still bad and they sometimes get worse. We don't hear much talk of a "crisis" or "epidemic" anymore, but from time to time these problems still "surge." Descriptors like "chronic" have become common. There is also considerable talk about the same problems in Chicago and Los Angeles, which have been dubbed the "gang capitals" of the United States. Indeed, a *Washington Post* story recently talked of a "crisis" of youth violence in both cities (10/7/09), a problem that largely comprises poverty and gangs. According to the story, although it isn't as bad as in the mid-1990s, it is still "tough to be a kid in Chicago." A letter to the editor in the *New York Times* (5/17/10) talks of the "bloody urban landscapes" of Chicago. Stories in late 2009 have provided statistics of the number of Chicago kids who have been killed since the beginning of the school year. The narrative of Derrion Albert symbolizes this problem facing Chicago's South and West Sides. Chicago, it seems, is a great American city with two sides. It has Michigan Avenue and its shops and the lakefront, where people live in high-rise condos and jog along the water. The other side of the city is where Derrion lived. Poverty erodes these neighborhoods. Guns and gangs are everywhere. Derrion and a number of other Windy City kids end up as so much collateral damage in the gang wars. Their deaths are tragic and occasion calls for a national discussion of youth violence, but the discussions are never sustained. Causal accounts of this big-city violence—whether in Chicago, New York, Washington, DC, or elsewhere—are still complex and variegated and quite familiar. It's true we don't hear as much about the drugs, but poverty and unemployment are still blamed, as are violent video games and easy access to guns.

There is also considerable talk of the problem of bullying. According to news stories, editorials, and letters to the editor, kids have always bullied other kids. Bullying is an interesting example of a social problem that began as an element in causal accounts of another social problem. In this case, as you will recall, bullying originally emerged as part of causal accounts of the late 1990s problem of small-town and suburban school shootings. In this talk, kids who were bullied brought guns to school to wreak revenge, strike a blow for all bullied kids, make a statement, or simply gain some measure of fame—or notoriety. Since 2000, bullying has become a social problem in its own right, and there is no shortage of talk about it. This talk seems to gather two distinct threads. According to one thread, bullying has always been an adolescent rite of passage: It prepares us for the rough-and-tumble adult world. For example, in a *New York Times* editorial, a professor of child development suggests, "For children of past eras, participating in the culture of childhood was a socializing process. They learned to settle their own quarrels and break their own rules, and to respect the rights of others. They learned that friends can be mean as well as kind, and that life was not always fair" (3/27/10).

Alternatively, there is another school of thought, according to which bullying has recently become a crisis. It has reached epidemic proportions. Its victims suffer physical and, more importantly, psychological damage. As the Prince narrative symbolizes, bullying now too often results in suicide. In this talk, bullying is a complex and variegated problem. It seems to have traditionally been something mostly done by boys to other boys, but now girls are said to bully in their own style—involving, for example, teasing and gossiping. Bullying is identified as yet another manifestation of the marginalization or stigmatization of certain groups. Gay, lesbian, and transgendered kids are all targets, as are obese kids. Bullying has been tied to hazing—from fraternities and sororities to sports teams—in ways that seem to have produced what is as yet a more inclusive but unnamed problem. Last, but certainly not least, we now have "cyber-bullying," in which the Internet or cell phones facilitate picking on others. According to an NPR story (3/23/10), "these days, of course, bullies don't just lurk on the playground but on Facebook and in chat rooms." As a complex problem, it is perhaps not surprising that talk about it produces dual—seemingly contradictory—images of bullies, which in turn shapes talk of solutions to the problem. Sometimes bullies are cast as classic victimizers—relentless and remorseless, stopping at nothing to humiliate their victims. Here, we are told, our responses to bullying should be swift and punitive. Schools should have more stringent policies, and states should have antibullying laws in place. However, other talk portrays bullies in ways that seems to mitigate our antipathy for them. Here, we are told, bullying is a manifestation of their social and personal troubles. Perhaps they suffer from low self-esteem or have a strong need for social acceptance. They might be a product of a culture that encourages such "nasty" behavior.

Features of Contemporary Talk

Although big-city violence remains a frequent topic of talk, violence in small towns and suburbs has largely fallen from our cultural radar. There is precious little talk of school violence in small towns or of psychologically disturbed kids murdering suburban children. But it's not quite that simple. Consider the Virginia Tech and Prince narratives. The Virginia Tech campus was typically referred to as a community, and Blacksburg was described in ways reminiscent of the small towns beset by school violence in the 1990s. Hadley, Massachusetts—the setting for the Prince narrative—was likewise a "community" or "small town." According to NBC (3/30/10), "South Hadley High School is in a Massachusetts college community known for its good schools. But today people are asking why the school failed to protect one student from being tormented to death by several others." Both communities reacted in ways reminiscent of the 1990s. There was initial shock and disbelief: How could this happen here? However, neither narrative was ultimately constructed as a symbol of some middle-class problem. Virginia Tech was often compared to Columbine or other college campus shootings, but they were always in the past. Thus, it was a historical problem rather than a contemporary one. For its part, the Prince narrative was set in a community and was cast as symbolic of a national problem of bullying. However, talk about the more general problem fails to unambiguously locate it with regard to place, race, and class. It might be reasonable to read this more general talk as constructing bullying as a middle-class problem. After all, the Prince narrative does so. Further, the problem originated in causal accounts of school violence in communities.

The Red Lake narrative occupies an interesting interstitial position with respect to place, race, and class. In some respects, the Red Lake narrative was set in a community. It was frequently referred to as one. It was small and its people close-knit. The violence was surprising. It seemed more than a paradox—it appeared to be cast as a mystery. Sure, there were problems on the reservation, but *this*? The answers were quickly provided in two causal accounts, one in the form of personal and family tragedy and the other in descriptions of the Red Lake Reservation. The first account seemed to mirror common accounts of community—a troubled teenage boy who was driven to violence as he struggled with his inner demons. Just as in the Manzie-Werner and West Paducah narratives, some members of the community were displeased with Louis's sentencing—they wanted a more complete accounting that might help in understanding this event. This narrative was also reminiscent of neighborhood narratives of the 1990s, however. Poverty and alcoholism, hopelessness and violence did already exist on the reservation, and they served as the basis for the second account for the shootings, one that cast the shooter as a product of local problems. Also, this place sounded familiar. Descriptions of Red Lake did not seem offered as some novelty. Rather, it appeared, Red Lake was like any other reservation that could be found in many other places. In this way, this place itself was a kind of paradox—a small and tranquil community beset with poverty and alcoholism and violence. Thus, it seems, cultural understandings of place, race, and class comprise more than bifurcated images of neighborhoods and communities. Our cultural understandings of Native American reservations may represent a complex—and paradoxical—blending of these two sets of images.

What of contemporary causal accounts and talk of solutions? As I've suggested above, causal accounts for big-city violence are almost identical to those of the 1990s. The Virginia Tech narrative ultimately crafted a psychological account for its main protagonist. Here, it seems not much has changed. Also, consider talk about popular culture and technology.

Television, movies, and video games were popular elements of causal accounts in the 1990s. The Internet occupied an important place in our talk of 1990s youth violence—principally in the narratives of community violence. In the Sam Manzie–Eddie Werner narrative, Sam was contacted by a pedophile in a chat room. It occasioned considerable talk about how to keep our kids safe from the potential dangers posed by this technology. In the West Paducah narrative (as well as other school shooting narratives), the Internet also played a causal role, and the Internet was a conduit through which middle-class school shooters vented their anger and communicated their plans. Today, technology plays a principal role in our talk of the bullying problem, which no longer occurs only face-to-face. Now bullies use Facebook and other social networking sites, chat rooms, cell phones, and other media to terrorize their targets. In this talk, technology has fundamentally transformed the problem such that the victims of bullying cannot escape their tormenters. Perhaps for that reason, victims take their own lives more often than they did in the past. Further, since bullying mostly happens off school grounds, it has rendered talk about solutions considerably more complex. Schools are limited in what they can do, but parents, it seems, are unable or unwilling to supervise their kids' online behavior. Once again, our anxiety about new popular culture and technology finds its way into our talk about problems of youth. Once Americans wrung our hands over the role played by the automobile and drive-in movies in youthful promiscuity or lamented how television and movies were leading to middle-class youthful rebellion. Now, we worry about how social networking sites and cell phones facilitate bullying.

No less important, the debates over solutions to youth violence that were waged in the 1990s are still being waged today. Much of this talk resides at the local level in places like New York City and Washington, DC. A *Washington Post* editorial on June 18, 2010, critiqued local correctional facilities as being "revolving doors." Despite reforms, the facilities "remain violent and punitive." Another *Post* editorial complained of "D.C.'s juvenile justice farce" (6/12/10). According to the editors, the city suffered from a chronic problem of youth violence that was not being effectively addressed by the current "anti-detention, community-based approach" of the Department of Youth Rehabilitation Services, which in effect has rendered local juvenile justice ineffective. Part of the problem, it seemed, had to do with political infighting that made it hard to implement needed changes. Another *Post* editorial talked of new solutions to the problem of school violence involving a multipronged approach that included violence and abuse prevention programs, training programs for teachers, expanded mental health services, and out-of-school services such as mentoring and employment training. Thus, on the one hand, local juvenile justice is critiqued as not being sufficiently punitive, but on the other hand, we see calls for more treatment and prevention.

Gun control emerges from time to time as a topic of talk. The Virginia Tech narrative called for stricter laws. According to one oft-repeated refrain, the Columbine shootings failed to produce such laws, but perhaps this new campus tragedy might provide the needed impetus. Once again, culture wars were implicated: It was Democrats versus Republicans, gun control advocates versus the NRA. However, in several *Washington Post* editorials, no small degree of pessimism was expressed: These two sides were so entrenched in their positions that nothing would get done. Such feelings were especially notable in the aftermath of the Virginia Tech shootings. According to a *New York Times* story (4/17/07), "Leaders of both parties voiced their sympathies, their outrage, and their prayers in the aftermath of the shootings at Virginia Tech. Advocates of gun control laws said they hoped for something more: a reopening of the debate over gun regulations." As the story proceeded, we learned that this "hope" might go wanting. The National Rifle Association remained a powerful force, and Democrats seemed to have little stomach for this battle. After all, we were told, Al Gore had lost the 2000 presidential election in part because of his support for gun control.

One of the most important features of our contemporary talk about causes and solutions is a seeming lack of urgency or immediacy. Admittedly, talk of the crisis of bullying generates a sense that we must do something about this problem. Otherwise, there seems to have emerged a subtle change in talk with regard to neighborhood violence. Yes, we are still shocked and angry when kids like Derrion Albert are killed, and admittedly there are calls for a national discussion about the problem. However, such events do not seem to generate a sustained dialogue. A strong sense of resignation seems to pervade our talk about the big city. Violence, we are told, has always been a part of living in the inner city, and past attempts to remedy the problem have largely failed. There may be small success stories, but the basic problem remains unchanged.

Where Do We Go from Here?

The debates and contests that animated much of the talk about solutions in the 1990s appear to have disappeared. From time to time, local solutions

192 The Paradox of Youth Violence

are critiqued or debated. However, our attention seems focused else-where. Perhaps it is due to the resignation I discussed above. Perhaps it is due to the lack of a sustained national crisis of youth violence. Perhaps our attention is drawn to terrorism or the recent recession. In any event, we—and our kids—might benefit from a return to a serious and sustained discussion about how to respond to violent youth.

Much of our solutions talk in the 1990s comprised a debate between punishment and treatment on the one hand and punishment and preven-tion on the other. This debate between seemingly incompatible solutions is not new. According to Bernard and Kurlychek (2010), these two ap-proaches have been vying for the heart and soul of the juvenile justice system throughout its history, and at any given point in time one or the other dominates. In the second half of the 1990s, advocates of the puni-tive approach won most of the battles, as we witnessed states reworking their statutes to make it easier to transfer to and try juvenile offenders in the adult criminal justice system. However, as we saw in Chapter 3, the punitive approach had its critics. Punishing youth may satisfy the desire of some for retribution, but beyond removing these youth from society for a period of time, this approach has not been shown to effectively deter future violent crime. We know this—it was part of our talk during the 1990s, and there is a considerable body of research that confirms it. Tra-ditional treatment programs, probation, and prevention programs have their own limitations, however, not the least of which includes their focus on the individual without making changes in the social system in which the individual lives. Further, these sorts of solutions do not seem to sat-isfy those who call for holding youth accountable.

What, then, might we do to extricate ourselves from this seemingly endless debate? I conclude this book with some thoughts on this question. First, I suggested in Chapter 5 that one of the lessons to be learned from this study was that we spend more time doing things *with* kids rather than *to* or *for* them. To be sure, there are times when punishment is appropriate and most certainly when protecting them is called for. However, an exclu-sive focus on one or the other—or even both—reinforces our tendency to keep kids at arm's length from adults and somewhat removed from the adult world. Doing things with kids can mean a multitude of practices. I like to tell the students in my juvenile delinquency class that we should spend time with our kids, but don't just spend time; spend time talking with them. But don't just talk to them; spend time talking to them about things that matter. It may seem like a simple thing, but in the hustle and bustle of our daily lives, we often feel we don't have the time or energy.

Taking time to do these simple things can go a long way toward establishing strong connections with our kids and mitigating the effects of the ordinary, and extraordinary, factors in kids' lives that push and pull them toward violent behavior.

Second, I also suggested that another way to connect violent youth with the adult world is through programs variously called restorative justice, mediation, and conflict management. Perhaps because these programs may not work as well with serious violent offenders, they have not been part of our public discussion of solutions. However, they should be a salient part of this discussion. Implementing these programs early and often in the lives of kids who run afoul of the law might go a long way toward reducing youthful violence in the long run. Involving community members in these proceedings may help connect them with offenders in ways that traditional juvenile justice is simply incapable of doing. Doing so may help reduce the need for retribution. However, making this part of our national discourse may be difficult for several reasons. It does not seem to be a salient part of our current talk about youth violence. Indeed, with the exception of gun control or bullying, there is little talk focused on solutions. Although this may be understandable in the absence of a crisis or epidemic of youth violence, and the salience of other problems such as the economy or international terrorism, it prevents us from seriously addressing the problem in the long run.

Creating Meaning: Working Toward a Better World

Some final thoughts seem in order that pertain to how we talk about youth violence and our broader cultural notions about kids. In an episode of the television police drama series *The Closer,* a young man is shot and killed. He was on parole but, as his mother suggests, trying to turn his life around. The detectives spend the hour trying to solve the killing in large part by searching for a motive that would lead them to a suspect. By the show's end, we find out that the young man was killed by a stray bullet from a gun that was shot several blocks away in a completely unrelated incident. The detectives were dismayed. In their opinion, since there was no "motive" in the death of this young man, it could only be seen as a tragic and random accident. Consider the following exchange between Father Jack, who had counseled the young man, and Deputy Police Chief Johnson:

Chief Johnson: Where there's no motive, there's no meaning.
    Father Jack: You only think there's no meaning because you're looking for it. But meaning isn't something you find, Chief Johnson. It's something you give. Making sense of Reggie's murder, well, that's up to us.

In the final scene of this episode, members of the police department set aside their uniforms and join neighborhood residents in giving such a meaning to Reggie's death by painting over gang-related graffiti on the front of the church where the young man lived and was counseled. Chief Johnson's suggestion that we find meanings in motives illustrates an important facet of talk about youth violence. The "meaning" of youth violence seems to hinge most of the time on the offenders' motives—or, more accurately, motivations, to stay true to C. Wright Mills's (1940) distinction. Simply put, the search for motivations seems to represent our collective way of trying to make sense of the problem. Based on the way we talk, it seems that if only we—like Chief Johnson—could discover what was going on in the killer's head at the time of the event, it would all make sense. Perhaps that is understandable. The problem was constructed in ways that may have doomed any other search for meaning. These were "unthinkable" or "senseless" crimes—children killing other children, children killing pregnant women—tragedies compounded by other tragedies. Whenever we thought we "found" the killer's motivation, it seemed of the most trivial sort. Eric Morse died when he refused to steal candy for two other boys. In another narrative, a young boy broke into the Bermudez's house to steal a tricycle and while he was there he beat a four-week-old infant almost to death. More recently, Phoebe Prince was bullied to death, it seemed, because of jealous rivalry over a boy.

Father Jack's response, however, suggests that meaning can be found outside an offender's motivations. More specifically, he suggests that meanings are attributed rather than residing in the events themselves. That, of course, is one of the foundational assumptions of this book. If we look at the talk about the problem, it would seem that whatever inroads were made into mitigating the problem of criminal violence by youth in the 1990s may have been made *in spite of* our collective searches for causes and solutions. By the time state legislatures were approving and implementing tougher legal responses (such as expanded waiver provisions to adult courts), most official measures of violent crime by youth had already begun to decline. To date, those rates are still lower than at any time in the 1990s. Perhaps it was conflict resolution training in schools. Perhaps it was more parents spending more time with their kids.

Perhaps it was zero-tolerance policies in schools. Perhaps it was all of them, and perhaps it was none of them. That is the stuff of other studies. However, our attempts might have been more "meaningful" if we had responded not by searching for causes but instead by setting about building a world in which children really mattered. David Orr (2002, p. 199) makes these points in *The Nature of Design: Ecology, Culture, and Human Intention,* a self-described "meditation on the larger patterns of our time and their effects on children." Focusing primarily on political and economic arrangements, he argues that youth violence is symptomatic of something much bigger, whose other symptoms include diffuse anger, despair, apathy, and youth suicide. For Orr, this "something bigger" is a political-economic system that fails to allow children to fully develop physically, emotionally, personally, socially, and spiritually. For Orr, the answer lies in protecting the biosphere for this and future generations of children. Perhaps he is correct, for the paths to that kind of world direct our attention to aspects of American society that are important to the well-being of our children. Regardless of the approach, providing meaning to the problem of youth violence means seriously addressing it rather than debating its underlying causes.

Gangs remain a fixture of the urban landscape, and the death toll from youth violence in neighborhoods remains unacceptably high. Suicide rates for teenagers are, likewise, unacceptably high. Based on what we know about suicide more generally, it is most likely the case that middle-class kids disproportionately contribute to these rates. Assuming alienation, isolation, and depression are major causal factors in suicide, it follows that living in the suburbs may not be a whole lot easier than living in the inner city. Seriously addressing these issues would mean critically examining some of the most fundamental cultural and structural aspects of American society. Structurally, it means confronting the sources of poverty, unemployment, and family instability. It means changing the way we fund public schools and child protection services. It means directly confronting race in our civic discourse. It also means examining the ways we orient to children. It requires taking a serious look at the factors that produce alienation and malaise among kids that in turn result in heavy drinking, unprotected sex, violence, and a host of other risky behaviors. Perhaps it means working fewer hours and placing less significance on material things. It means frank and serious talk that asks, for example: Do we really treat children as second-class citizens? Do we really keep them at arm's length from adults and the adult world? If those questions partially express the cultural status of youth, it would help to

explain our tendency to search for solutions to youth violence by looking for ways to do things *for* kids or *to* them rather than *with* them. It
would help to explain why despite all our attempts to discover what kids
thought about the problem, we never really seemed to *hear* what they
had to say. It would explain why after decades of collective searching, it
seemed we are as far away as ever from finding durable or lasting solutions not only to youth violence but to a host of other problems involving youth. Youth violence may no longer be the "crisis" or "epidemic"
that it was fifteen years ago, and we may not have the same sense of urgency when we talk about youth violence. In some ways, that is a shame.
Youth violence is still populated by a multitude of victims—those who
are killed and injured and their families, neighborhoods, and communities, as well as the youth who perpetrate the violence and their families.
Ultimately, perhaps, the best way we can memorialize all those who suffer from youth violence is to work toward creating a world for children
as if they *did* matter.

References

Abrams, Laura S. 2000. "Guardians of Virtue: The Social Reformers and the 'Girl Problem,' 1890–1920." *Social Service Review* (September): 436–454.

Adorjan, Michael. 2009. "Discord and Ambiguity Within Youth Crime and Justice Debates." PhD diss., McMaster University.

———. Forthcoming. "Emotions, Contests, and Reflexivity in the News: Examining Discourse on Youth Crime in Canada." *Journal of Contemporary Ethnography.*

Altheide, David. 2002. *Creating Fear: News and the Construction of Crisis.* New York: Aldine de Gruyter.

Aries, Phillippe. 1962. *Centuries of Childhood: A Social History of Family Life.* Translated by Robert Baldick. New York: Random House.

Asbury, Herbert. 1927. *The Gangs of New York.* New York: Knopf.

Bakan, David. 1971. "Adolescence in America: From Idea to Social Fact." *Daedalus* (Fall): 979–995.

"Balanced Juvenile Justice and Crime Prevention Act." 1996. H.R. 3445, 104th Congress, 2nd session.

Barker, Chris. 2003. *Cultural Studies: Theory and Practice.* London: Sage.

Barthes, Roland. 1972. *The Elements of Semiology.* London: Cape.

Beckett, Katherine, and Theodore Sasson. 2000. *The Politics of Injustice.* Thousand Oaks, CA: Pine Forge.

Bennett, William, John J. DiIulio, Jr., and John P. Walters. 1996. *Body Count: Moral Poverty . . . and How to Win America's War Against Crime and Drugs.* New York: Simon and Schuster.

Bernard, Thomas, and Megan Kurlychek. 2010. *The Cycle of Juvenile Justice*. New York: Oxford University Press.

Best, Joel. 1990. *Threatened Children: Rhetoric and Concern About Child-Victims*. Chicago: University of Chicago Press.

———. 1999. *Random Violence: How We Talk About New Crimes and New Victims*. Berkeley: University of California Press.

Blumer, Herbert. 1971. "Social Problems as Collective Behavior." *Social Problems* 18: 298–306.

Bonta, James, Suzanne Wallace-Capretta, and Jennifer Rooney. 1998. *Restorative Justice: An Evaluation of the Restorative Resolutions Project*. Ottawa: Solicitor General.

Branton, Regina P., and Johanna Dunaway. 2009. "Spatial Proximity to the US-Mexico Border and Newspaper Coverage of Immigration Issues." *Political Research Quarterly* 62: 289–302.

Bromley, David G. , Anson D. Shupe, and J. C. Ventimiglia. 1979. "Atrocity Tales, the Unification Church, and the Social Construction of Evil." *Journal of Communication* 29: 242–254.

Brown, Gillian. 2003. "Child's Play." Pp. 13–39 in *The American Child*, edited by Caroline F. Levander and Carol J. Singley. Piscataway, NJ: Rutgers University Press.

Bulman, Robert C. 2005. *Hollywood Goes to High School: Cinema, Schools, and American Culture*. New York: Worth.

Cappella, Joseph, and Kathleen Jamieson. 1997. *Spiral of Cynicism: The Press and the Public Good*. Boulder, CO: NetLibrary.

Cavaglion, Gabriel. 2009. "Fathers Who Kill and Press Coverage in Israel." *Child Abuse Review* 18: 127–143.

Cerulo, Karen. 1998. *Deciphering Violence: The Cognitive Structure of Right and Wrong*. New York: Routledge.

"The Changing Nature of Youth Violence." 1996. 104th Congress, 2nd session, testimony of John J. DiIulio, Jr.

Chesney-Lind, Meda. 1999. "Media Misogyny: Demonizing 'Violent' Girls and Women." Pp. 115–140 in *Making Trouble: Cultural Constructions of Crime, Deviance, and Control*, edited by J. Ferrell and N. Websdale. Hawthorne, NY: Aldine de Gruyter.

Clark, Candace. 1987. "Sympathy Biography and Sympathy Margin." *American Journal of Sociology* 92: 290–321.

Cohen, Stanley. 1980. *Folk Devils and Moral Panics*. New York: St. Martin's.

Colomy, Paul, and Laura Ross Greiner. 2000. "Making Youth Violence Visible: The News Media and the Summer of Violence." *Denver University Law Review* 77: 661–688.

————. 2004. "Criminalizing Transgressing Youth: A Neofunctionalist Analysis." Pp. 125–156 in *Illuminating Social Life: Classical and Contemporary Social Theory,* edited by P. Kivisto. Thousand Oaks, CA: Pine Forge.

Conrad, Peter, and Joseph Schneider. 1992. *Deviance and Medicalization: From Badness to Sickness.* Philadelphia: Temple University Press.

Corsaro, William. 1997. *The Sociology of Childhood.* Thousand Oaks, CA: Pine Forge.

Crook, Amy. 1996. "From 'Pint-Size Drug Runners' to 'Murder in Miniature': Media Constructions of Juvenile Delinquency." Master's thesis, Purdue University.

Denzin, Norman K. 1991. *Hollywood Shot by Shot: Alcoholism in American Cinema.* New York: Aldine de Gruyter.

————. 1995. *Cinematic Society: The Voyeur's Gaze.* London: Sage.

DiIulio, John J., Jr. 1995. "The Coming of the Superpredators." *Weekly Standard,* November 27.

Edelman, Murray J. 1988. *Constructing the Political Spectacle.* Chicago: University of Chicago Press.

Empy, LaMar T., and Mark C. Stafford. 1991. *American Delinquency: Its Meaning and Construction.* Belmont, CA: Wadsworth.

Eron, Leonard D., Monroe M. Lefkowitz, L. Powell Huesman, and Leopold O. Walder. 1972. "Does Television Violence Cause Aggression?" *American Psychologist* (April): 253–263.

Fine, Gary Alan, and Ryan D. White. 2002. "Creating Collective Attention in the Public Domain: Human Interest Narratives and the Rescue of Floyd Collins." *Social Forces* 81: 57–85.

Fishman, Mark. 1978. "Crime Waves as Ideology." *Social Problems* 25: 531–543.

————. 1980. *Manufacturing the News.* Austin: University of Texas Press.

Flanagan, Maureen A. 1986. "Charter Reform in Chicago: Political Culture and Urban Progressive Reform." *Journal of Urban History* 12 (2): 109–130.

Galinsky, Ellen. 2000. *Ask the Children.* New York: HarperCollins.

Gamson, William A., and Andre Modigliani. 1989. "Media Discourse and Public Opinion on Nuclear Power: A Constructionist Approach." *American Journal of Sociology* 95: 1–37.

Garbarino, James. 2001. "Lost Boys: Why Our Sons Turn Violent and How We Can Save Them." *Smith College Studies in Social Work* 71: 169–181.

Garfinkel, Harold. 1956. "Conditions of Successful Degradation Ceremonies." *American Journal of Sociology* 61: 420–424.

Gilbert, James. 1986. *A Cycle of Outrage*. New York: Oxford University Press.

Gorelick, Stephen. 1989. "'Join Our War': The Construction of Ideology in a Newspaper Crimefighting Campaign." *Crime and Delinquency* 35: 421–436.

Graber, Doris A. 1980. *Crime News and the Public*. New York: Praeger.

Gubrium, Jaber, and James A. Holstein. 1998. "Narrative Practice and the Coherence of Personal Stories." *Sociological Quarterly* 39 (1): 163–187.

Gusfield, Joseph. 1981. *The Culture of Public Problems: Drinking, Driving, and the Symbolic Order*. Chicago: University of Chicago Press.

Hadden, Jeffrey, and Josef J. Barton. 1973. "An Image That Will Not Die: Thoughts on the History of Anti-Urban Ideology." Pp. 79–119 in *The Urbanization of the Suburbs*, edited by L. Masotti and J. Hadden. Beverly Hills: Sage.

Hagan, John, and Jeffrey Leon. 198277. "Rediscovering Delinquency: Social History, Political Ideology, and the Sociology of Law." *American Sociological Review* 42: 587–598.

Hall, Stuart, Chas Critcher, Tony Jefferson, John Clarke, and Brian Roberts. 1978. *Policing the Crisis: Mugging, the State, and Law and Order*. London: Macmillan.

Haydon, Deena, and Phil Scraton. 2000. "'Condemn a Little More, Understand a Little Less': The Political Context and Rights Implications of the Domestic and European Rulings in the Venebales-Thompson Case." *Journal of Law and Society* 27 (3): 416–448.

Henderson, Lesley, and Jenny Kitzinger. 1999. "The Human Drama of Genetics: 'Hard' and 'Soft' Media Representations of Inherited Breast Cancer." *Sociology of Health and Illness* 21: 560–578.

Herda-Rapp, Ann. 2003. "The Social Construction of Local School Violence Threats by the News Media and Professional Organizations." *Sociological Inquiry* 73: 545–574.

Hilgartner, Stephen, and Charles L. Bosk. 1988. "The Rise and Fall of Social Problems: A Public Arenas Model." *American Journal of Sociology* 94: 53–78.

Hine, Thomas. 1999. *The Rise and Fall of the American Teenager*. New York: Bard.

Holstein, James A., and Gale Miller. 1990. "Rethinking Victimization: An Interactional Approach to Victimology." *Symbolic Interaction* 13: 103–122.

Hunter, James Davison. 1991. *Culture Wars: The Struggle to Define America*. New York: Basic Books.

Ibarra, Peter, and John Kitsuse. 1993. "Vernacular Constituents of Moral Discourse: An Interactionist Proposal for the Study of Social Problems." Pp. 21–54 in *Constructionist Controversies: Issues in Social Problems Theory*, edited by G. Miller and J. Holstein. New York: Aldine de Gruyter.

Jenkins, Philip. 1992. *Intimate Enemies: Moral Panics in Contemporary Great Britain*. Hawthorne, NY: Aldine de Gruyter.

———. 1994. *Using Murder: The Social Construction of Serial Homicide*. New York: Aldine de Gruyter.

Jensen, Gary, and Dean Rojek. 2000. *Delinquency and Youth Crime*. Prospect Heights, IL: Waveland.

Johnson, David R. 1979. *Policing the Urban Underworld: The Impact of Crime on the Development of the American Police, 1800–1887*. Philadelphia: Temple University Press.

Johnson, John. 1995. "Horror Stories and the Construction of Child Abuse." Pp. 17–31 in *Images of Issues: Typifying Contemporary Social Problems*, edited by Joel Best. New York: Aldine de Gruyter.

Kappeler, Victor E., Mark Blumberg, and Gary W. Potter. 2000. *The Mythology of Crime and Criminal Justice*. Prospect Heights, IL: Waveland.

Kotlowitz, Alex. 1992. *There Are No Children Here*. New York: Anchor.

Kupchik, Aaron. 2006. *Judging Juveniles: Prosecuting Adolescents in Adult and Juvenile Courts*. New York: New York University Press.

Leach, Penelope. 1994. *Putting Children First: What Our Society Must Do—and Is Not Doing—for Our Children Today*. New York: Knopf.

Lester, Marilyn. 1980. "Generating Newsworthiness: The Interpretive Construction of Public Events." *American Sociological Review* 45: 484–494.

Levander, Caroline F. , and Carol J. Singley. 2003. *The American Child: A Cultural Studies Reader*. New Brunswick, NJ: Rutgers University Press.

Lichter, S. Robert, and Linda S. Lichter. 1994. *Media Monitor: 1993—The Year in Review, VIII*. Washington, DC: Center for Media and Public Affairs.

Lofland, Lynn H. 1998. *The Public Realm: Exploring the City's Quintessential Social Territory*. Hawthorne, NY: Aldine de Gruyter.

Loseke, Donileen. 1992. *The Battered Woman and Shelters*. Albany: SUNY Press.

———. 1993. "Constructing Conditions, People, Morality, and Emotion." Pp. 207–216 in *Constructionist Controversies: Issues in Social Problems Theory,* edited by G. Miller and J. Holstein. New York: Aldine de Gruyter.

Loseke, Donileen, and Joel Best. 2003. *Social Problems: Constructionist Readings.* Hawthorne, NY: Aldine de Gruyter.

Lowney, Kathleen S., and Joel Best. 1995. "Stalking Strangers and Lovers: Changing Media Typifications of a New Crime Problem." Pp. 33–58 in *Images of Issues: Typifying Contemporary Social Problems,* edited by J. Best. Hawthorne, NY: Aldine de Gruyter.

Menifield, Charles, Winfield Rose, John Homa, and Anita Brewer Cunningham. 2000. "The Media's Portrayal of Urban and Rural School Violence: A Preliminary Analysis." *Deviant Behavior* 22: 447–464.

Mills, C. Wright. 1940. "Situated Actions and Vocabularies of Motive." *American Sociological Review* 5: 904–913.

Molotch, Harvey, and Marilyn Lester. 1974. "News as Purposive Behavior: On the Strategic Use of Routine Events, Accidents, and Scandals." *American Sociological Review* 39: 101–112.

Newman, Katherine. 2004. *Rampage: The Social Roots of School Shootings.* New York: Basic.

Novotney, Lawrence C., Elizabeth Mertinko, James Lange, and Tara Kelley Baker. 2000. "Juvenile Mentoring Program: A Progress Review." Washington, DC: US Department of Justice.

Ogle, Jennifer Paff, Molly Eckman, and Catherine Amoroso Leslie. 2003. "Appearance Cues and the Shootings at Columbine High: Construction of a Social Problem in the Print Media." *Sociological Inquiry* 73: 1–27.

Orr, David W. 2002. *The Nature of Design: Ecology, Culture, and Human Intention.* New York: Oxford University Press.

Patterson, Thomas E. 1993. *Out of Order.* New York: Random House.

Pfhol, Stephen J. 1977. "The 'Discovery' of Child Abuse." *Social Problems* 24: 310–323.

Platt, Anthony. 1977. *The Child Savers.* Chicago: University of Chicago Press.

Rafter, Nicole. 1992. "Claims-Making and Socio-Cultural Context in the First US Eugenics Campaign." *Social Problems* 39 (1): 17–34.

Reiman, Jeffrey H. 1997. *The Rich Get Richer and the Poor Get Prison.* Boston: Allyn and Bacon.

Reinarman, Craig, and Harry G. Levine. 1995. "The Crack Attack: America's Latest Drug Scare, 1986–1992." Pp. 147–186 in *Images of Is-*

sues: Typifying Contemporary Social Problems, edited by J. Best. Hawthorne, NY: Aldine de Gruyter.

Rodriguez, Nancy. 2007. "Restorative Justice at Work: Examining the Impact of Restorative Justice Resolutions on Juvenile Recidivism." *Crime and Delinquency* 53 (3): 355–379.

Sasson, Theodore. 1995. *Crime Talk: How Citizens Construct a Social Problem.* Hawthorne, NY: Aldine de Gruyter.

Scheingold, Stuart A. 1991. *The Politics of Street Crime: Criminal Process and Cultural Obsession.* Philadelphia: Temple University Press.

Schlossman, Steven L. 1977. *Love and the American Delinquent: The Theory and Practice of "Progressive" Juvenile Justice, 1825–1920.* Chicago: University of Chicago Press.

Schudson, Michael. 1992. *Watergate in American Memory: How We Remember, Forget, and Reconstruct the Past.* New York: Basic.

Schwartz, Ira M. 1992. "Juvenile Crime-Fighting Policies: What the Public Really Wants." Pp. 214–248 in *Juvenile Justice and Public Policy: Toward a National Agenda,* edited by Ira M. Schwartz. New York: Lexington Books.

Shaw, Clifford, and Henry D. McKay. 1942. *Juvenile Delinquency and Urban Areas.* Chicago: University of Chicago Press.

Sheley, Joseph F., and Cindy D. Ashkins. 1981. "Crime, Crime News, and Crime Views." *Public Opinion Quarterly* 45: 492–506.

Shepherd, Robert E. 1997. "One Hundred Years of Juvenile Justice." *Maryland Bar Review* 30: 12–18.

Sherizen, Sanford. 1978. "Social Creation of Crime News." Pp. 203–224 in *Deviance and Mass Media,* edited by Charles. Winick. Thousand Oaks, CA: Sage.

Sibley, David. 1995. *Geographies of Exclusion.* London: Routledge.

Sisco, Tauna. 2008. "The Changing Face of Homelessness: Federal Policy, Gender, the Media, and the Emergence of an 'Invisible' Population." PhD diss., Purdue University.

Snow, David, and Robert Benford. 1988. "Ideology, Frame Resonance, and Participant Mobilization." *International Social Movement Research* 1: 197–217.

Snyder, Howard N. 2000. "Juvenile Arrests, 1999." Washington, DC: US Department of Justice.

Snyder, Howard N., and Melissa Sickmund. 1999. *Juvenile Offenders and Victims: A 1999 National Report.* Rockville, MD: Juvenile Justice Clearinghouse.

Spector, Malcolm, and John J. Kitsuse. [1977] 1987. *Constructing Social Problems*. Hawthorne, NY: Aldine de Gruyter.

Spencer, J. William. 1996. "From Bums to the Homeless: Media Constructions of Persons Without Homes from 1980 to 1984." Pp. 39–58 in *Perspectives on Social Problems,* vol. 8, edited by James A. Holstein and Gale. Miller. Greenwich, CT: JAI.

———. 1997. "Homeless in River City: Client Work in Human Service Encounters." Pp. 149–166 in *Social Problems in Everyday Life,* edited by Gale Miller and James A. Holstein. Greenwich, CT: JAI.

———. 2000. "Appropriating Cultural Discourses: Notes on a Framework for Constructionist Analyses of the Language of Claims-Making." Pp. 25-40 in *Perspectives on Social Problems (12),* edited by James A. Holstein and Gale Miller. Greenwich, CT: JAI.

———. 2005. "It's Not as Simple as It Seems: Ambiguous Culpability and Ambivalent Affect in Media Representations of Violent Youth." *Symbolic Interaction* 28 (1): 47–65.

Spencer, J. William, and Glenn W. Muschert. 2009. "The Contested Meanings of the Crosses of Columbine." *American Behavioral Scientist* 52 (10): 1371–1386.

Stallings, Robert. 1995. *Promoting Risk: Constructing the Earthquake Threat.* Hawthorne, NY: Aldine de Gruyter.

Tierney, Joseph P., Jean B. Grossman, and Nancy Resch. 2000. *Making a Difference: An Impact Study of Big Brothers Big Sisters.* Philadelphia: Public Private Ventures.

Tuchman, Gaye. 1978. *Making the News.* New York: Free Press.

US Department of Labor, Office of Planning and Research. 1965. *The Negro Family: The Case for National Action.* Washington, DC: US Department of Labor.

"Violent Youth Predator Act." 1996. H.R. 3565, 104th Congress, 2nd session.

Warr, Mark. 1995. "Poll Trends: Public Opinion on Crime and Punishment." *Public Opinion Quarterly* 59: 296–310.

Websdale, Neil. 1999. "Predators: The Social Construction of 'Stranger-Danger' in Washington State as a Form of Patriarchal Ideology." Pp. 91–114 in *Making Trouble: Cultural Constructions of Crime, Deviance, and Control,* edited by Jeff Ferrell and Neil Websdale. New York: Aldine de Gruyter.

Websdale, Neil, and Alexander Alvarez. 1998. "Forensic Journalism as Patriarchal Ideology: The Newspaper Construction of Homicide-Suicide." Pp. 123–141 in *Popular Culture, Crime, and Justice,* edited by Frankie Y. Bailey and Donna C. Hale. Belmont, CA: Wadsworth.

Welch, Michael, Eric A. Price, and Nana Yankey. 2002. "Moral Panic over Youth Violence: Wilding and the Manufacture of Menace in the Media." *Youth and Society* 34 (1): 3–30.

Zelizer, Viviana A. 1985. *Pricing the Priceless Child: The Changing Value of Children.* New York: Basic.

Index

About the Book

Is a teenage violent offender a dangerous predator—or a vulnerable innocent that we should rescue from a life of crime? J. William Spencer probes our ambivalent response to youth violence to show how deeply entwined issues of crime, age, race, and class distort our understanding of an important social problem.

Spencer's pointed yet nuanced analysis traces how misconceptions about youth violence—whether in the form of gangs, school violence, "superpredators," or cyberbullying—take root in our national consciousness and undercut our attempts to remedy the problem. Equally, it offers a new understanding both of the nature of juvenile delinquency and of the role of cultural politics in shaping criminal justice and social services policy.

J. William Spencer is associate professor of sociology at Purdue University.

211